PARALLEL LIVES

BOOKS BY JEFFREY MEYERS

Painting and the Novel
Homosexuality and Literature
D. H. Lawrence and the Experience of Italy
Disease and the Novel
The Spirit of Biography
Hemingway: Life into Art
Orwell: Life and Art
Thomas Mann's Artist-Heroes
James Salter: Pilot, Screenwriter, Novelist

BIBLIOGRAPHY

T. E. Lawrence: A Bibliography
Catalogue of the Library of the Late Siegfried Sassoon
George Orwell: An Annotated Bibliography of Criticism

EDITED COLLECTIONS

George Orwell: The Critical Heritage
Hemingway: The Critical Heritage
Robert Lowell: Interviews and Memoirs
The Sir Arthur Conan Doyle Reader
The W. Somerset Maugham Reader

EDITED ORIGINAL ESSAYS

Wyndham Lewis: A Revaluation
Wyndham Lewis, by Roy Campbell
D. H. Lawrence and Tradition
The Legacy of D. H. Lawrence
The Craft of Literary Biography
The Biographer's Art
T. E. Lawrence: Soldier, Writer, Legend
Graham Greene: A Revaluation

EDITED LETTERS

Remembering Iris Murdoch: Letters and Interviews, with a Memoir
*The Mystery of the Real: Letters of the Canadian Artist Alex Colville and
Biographer Jeffrey Meyers. Edited, with Four Essays, by Jeffrey Meyers*

PARALLEL LIVES

FROM FREUD AND MANN TO ARBUS AND PLATH

JEFFREY MEYERS

LOUISIANA STATE UNIVERSITY PRESS

BATON ROUGE

Published by Louisiana State University Press
lsupress.org

LSU Press Paperback Original

Designer: Barbara Neely Bourgoyne
Typeface: Whitman

Cover illustration: *The Ambassadors*, by Hans Holbein
the Younger, 1533. National Gallery, London.

Earlier versions of these chapters appeared in *Salmagundi, Kenyon Review,
Virginia Quarterly Review, American Scholar, Antioch Review, London Magazine,
Studies* (Dublin), *The Article* (London), and in *T. E. Lawrence: Soldier, Writer,
Legend* (1989) and *Serendipitous Adventures in Britannia* (2019).

Library of Congress Cataloging-in-Publication Data
Names: Meyers, Jeffrey, author.
Title: Parallel lives : from Freud and Mann to Arbus and Plath / Jeffrey Meyers.
Other titles: From Freud and Mann to Arbus and Plath
Description: Baton Rouge : Louisiana State University Press, [2024] |
    Includes bibliographical references and index.
Identifiers: LCCN 2024002000 (print) | LCCN 2024002001 (ebook) | ISBN
    978-0-8071-8226-0 (paperback) | ISBN 978-0-8071-8269-7 (epub) | ISBN
    978-0-8071-8270-3 (pdf)
Subjects: LCSH: Biography—19th century. | Biography—20th century. |
    Intellectual life—History.
Classification: LCC CT119 .M53 2024 (print) | LCC CT119 (ebook) | DDC
    920—dc23/eng/20240315
LC record available at https://lccn.loc.gov/2024002000
LC ebook record available at https://lccn.loc.gov/2024002001

CONTENTS

PREFACE

The sharp intelligence and original method of Plutarch's *Parallel Lives*, written in Greek in the second century A.D., have been admired by major authors from the Renaissance to the modern era. Montaigne wrote: "In his parallels (which are the most admirable part of his work, and in which, in my opinion, he took particular satisfaction), the fidelity and sincerity of his judgments equal their depth and weight." Rousseau's biographers note that the *Lives* "had served to fire both his enthusiasm as a boy for the republics of the ancient world and his pride in being Genevan. . . . Rousseau's love for 'my master and my comforter Plutarch' never waned; a friend said that he knew Plutarch by heart and could have found his way in the streets of Athens better than in Geneva." Beethoven said that Plutarch, his favorite ancient writer, "taught him resignation" in troubled times.

In the *Life of Johnson* (1791), James Boswell quoted Plutarch's "Life of Alexander" as an example of his own biographical method: "Nor is it always in the most distinguished achievements that men's virtues or vices may be best discerned; but very often an action of small note, a short saying, or a jest, shall distinguish a person's real character more than the greatest sieges, or the most important battles." Lytton Strachey's Preface to *Eminent Victorians* (1918) also adopted Plutarch's approach. The wise biographer, he stated, "will attack his subject in unexpected places; he will fall upon the flank, or the rear; he will shoot a sudden, revealing searchlight into obscure recesses, hitherto undivined."

Hamlet tells the players "to hold as 'twere the mirror up to nature" and like Polonius "by indirections find directions out." Hemingway, adopting this indirect technique and using a jai alai term for a two-wall shot, said he wrote his autobiography *A Moveable Feast* by *remate*, by reflection of himself in relation to other people. By using mirror images, my *Parallel Lives* reveals a new way to perceive these illustrious men and women.

The characters described in *Parallel Lives* cover the century from the birth of Sigmund Freud in 1856 to the death of Sylvia Plath in 1963. This book includes Austrian, German, Dutch, French, English, American and Russian authors and artists, directors and actors, children and soldiers, friends and lovers, rivals and enemies. Like the bifocal principle of dual composition in Plutarch, these brief lives are arranged in pairs to interact with each other and illuminate their similarities, characters and friendships. Like horses yoked together, they have greater strength and power when they complement each other.

In the linked structure of *Parallel Lives* Freud, Waugh, Wilson, Nabokov, Hemingway and Heaney appear in several chapters. The most violent friendship ended when Verlaine shot Rimbaud and went to prison, and Rimbaud crawled back from Africa to die miserably in France. The most brilliant friendship broke up when Wilson attacked Nabokov's edition of Pushkin. The most moving connection was Audrey Hepburn's tender and sympathetic attachment to her soul-sister Anne Frank.

Each chapter in this book shifts the focus back and forth between two subjects, comparing them, changing perspective, reevaluating similarities and contrasts. With vivid details and dramatic events, it emphasizes the backgrounds, intellectual influences and personality traits. By examining the complex motives for irrational behavior ranging from deep affection and intense hostility, warm encouragement and bitter rivalry (sometimes together in the same chapter) this book offers insights into the dynamics of complementary characters.

PARALLEL LIVES

I

SIGMUND FREUD

—— AND ——

ADOLF HITLER

Conscience is a Jewish invention.

—HITLER

I

In Vienna, during the decade before the Great War, an astounding concentration of creative genius coincided with the final stages of political collapse. The work of Hofmannsthal, Musil, Broch, Schnitzler, Kraus, Werfel and Zweig in literature; Mahler, Wolf and Schönberg in music; Krafft-Ebing, Adler and Rank in psychology; Wittgenstein and Buber in philosophy, suggested that Austria had achieved self-awareness only at the moment of dissolution. As Musil wrote, "Yes, maybe Kakania [Austria] was, despite much which speaks to the contrary, a country for geniuses; and probably that is another reason why it succumbed."

Freud and Hitler also lived in Vienna during these formative years of psychoanalysis, logical positivism, atonal music, abstract painting and functional architecture, and they represented two radical ways of diagnosing and curing the psychological and political illnesses of the capital. "Politics is magic," said Hofmannsthal. "He who knows how to summon the forces from the deep, him they will follow." Both Freud and Hitler, who were profoundly influenced by Viennese culture and politics, rejected rationalism and recognized the importance of subconscious forces. But while Freud attempted to understand and control the forces from the deep, Hitler unleashed and exploited them—with tragic consequences for Freud (when Hitler triumphantly returned to Vienna in 1938) as well as for all the Jews of Europe.

The Austro-Hungarian Empire had been created in the seventeenth century to protect Europe from the infidel invasions of the Turks, who had reached the gates of Vienna in 1683. At the turn of the twentieth century, Vienna was still the capital of an empire of nearly fifty million people that stretched from the Rhine to the Dneister, from the Po Valley to the Carpathians and from Saxony to Montenegro. Like its Ottoman rival, the Hapsburg Empire was a political fossil that preserved, well into modern times, many of the ideas and institutions that had been destroyed elsewhere in Europe by the revolutions of 1848. In the final years of Hapsburg power conditions were characteristically described as "always desperate, but never serious."

Vienna represented a state of mind in a state of siege. The lack of political reality was expressed in a social artificiality and pretense that emphasized external appearances and adornments, elaborate titles and gradations. The traditional Austrian Biedermeier attitudes: sentimentality, nostalgia for the past, lighthearted aestheticism, love of spectacle, fondness for the countryside, indifference to reform and passivity toward bureaucracy mingled uneasily with more modern currents: the protests against censorship and rigid sexual conventions, the alienation of intellectuals and high suicide rate, the nationalist and anti-Semitic movements. Those who lived blindly and happily in the past could agree with the music critic, Max Graf, that "we who were born in Vienna, and grew up there, had no idea, during the city's brilliant period before the first world war, that this epoch was to be the end and still less did we suspect that the Hapsburg Monarchy was destined to decline."

But more apocalyptic artists, like Oskar Kokoschka and the satirist Karl Kraus, recognized the impending doom during "the last days of mankind." The painter wrote that "My early black portraits arose in Vienna before the World War; the people lived in security, yet they were all afraid. I felt this through their cultivated form of living, which was still derived from the Baroque; I painted them in their anxiety and pain." On the death of Franz Josef in 1916, Kraus remarked that he could believe the Emperor had died, but could not convince himself he had ever lived. He ironically called Austria, with its quixotic mixture of repression and freedom, "an isolation cell in which one was allowed to scream."

II

In this contradictory and stimulating atmosphere of Vienna, Jewish genius flowered as richly as it had under the Muslim caliphs of Granada. The Austrian Jews were not completely freed from legal constraints until 1867, but as William Johnston writes in *The Austrian Mind*, "No other ethnic group produced so many thinkers of transcendent originality."

In 1910 the 175,000 Jews of Vienna comprised nearly 9 percent of the population, and the city had, after Warsaw and Budapest, the largest Jewish community in Europe. Jews controlled the great financial houses as well as the Marxist Social Democratic party, which in 1907 had won the largest number of seats in the Reichsrat. Jews dominated artistic and cultural life, and formed the majority in the professions of medicine, law and journalism.

Jewish success, as well as Jewish failure, stimulated the deeprooted political anti-Semitism, and Jews became the obvious scapegoats during the twenty years of economic depression that followed the great Bourse crash of 1873. This political anti-Semitism, which first developed in modern Austria, was fed by the racial theories of men like Houston Stewart Chamberlain (who lived in Vienna from 1889 until 1909), and by fear of Jewish fecundity, economic envy, *volkisch* rejection of materialism and, as Freud adds in *Moses and Monotheism*, by the Jews' traditional resistance to persecution and oppression, and their role as "parricides" who reject the Christian God.

Anti-Semitism was also exacerbated by the intense self-hatred that afflicted many assimilated and converted Jews, and by the heavy migration of orthodox rural Jews into Vienna. After 1900, the Jews and the Turks were the only minorities whose people wore their traditional clothing on the streets of the city. These, and other irrational factors, inspired an abundance of journals like the Social Catholic *Deutsches Volksblatt*, edited by Ernst Vergani, which combined crude sex and anti-Semitic prejudice with a popular version of current racial theories.

The two most powerful advocates of political anti-Semitism were the Pan-German Georg von Schönerer and the Christian Socialist mayor of Vienna, Karl Lueger. Both men had an immense influence on the young Adolf Hitler, who absorbed their ideas and learned how to exploit their prejudices, how to appeal to a mob and how to deal violently with political opponents. Schönerer was elected to the Reichsrat in 1873, the year of the financial crash, represented the very district where Hitler was born in 1889 (at the height of Schönerer's

anti-Semitic fulminations), and was defeated in 1907, when Hitler first came
to Vienna. Besides Pan-Germanism, Schönerer's virulent and largely negative
program included hostility toward Czechs and other minorities, hatred of the
Jews and the Catholic Church, fear of socialism and contempt for liberalism.

As early as 1887 Lueger made the macabre but novel proposal of putting "all
the Jews upon a large ship, to be sunk on the high seas with loss of all aboard,
as a great service to the world." Despite the opposition of the Emperor, Lueger
became mayor of Vienna in 1897 and died in office in 1910, while Hitler was
living in the capital. When criticized for his social relations with his political
scapegoats, Lueger made the characteristic remark, "I decide who is a Jew,"
which epitomized the split between his ruthless public character and his genial
informality in private. In his posthumously published autobiography, *The World
of Yesterday*, Stefan Zweig provided an extremely naive expression of the Jews'
ambivalent attitude toward Lueger:

> An able and popular leader was Dr. Karl Lueger, who mastered this un-
> rest and worry and, with the slogan "the little man must be helped,"
> carried with him the entire small bourgeoisie and the disgruntled middle
> class. . . . It was exactly the same worried group which Adolf Hitler later
> collected around him as his first substantial following. Karl Lueger was
> also his prototype in another sense, in that he taught him the usefulness
> of the anti-semitic catchword, which put an opponent before the eyes of
> the broad classes of the bourgeoisie. . . . [But] his official anti-semitism
> never stopped him from being helpful and friendly to his former Jewish
> friends. . . . The Jews, who had trembled at this triumph of the anti-semitic
> party, continued to live with the same rights and esteem as heretofore.

Thirty years later, when Lueger's "helpful and friendly" anti-Semitism had
led directly to Hitler and the Anschluss, Zweig went into exile and killed himself in Brazil, "exhausted by long years of homeless wandering." Hitler eventually became more nationalistic and anti-Semitic than Schönerer, and more
popular and powerful than Lueger. The Nazi reign of terror, as well as Theodor
Herzl's idea of Zionism, which provided a persuasive political response for
many of Hitler's victims, both had their origins in Vienna.

III

Freud was born in Moravia in 1856, came to Vienna at the age of four and lived there until the penultimate year of his long life. Though Freud was irritated by Pierre Janet's remark that "the idea of a sexual aetiology for the neuroses could only arise in the atmosphere of a town like Vienna," this *aperçu* contained an element of truth. For the rigid convention of silence about sex in a society of libertine men and frequently repressed, neurotic and frigid women led to an overt inhibition and a covert emphasis on sexual matters. The psychoanalytic investigation of the subconscious emerged in a city where the superficial calm concealed a hidden volcano.

Johnston has some very illuminating ideas about the relation of Freud's thought to the concepts of memory, repression, fatherfigures, duplicity and helplessness in his Viennese environment:

Freud's psychotherapy mirrors the fact that Vienna was a stronghold of memory. In Vienna everyone exemplified what in 1895 Freud ascribed to hysterics: they suffer largely from reminiscences. In this citadel of memory, Freud exploited Breuer's discovery that reliving a trauma could dispel its symptoms. . . .

A public life veiled in dissimulation paralleled the repression that Freud discerned in individuals. In this schema of neurosis we see Hapsburg society writ small. . . .

When Freud spoke of father-figures, he could have had in mind this macrocosmic father [the Emperor], whose deportment both the ambitious and the lethargic emulated. Secretiveness blanketed public life, prompting a search for latent meanings behind every event. . . . Duplicity aggravated the mechanisms of neurosis which Freud was seeking. When he spoke of superego censoring id, he knew what press censorship meant: a story would be missing from the front page, unleashing a fresh spate of rumors. Helpless—Freud would say castrated—before the bureaucracy, the populace indulged in fantasies that belittled the omnipotent personages who manipulated them. Austrians harbored feelings of paranoia towards the state.

Though Freud's seminal works were written in the early 1890s, he was at the height of his powers during the years before the Great War, which marked the beginning of his international recognition. The First International Psychoanalytical Congress took place in Salzburg in 1908, he delivered the influential lectures at Clark University in Worcester, Massachusetts, in 1909, founded four psychoanalytical journals, including *Imago*, between 1909 and 1913, and published *Leonardo da Vinci* in 1910, *The Psychology of Love* in 1910–12, *Totem and Taboo* and *The History of the Psychoanalytical Movement* in 1913.

The prevalence of official anti-Semitism in professional, academic and governmental circles, and a violent hostility to his ideas, were primarily responsible for Freud's profound dislike of Vienna. In the months before his marriage in 1886 he doubted if he could earn a living in the capital and seriously thought of moving either to a provincial city or to another country. Ernest Jones quoted Freud saying, "I hate Vienna almost personally. . . . It is a misery to live here: this is no atmosphere in which one can maintain the hope of achieving anything difficult." He even stated, quite unreasonably, "I have lived here for fifty years and have never come across a new idea here." But there was an element of ambivalence in Freud's hatred, for he was very reluctant to leave the city, even when his life was threatened by the Nazis, and he once admitted, "I feel an unrestrained affection for Vienna and Austria, although I know her abysses."

Freud's insistence on the sexual etiology of neurosis and his claim that psychoanalytic sessions could often cure hysteria conflicted with the traditional concepts of therapeutic nihilism in Viennese psychiatry, and the fact that almost all of his followers were Jewish made his ideas and his movement a special target of anti-Semitism. Despite his international recognition, Freud was not made a full Professor—in a field where the hierarchy of titles was particularly important—until 1919, and even then he called it an "empty title" because it did not include membership on the Board of the Faculty.

Freud never voted in elections until the end of Lueger's tenure, and in 1926 he told Max Eastman, "Politically I am—just nothing." Though Freud was an atheist who felt that religion was merely an infantile indulgence, his sense of Jewish identity inevitably sharpened with the intensification of anti-Semitism after the Austrian defeat in the Great War. In the late 1920s he wrote: "My language is German. My culture, my attainments are German. I considered myself a German intellectual, until I noticed the growth of anti-semite prejudice in

German Austria. Since that time, I considered myself no longer a German. I prefer to call myself a Jew."

In a famous letter to his fellow members of the Vienna B'nai B'rith Lodge, he defined his Jewish characteristics in terms of intellectual freedom and ideological independence and ended with a reference to Ibsen's *Enemy of the People*: "It was only to my Jewish nature that I owed the two qualities that have become indispensable to me throughout my difficult life. Because I was a Jew I found myself free of many prejudices which restrict others in the use of the intellect: as a Jew I was prepared to be in opposition and to renounce agreement with the 'Compact majority.'"

IV

Freud belonged to the comfortable and cultured middle class of Vienna, while Hitler dwelled among the homeless and uprooted outcasts at the very bottom of society. Hitler lived in Vienna for five and a half years between 1907 and 1913, during the most impressionable and formative period of his life; and like Freud, his character and opinions were profoundly marked and molded by the city.

Hitler emphasizes the importance of the years in Vienna in a long section in *Mein Kampf*, which he wrote in a German prison after the failure of the *putsch* in 1924, and categorically states: "In this period there took shape within me a world picture and a philosophy which became the granite foundation of all my acts. In addition to what I then created, I have had to learn little; and have had to alter nothing." He then adds, with an element of self-pity, that his experiences in "this city of lotus-eaters" was almost entirely negative and was (for a man who lacked a formal education) "the hardest, the most thorough, school of my life. To me Vienna represents, I am sorry to say, merely the living memory of the saddest period of my life. Even today this city can arouse in me nothing but the most dismal thoughts. . . . Five years of hardship and misery. Five years in which I was forced to earn a living, first as a day labourer, then as a smaller painter; a truly meager living which never sufficed to appease even my daily hunger."

Hitler first visited Vienna in May 1906 and sent home enthusiastic postcards about his youthful passions, Wagnerian music and Baroque architecture. He came to live in the capital in October 1907, full of illusory expectations, but soon began his descent into poverty and degradation. He was refused admission as a student of painting to the Vienna Academy of Fine Arts in 1907 and again in 1908. He still had not recovered from that shock when, sixteen years later, he described the traumatic incident with a characteristic combination of astonishment, rage and violence: "I was so convinced that I would be successful that when I received my rejection, it struck me as a bolt from the blue. . . . They rejected me, they threw me out, they turned me down. . . . The whole Academy ought to be blown up." Hitler was so ashamed of his failure that he never revealed it to his family and tried to keep it hidden from his roommate, August Kubizek. Shattered by his rejection, Hitler wandered aimlessly around the city, from the impressive new buildings on the Ring to the brothel district, until he ran out of money in December 1909.

The furnished room that Hitler first shared with Kubizek was rather grim, and his friend relates that "It was not necessary for us to go out to study the mass misery of the city—it was brought into our own home. Our own damp and crumbling walls, bug-infested furniture and the unpleasant odor of kerosene were typical." Hitler states that in the "socially backward" Vienna, "dazzling riches and loathsome poverty alternated sharply." He was clearly in the "loathsome" camp and came to hate the rich as his hunger and filth intensified. His description of the poor in Vienna is a clear portrayal of his own shameful decline: "He walks the streets, hungry; often he pawns and sells his last possessions; his clothing becomes more and more wretched; and thus he sinks into eternal surroundings which, on top of his physical misfortune, also poison his soul. . . . The more I witnessed it, the greater grew my revulsion for the big city which avidly sucked men in and then so cruelly crushed them."

By the end of 1909 Hitler was forced to give up his room, disappeared without even notifying Kubizek and was desperate enough to join the ranks of the city's tramps. He slept in doss-houses, park benches or (wrapped in newspapers) on the streets; and eked out a meager subsistence by running errands, beating carpets, carrying luggage at the Bahnhof and shoveling snow. In June 1910 he entered the prison-like Home for Men on the Meldemannstrasse, with its "sordid scenes and repulsive filth." He spent his last three Viennese years in the Home, where he eventually took up the trade of watercolor copyist. Hitler describes this period of his life as years of great loneliness. He avoided contact with the Viennese, whom he condemned as too easygoing and frivolous, made no friends and lived in solitude among the homeless tramps and drunkards.

It was almost inevitable that Hitler, who experienced poverty and misery in an intensely anti-Semitic atmosphere, and who longed for and envied both wealth and culture, should enthusiastically adopt the prevailing hostility to Jews. But there was also a personal reason. Hitler, who once said "The Jew is always within us," was haunted by the fear that he might be partly Jewish. His crude friend, Reinhold Hanisch, reports, "Hitler at that time looked very Jewish, and I often joked with him that he must be of Jewish blood."

Hitler wrote in *Mein Kampf* that he was converted to anti-Semitism (which he relates to Jewish politics) while living in Vienna: "In this period my eyes were opened to two menaces of which I had previously scarcely known the names . . . Marxism and Jewry." And in a notorious passage he describes his first meeting with a Jew, whose strange appearance made him stand out in the urban crowd: "One day I suddenly encountered an apparition in a black caftan and black hair locks. Is this a Jew?, was my first thought. For, to be sure, they had not looked like that in Linz. I observed the man furtively and cautiously, but the longer I stared at this foreign face, scrutinizing feature for feature, the more my first question assumed a new form: Is this a German? As always in such cases, I now began to try to relive my doubts by books. For a few hellers I bought the first anti-Semitic pamphlets of my life."

Hitler added nothing new to the abundant anti-Semitic literature that expressed the racial theories of men like Count Gobineau and Houston Chamberlain, which were adopted by Schönerer and Lueger, but like his political mentors he made it a cornerstone of his party program. During these repressed and ascetic years he was particularly fascinated by the sexual activities of the Jews. He states that "the relation of the Jews to prostitution, and even more to white-slave traffic, could be studied in Vienna as perhaps in no other city of western Europe," and he was outraged by the fantastic "nightmare vision of the seduction of hundreds of thousands of girls by crookedlegged Jew bastards." As Alan Bullock observes, "Hitler's Jew is no longer a human being, he has become a mythical figure, a grimacing, leering devil invested with infernal powers, the incarnation of evil, into which Hitler projects all that he hates and fears—and desires."

It is possible to see Hitler's attitude toward Austria and Germany, as well as toward Jews, in terms of Freudian psychology. Hitler called Vienna, with its extraordinary mixture of races, "the symbol of incest." He identified his aged, exhausted yet tyrannical father, whom he intensely disliked, with the Emperor and the city from which "the last flush of life flowed out into the sickly, old body of the crumbling empire." Hitler had succeeded in usurping his young mother's affection for his father by becoming the spoiled darling of the only person he ever loved, and he wished to extinguish the authority and power of the threatening Austrian fatherland by the triumph of the more potent German motherland:

> The protection of the German race presumed the destruction of Austria . . . above all else, the Royal House of Hapsburg was destined to bring misfortune upon the German nation. . . . Since my heart had never beaten for an Austrian monarchy but only for a German Reich, the hour of this state's downfall could only seem to me the beginning of the redemption of the German nation.

In another crucial passage, despite his confused and inconsistent use of the words "fatherland" and "mother country," Hitler—who was strengthened by his mother and oppressed by his father—describes the political opposition of Austria and Germany in terms of parental conflict:

> My most ardent and heartfelt wish: the union of my beloved homeland with the common fatherland: the German Reich. . . . I address myself to all those who, detached from their mother country . . . are persecuted and tortured for their loyalty to the fatherland, and who now, with poignant emotion, long for the hour which will permit them to return to the heart of their faithful mother.

Hitler's forcible annexation of Austria to Germany was a political expression of his subconscious desire for a "return to the heart of his faithful mother'"—who had died of breast cancer in December 1907 while he was separated from her and living in Vienna. Hitler's Anschluss, which was specifically prohibited by the Treaty of Versailles, symbolically absorbed and replaced the

Austrian father-image through a forbidden and "incestuous" union with the German mother-image.

The extraordinary transformation of Hitler from the young tramp of Vienna to the conqueror of Europe suggests the demonic possibilities of mediocrity. When Hitler moved to Munich in May 1913 in order to avoid military service in Austria, his political beliefs—which had evolved from his personal guilt, fear, anger and destructiveness—were fully developed. His intense German nationalism, his contempt for Viennese cosmopolitanism, his hatred of parliamentary democracy, Marxist Socialism, Jews and Jewish thought, were to dominate his actions for the rest of his life.

V

According to Nazi ideology, psychoanalysis had soul-destroying consequences; it was alien to the German nature and had been refuted by German science. The Nazis lost no time in attacking Freud, and his books were burned in Berlin as early as May 1933. The following year, Freud wrote with foreboding to his son, Ernst: "The future is uncertain; either Austrian fascism or the swastika. In the latter event we shall have to leave; native fascism we are willing to take in our stride up to a certain point; it can hardly treat us as badly as its German cousin." Freud was more aware than most Viennese Jews of Hitler's overwhelming need for revenge, self-justification and self-redemption, of his urge to dominate and subdue the city that had once "sucked him in and cruelly crushed him."

The annexation of Austria was inevitable after the remilitarization of the Rhineland and the establishment of the Rome-Berlin axis. Despite, or perhaps because of the humiliation of the Austrian government, there was a spontaneous and enthusiastic welcome when the Nazi troops crossed the border on March 11, 1938, and when Hitler himself drove through the cheering crowds of Linz. (He immediately transformed the cemetery where his family was buried into an artillery range to destroy any possible evidence of his Jewish blood.) During his reception at the Hapsburg palace twenty-five years after his undignified departure from the city, Hitler proudly told the Burgermeister of Vienna: "Be assured that this city is in my eyes a pearl. I will bring it into that setting which is worthy of it and I will entrust it to the care of the whole German nation."

This "care," needless to say, did not extend to the Jews. Two nights after the Anschluss, as Hitler complacently observed that "a good political action saves blood," the swastika was hoisted above St. Stephen's Cathedral and the first of the 76,000 arrests began. The street named for Heine was appropriately renamed for Schönerer; the atrocities of the Austrian Nazis—a prolonged Kristallnacht—exceeded anything that had happened in the Reich; and after three months in Austria the Nazis accomplished what had taken five years to do in Germany. Rabbis were forced to scrub the pro-Schuschnigg slogans off the pavements, synagogues were desecrated, Jewish homes and shops were wrecked and looted, and Jews were driven out of governmental and industrial positions, the public schools and even the public parks.

Though shocked and threatened by these outrages, Freud was not surprised by them, for he had little reason to change his "judgment of human nature, above all the Christian-Aryan variety." His denial, in *Civilization and Its Discontents*, of the supremacy of culture over instinct, and his belief in the elemental destructive urge in the human soul, had been tragically confirmed when, as he said in *Moses and Monotheism*, "The German people retrogressed into all but pre-historic barbarism."

Even the Nazis hesitated to condemn a man of Freud's fame and stature, and the personal intervention of both Roosevelt and Mussolini (through Freud's Italian translator) helped to secure his eventual release. Before he left, the Nazis confiscated Freud's substantial bank account and forced him to pay an exit tax of 12,000 Dutch gulden. Freud's Psychoanalytic Society was dissolved; his publishing company was destroyed; his books banned, confiscated and reduced to pulp; another stock of books recalled from Switzerland for destruction; his children expelled from their professions. In a moving letter of May 12 Freud wrote to his son, Ernst, in London and likened himself to a biblical patriarch: "Two prospects keep me going in these grim times: to rejoin you all and—to die in freedom. I sometimes compare myself with the old Jacob who, when a very old man, was taken by his children to Egypt, as Thomas Mann is to describe in his next novel." On June 4, 1938, after continuous persecution, the old and frail Freud signed the absurd statement that he had been well treated by the Nazis, adding the superb postscript: "I can heartily recommend the Gestapo to anyone." Escorted by Ernest Jones, he was allowed to leave the city where he had lived and worked for seventy-eight years. Freud was forced to leave his four aged sisters in Vienna, and they were all killed in concentration camps in 1943.

A few days after he arrived in his London refuge (where he died in 1939 from the cancer of the jaw that had tormented him during the last two decades of his life), Freud wrote with defensive irony to his lifelong friend and disciple, Max Eitingon: "The feeling of triumph on being liberated is too strongly mixed with sorrow, for in spite of everything I still greatly loved the prison from which I have been released. The enchantment of the new surroundings (which make one want to shout 'Heil Hitler!') is blended with discontent caused by little peculiarities of the strange environment."

Thomas Mann, the first and most brilliant exponent of Freudian thought in literature, has made an illuminating speculation about the final, tragic conjunction of Freud and Hitler in Vienna: "I have a private suspicion that the élan of the march on Vienna had a secret spring: it was directed at the venerable Freud, the real and actual enemy, the philosopher and revealer of neuroses, the great disillusioner, the seer and sayer of the laws of genius." Hitler saw Freud, who was nourished by the same ambivalent and cosmopolitan atmosphere and who recognized, but could not cure, the disease of modern civilization that Hitler represented, as the personification of Jewish culture and conscience, intellect and insight, that he hated, feared—and destroyed—in Vienna.

2

FREUD

———— AND ————

THOMAS MANN

I

Thomas Mann's international fame as a novelist ran parallel to the equally celebrated career of Sigmund Freud. He respected Freud's courage and genius, praised Freud (nineteen years his senior) in his public speeches and correspondence, acknowledged Freud's influence on his work and visited him four times in Vienna. The third occasion, on Freud's eightieth birthday, was a deeply moving experience for both of them. Despite their contrasting personalities—the stiff German and the *gemütlich* Viennese—they transcended the emotional barriers and became quite close. Mann was strongly attracted to Freud's theory about the danger of suppressing sexual desires, yet was ambivalent about Freud's ideas. He was suspicious about psychoanalysis and satirized Freud's analytic theories in *The Magic Mountain*. His two essays on Freud emphasized the value of instinct over reason, which reflected his own views rather than Freud's.

They honored each other's work, and Mann was unusually deferential and flattering, but he disguised his intellectual doubts about Freud. Mann could exploit in his fiction Freud's concepts of the meaning of dreams, the role of the unconscious and the effects of sexual repression, even though he didn't actually believe in them. Freud's theories enabled him to write about homosexual feelings, then a taboo subject, and hide his own attraction to handsome young boys and men, including (as we shall see) his own son.

Most significantly, these friends had two amazingly similar biographical experiences. During the Nazi persecution of the 1930s, both managed to suppress incriminating personal documents that could have destroyed their reputations and ruined their lives. The tragic death of Freud's beloved young grandson in 1923 and Mann's fictional portrayal of the horrific death of Adrian Leverkühn's nephew Nepo in *Doctor Faustus* revealed that both men had the same emotional response, real and imagined, to that traumatic situation.

In a 1925 interview with *La Stampa* in Turin, Mann told an Italian journalist that Freud had influenced *Death in Venice* (1912), in which the author Gustav von Aschenbach, infatuated by the beautiful boy Tadzio, lingers in cholera-infested Venice and dies in that city. He said, "The death wish is present in Aschenbach's consciousness though he's unaware of it, and the word *Ich* [Ego] is used in the Freudian way to indicate a part of the personality that makes demands in conflict with instinct." He gave Freud more credit than he deserved by disingenuously claiming, "without Freud I would never have thought of treating this erotic motif; or I would certainly have treated it differently." But since the novella was closely based on Mann's actual experience in Venice, he didn't need Freud to inspire the story. He was intimidated by Freud's "X-ray" invasion of the artist's soul and suspicious of probing psychoanalysis. He felt that when an author's mind is invaded, and all his secrets exposed and wasted in talk, "the source of creativity fritters away."

While *Death in Venice* uses Freud as a means of articulating Mann's personal feelings, *The Magic Mountain* (1924) treats Freud's ideas with black humor. Dr. Krokowski, who glows with an eerie phosphorescent pallor, advocates the psychoanalytic point of view and probes the unconscious. He suppresses the pathological origins of epilepsy and calls it an "orgasm of the brain." He believes that organic disease is always a secondary phenomenon, a morbid growth upon the spirit. He argues in a series of lectures on "Love as a force contributing to disease" that illness results from the conflict between the powers of love and of chastity—between instinct and repression, the id and the ego. He thinks that when love is held in chains by purity, fear, morality or aversion, it reappears in the form of illness: "Symptoms of disease are nothing but a disguised manifestation of the power of love; and all disease is only love transformed." Krokowski's theories about disease and love suggest that sexual freedom, though discouraged by the medical authorities because of its adverse effect on tubercular lungs, would cure the disease. When Hans Castorp finally makes love to Clavdia Chauchat his fever increases and health deteriorates. Though this decline could be attributed to her sudden departure and his consequent sexual deprivation, the disease is both the expression of and the penalty for love.

Castorp's mentor, the Italian humanist Ludovico Settembrini, opposes Krokowski's views. He exclaims that psychoanalysis, with the patient recumbent on a couch, is bad insofar as it encourages passivity: "It stands in the way of action, cannot shape the vital forces, maims life at the roots." Mann's biographer Anthony Heilbut states that "Mann treats psychoanalysis with skepticism. He captures the moment when it was still regarded as half-quackery, and he makes it a part of commercial history, a tourist's entertainment along with mountain hikes and afternoon tea. . . . Dr. Krokowski conducts a séance, a reminder that psychoanalysis shares its origins with such spurious pursuits as phrenology and clairvoyance."

Mann praised the liberating effects of the instincts in his essays on Freud while portraying their disastrous effects in his fiction. Despite Mann's satiric and sceptical portrait of Krokowski, he publicly praised Freud during the last decade of the analyst's life (1929–39), when his leading disciples were still alive and spreading his gospel, and as Mann's reputation continued to soar. Mann's rather abstract and repetitive essay, "Freud's Position in the History of Modern Thought" (1929)—published the year Mann won the Nobel Prize—focused more on his heroes in the German Romantic tradition, Novalis, Schopenhauer and Nietzsche, than on the ostensible subject of Freud. Mann rather ponderously described it in a letter of May 3, 1929 (not included in the English edition of his *Letters*), to the French writer Charles Du Bos: "At this moment I'm thinking about an essay on 'Freud's Position in the History of Modern Thought,' an extensive treatise on the problem of revolution, full of educational purpose and particularly intended for those who recognize psychoanalysis as the only phenomenon of modern anti-rationalism which does not lend itself to reactionary misuse" (my translation).

In this subtly autobiographical essay Mann placed Freud in his own literary tradition and described him as the advocate of dark gods. Mann wrote: "As a delver into the depths, a researcher in the psychology of instinct, Freud unquestionably belongs with those writers of the nineteenth century who . . . stand opposed to rationalism, intellectualism, classicism . . . emphasising instead the night side of nature and the soul as the actually life-conditioning and life-giving element." He represents in the "most revolutionary sense the divinity of earth, the primacy of the unconscious, the pre-mental, the will, the passions, or, as Nietzsche says, the 'feeling' above the 'reason.'" Mann exalted the "night side" of man, but the second sentence on the "primacy of the unconscious" does not logically follow from the first, and his evidence from the German Romantics seems to contradict his conclusion. The opposition to reason and intellect, the domination of Nietzsche's passionate will to power, have not been "life-giving," but have led straight to the horrors of the twentieth century.

Mann's observations illuminated his own work rather than Freud's. Mann's comment, "Schopenhauer humbles the intellect far below the will, before prescribing to it a means of moral conversion and self-regeneration," alluded to Thomas Buddenbrook's reading the chapter "On Death" in *The World as Will and Idea* before he collapses in the gutter and dies. Mann's phrase, "the neurotic symptom . . . is the pathological consequence of suppression," explained Aschenbach's illness after he has repressed his love for Tadzio. Mann's description of Freud as "a psychologist of the depths, an investigator of the unconscious, that makes him understand life through disease," reprised his portrayal of Krokowski's ideas in *The Magic Mountain*. The "mischievous guilelessness, the frightful, equivocal, oracular obscurantism of music" prefigured the diabolical source of Leverkühn's musical creation in *Doctor Faustus*.

Freud, an astute reader, made an extremely shrewd analysis of the etiology of Mann's patched-together essay. He saw that when Mann was invited to turn out an encomiastic piece on Freud he reached for the old papers in his bottom drawer. On July 28, 1929, Freud wrote to his devoted follower, the femme fatale Lou Andreas-Salomé, who'd been an intimate friend of Nietzsche: "Thomas Mann's essay is no doubt quite an honour. He gives me the impression of having just completed an essay on romanticism when he was asked to write about me, and so he applied a veneer, as the cabinetmaker says, of psychoanalysis to the front and back of this essay: the bulk of it is of a different wood." But he didn't dispute Mann's friendly thesis and concluded, "Nevertheless, whenever Mann says something it is pretty sound"—even if Mann was talking about himself.

In January 1930, soon after his first essay, Mann effusively wrote to Freud—calling him a courageous genius—and thanked him for an unidentified short work, probably one of Freud's best books, *Civilization and Its Discontents*. He was grateful "for the extraordinary gift of your book, whose range so formidably surpasses its outer dimensions. I read it at one sitting, deeply moved by a courageous search for truth which, the older I grow, I see more and more as the source of all genius."

Freud's biographer Ernest Jones records that in March 1932, between his first and second essays on Freud, Mann paid his first visit to Vienna and they established an immediate rapport, what Goethe called an "elective affinity." Jones writes, "Freud at once got on to intimate terms with him: 'what Mann had to say was very understanding; it gave the impression of a [cultured] background.' His wife and her sister, who were enthusiastic readers of Mann, were still more delighted."

In May 1935 Freud told their mutual friend, the German antiwar novelist Arnold Zweig, that he'd followed the suggestion of Mann's publisher Fischer Verlag, sent Mann in Zurich a customary tribute on his sixtieth birthday and "into it slipped a warning which I trust will not go unnoticed." He wrote: "in the name of countless numbers of your contemporaries I wish to express the confidence that you will never do or say anything—an author's words, after all, are deeds—that is cowardly or base, and that even at a time which blurs judgment you will choose the right way and show it to others." There was certainly no need to warn the brave and upright Mann not to be cowardly nor compromise with the Nazi regime. But he wanted to continue their mutual flattery and emphasize, as Mann well knew, that Mann was speaking for all the prominent anti-Hitler exiles.

In his laudatory speech "Freud and the Future" (1936) Mann again widened the focus to include Schopenhauer and Nietzsche. Writing to celebrate Freud's eightieth birthday on May 6—at a time when books by Freud and Mann had been burned in Germany—Mann praised him as a master, great scientist and wise genius. He saw Freud as scientifically validating the philosophical insights of the German Romantics—though there was no scientific basis for psychoanalysis—and dubiously claimed that Freud's work "shall be the future dwelling of a wiser and freer humanity . . . productive of a riper art than any possible in our neurotic, fear-ridden, hate-ridden world."

But neither Freud's theories nor Mann's public approval ever explained how the triumph of instinct over reason would regenerate humankind and lead to a better world. In a letter of January 1944 to the American literary critic Frederick Hoffman, Mann alluded to Plato's charioteer with the tamed and wild horses and to the Dionysian-Apollonian opposition in Nietzsche's *The Birth of Tragedy*, and stated that Freud "knows well the abyss of the unconscious and the instincts which by far exceed the power and the influence of intellect and reason." He quoted Freud's optimistic proclamation in his *New Introductory Lectures on Psychoanalysis*, "where Id was, there shall Ego be," but seemed to reverse it by suggesting where reason was, there shall instinct be. Nevertheless, he generously acknowledged Freud's powerful influence on his work from the sexual humiliation in "Little Herr Friedemann" to *Death in Venice*, *The Magic Mountain* and the *Joseph* novels: "it made me aware . . . of my own latent, preconscious sympathies."

Mann's *Diary* described the rapturous reception of his speech on May 8, 1936, which took place less than two years before the German annexation of Austria and Freud's flight to England: "In the evening the tumultuous success of the Freud lecture in the packed hall of the [Vienna] Konzerthaus. That morning a visit to Freud's apartment, bringing him the portfolio and the manuscript; deeply moving impressions. After the lecture a banquet at the Imperial [Hotel], I seated between Freud's son and daughter," Ernst and Anna. Though Mann was the guest of honor, he felt proud to be placed next to Freud's children.

Max Schur, Freud's close friend and personal physician during his thirty-three agonizing operations for cancer of the jaw, was delighted to hear Mann's praise and confirmed that it was indeed a splendid occasion. He agreed that it was a "deeply moving" event, said that Mann gave a poignant performance (which disguised Freud's dubious ideas) and noted that Freud felt it verified the truth of his controversial theories:

> Mann's address was thus a tribute not only to Freud but to the power of the spirit, to the rights of the individual . . . a ringing challenge to the forces of unreason and evil. Mann, who usually was rather detached and distant as a reader or speaker, rose to the occasion in the delivery of his address as well as in its content. It was a deeply moving experience for everyone present, giving us the feeling, which was rare in those days, that all was not yet lost. . . . It was to Freud a summary of his life's work, a vindication for the years of calumny and misunderstanding he had endured, and a confirmation that it really had been worthwhile to have lived that long.

Since Freud was too old and too ill with cancer to attend the festivities, Mann enhanced his tribute by personally repeating his oft-repeated talk in Freud's holiday house in Grinzing, a wine village outside Vienna. After delivering his lecture in several European cities, he returned to Vienna five weeks later on June 14. Schur recalled that "Freud and Mann were poles apart in looks, behavior and even attire. Freud, the Jew who had absorbed the good aspects of Viennese culture and civilization, and Mann, the typical North German, in some ways as stiff as the collar he was wearing."

The contrast in their personalities (which contradicts Jones' account of their congenial meeting in 1932) was mitigated by Mann's Jewish wife Katya. Freud was well pleased by the encounter and recalled, "this was a great joy for me and for all my family who were present. A noble *goy!*" Freud's son Ernst deleted and Schur restored the last three words, which conceded that Mann, though not Jewish, had a noble character. (Mann had offended Katya's family by having fictional characters modeled on them using Yiddish words—"We've *beganeffed* him—the *goy!*"—in the journal version of his story "The Blood of the Walsungs," which he suppressed.) Mann's biographer Donald Prater adds that Freud "was near to tears as he listened to his personal reading of the lecture and eagerly discussed his idea of myth constantly relived. . . . He embraced him warmly, and sent to his hotel a bottle of old Tokay with fruit and cakes, which made an excellent lunch for them on the train back" to Zurich. Freud was accustomed to constant veneration from his Jewish admirers. But he was deeply moved by the intellectual endorsement and personal tribute from the gentile Thomas Mann, the greatest living German writer.

In "Freud and the Future" Mann remarked, "how often have we not been told that the figure of Napoleon was cast in the antique mould!" Freud took up this idea in a comical tailpiece to their meeting. A few months later, in a letter of November 1936, he retaliated by subjecting Mann to a ridiculous notion: "I keep wondering if there isn't a figure in history for whom the life of Joseph was a mythical prototype, allowing us to detect the phantasy of Joseph as the secret daemonic motor behind the scenes of his complex life? I am thinking of Napoleon I." He then launched into a truly absurd speculation about the name of Napoleon's wife, slyly changing en route "probably" to "undoubtedly": "There were a number of things to be said against her, but what probably decided him [to marry her] was that her name was Josephine. . . . The infatuation for Josephine was undoubtedly brought about by the name." He then recalled that he'd previously subjected his trapped victim to this fantasy: "My daughter reminds me that I already divulged to you this interpretation of the daemonic after you read your essay here." Poor Mann, too polite to object, had to hear this absolute rubbish twice.

The patrician Mann, responding to Freud's letter the following month, quite uncharacteristically continued to bow down before him: "How vividly your letter has recalled to me the afternoon with you, which belongs among the finest memories of my life, when I had the privilege of reading my festival lecture to you." Ignoring Freud's boring repetition of his Napoleon conceit, he continued his flattery: "this letter is a stirring example of your genius, your incredible perspicacity in matters of the unconscious psychic life and the effects produced from its depths, and I take pride in being the recipient." Though Freud's eightieth-birthday *jubilatio* required undiminished praise, these words—usually reserved for Mann himself—seem insincere and excessive. He did not kowtow in this way to his older brother Heinrich and to such towering friends as Gerhart Hauptmann and Albert Einstein.

Mann also put the icing on the cake in 1936. Incited by Freud's follower Princess Marie Bonaparte (who'd inspired Freud's free association about her distinguished ancestor) Mann unsuccessfully recommended Freud for the Nobel Prize in Literature. Since Freud had an elegant style and influential ideas, this was not a far-fetched possibility. The historian Theodor Mommsen in 1902 and the philosopher Henri Bergson in 1907 had won the prize; and the nonfiction prose writers Bertrand Russell, Winston Churchill and Svetlana Alexievich would later win it.

Mann's four *Joseph and His Brothers* novels (1933–43) and Freud's *Moses and Monotheism* (1939) were both completed during their exile from Hitler's regime. In a letter to Freud in December 1936, Mann wrote that he'd been depressed by recent events. His days were clouded by the retraction of his honorary doctorate from the University of Bonn and "by the Berlin decree pronouncing me an outcast" and depriving him of German citizenship. In "The Theme of the *Joseph* Novels" Mann observed that the choice of an Old Testament subject was certainly not accidental. It was written during "the growing vulgar anti-semitism which is an essential part of the Fascist mob-myth." Both Mann and Freud did prodigious research and must have read some of the same books on ancient religion, history and archeology. Mann made two trips to Egypt. Freud, who had a superb collection of Middle Eastern artifacts, longed to go there but was prevented from traveling by old age and illness.

In Mann's novel, based on the Bible story and influenced by Freud's *Interpretation of Dreams*, Joseph has amazing premonitions and clairvoyant power, and reveals that the dreams of Potiphar's wife express her sexual wish-fulfillment. After Joseph demonstrates his ability to interpret dreams and divine the future, he is released from prison and brought to Pharaoh. Recreating Genesis 41, Mann has Pharaoh gratefully declare: "'My king-dreams are now interpreted to me. . . . Now, thanks to this prophetic youth, I know the truth. . . . My majesty has been shown that seven fat years will come in all Egypt and after that seven years of dearth, such that one will quite forget the previous plenty, and famine will consume the land.'"

In July 1936, a month after Mann's visit to Grinzing, Arnold Zweig eagerly asked Freud about Mann's *Young Joseph*, the second novel in his tetralogy: "What do you think of his Joseph novel? What is your opinion of it as a whole and in parts, as to subject-matter, style and form?" Unfortunately Freud, who may not have read the novel or did not want to disturb the ballet of flattery by expressing a negative opinion, did not answer.

Freud's last book, *Moses and Monotheism* (1939), concerns the origins of the Jewish religion. His convoluted and wildly unconvincing argument (defended, of course by the faithful Ernest Jones) stated that Moses was not a Jewish patriarch, but an Egyptian who led a small band of Jewish rebels out of Egypt during a civil war. These people killed Moses, and their original sin has haunted the tribe of Israel since then. Freud thought the "embryonic experience of the race, the influence of the man Moses and the exodus from Egypt conditioned the entire further development [of the Jews] up to the present day." Contemporary Jewish readers, however, were not at all pleased by Freud's denigration of their great hero into an Egyptian nobody.

Freud reinterpreted the story of Moses; Mann dramatically retold it after Freud's death, so he would not compete with or contradict the master. In Mann's *The Tables of the Law* (1943) Moses is a heroic Jewish leader, not an Egyptian rebel. Mann related the early life of Moses, his preparations for leading his people out of Egypt, the exodus itself and his engraving of the stone tablets of the law at Sinai. Mann wrote that when Moses broke the tablets before the Golden Calf in Exodus 32:19, "He lifted high one of the tables of the law in his mighty arms and smashed it down upon the ridiculous animal until it buckled at the knees; struck again and again with such fury that the tablet itself flew into pieces."

II

The most traumatic personal parallel between Freud and Mann was their attempt to hide their most intimate secrets, which during the Nazi period were in danger of being publicly exposed. Luckily, the potentially damaging papers were rescued by Mann's son and by one of Freud's disciples. When Mann went into exile after Hitler took power in January 1933, he asked his son Golo to go to his house in Munich, pack his diaries in a suitcase and send them to him in Switzerland. He then warned Golo: "I am counting on you to be discreet and not read any of these things!" Golo naively handed the suitcase over to their chauffeur, who offered to take it to the train station but gave it instead to the Gestapo. Fearing the worst about his homosexual revelations and early love for Paul Ehrenberg, Mann exclaimed that the Nazis would publish excerpts in their newspaper: "they will ruin everything, they will ruin me. My life will never be right again. . . . My fears now revolve first and foremost almost exclusively about this threat to my life's secrets. They are deeply serious. The consequences could be terrible, even fatal."

The *Diary* recorded that in May 1918, when Klaus was eleven years old and struggling with the changes of puberty, Mann seemed to possess a precious in-house Tadzio who matched Aschenbach's idealized adolescent in *Death in Venice*. Mann rapturously wrote, "I am really pleased to have such a beautiful boy as a son. . . . His naked bronzed body left me unsettled." Two years later, from May to July 1920, Mann revealed his forbidden feelings for Klaus. The normally undemonstrative Mann described using physical gestures and soothing words about platonic man-to-man love to justify his own rash behavior and persuade his son to accept it: "I made Klaus aware of my inclination with my caresses and by persuading him to be of good cheer." Using Klaus's nickname Mann blissfully wrote, "Eissi at the moment enchants me." Intruding on Klaus when he was naked and washing himself, he noted in an astonishing entry, "Am enraptured with Eissi: frighteningly handsome in the bath. Find it very natural that I should be in love with my son. . . . I came upon Eissi totally nude and up to some [masturbation] nonsense in Golo's bed. Deeply struck by his radiant adolescent body, overwhelming."

In the end, Mann's lawyer managed to recover the diaries that expressed his incestuous desires; they were finally published in 1977–80. When Golo read them, he learned that the homosexual attraction and longing described in Mann's fiction were based on his secret feelings. Mann's three homosexual children—Golo, Erika and Klaus—had much more in common with their father than they had ever realized.

Freud's closest friend from 1887 to 1904 was Wilhelm Fliess, a German-Jewish doctor, two years younger than he, who practiced in Berlin. Freud's unusually frank letters to Fliess—when he was analyzing himself and trying to formulate his pioneering ideas—contained grave indiscretions, mentioned his cocaine addiction and revealed his innermost thoughts. When Fliess told Freud that some of his ideas "smacked of magic, not science," their friendship was traumatically ruptured.

A review of Freud's letters to Fliess in the *New York Times* of March 17, 1985, said that Freud "held nothing back from Fliess, sharing with him fears so deep he would not tell them to his wife, confessing to Fliess his weaknesses, sexual frustrations, anxieties and hatreds. . . . The man revealed in them is as unabashedly neurotic as he is brilliant." Fliess' weird theories about the effect of rhythmical cycles on daily lives and his far-fetched connection between the nose and the genitals have been completely discredited. Frederick Crews declares that "Freud had embraced all of Fliess' ideas without showing even a flicker of critical judgment. Some of those ideas [later] struck Anna Freud and her colleagues as ridiculous. . . . His letters to Fliess suggested a mind in turmoil, lurching among half-articulated brainstorms without engagement in consecutive reasoning."

In December 1936—the year of Mann's second essay and his two congenial visits to Freud—Marie Bonaparte announced that she had purchased the 250 letters from Freud to Fliess, from the collector who'd bought them from Fliess' widow, for $480. Grateful and relieved, Freud poured out his feelings to Marie in two letters of January 1937:

Our correspondence was of the most intimate nature, as you can surmise. It would have been most painful to have it fall into the hands of strangers. It is therefore an extraordinary labor of love that you have gotten hold of them and removed them from danger. . . .

They indicate all the presentiments and blind alleys of the budding psychoanalysis, and are also quite personal in this case [his self-analysis]. There are also not a few mentions of intimate processes and relationships; things like the reproaches through which the friendship went to pieces are especially distressing in retrospect.

When Marie told Freud that she had the letters, he asked her (as Mann had asked Golo) not to read them. He offered to pay half the sale price, but she feared he would destroy them and refused payment. They are now with Marie's papers in the Library of Congress.

Freud expressed his deepest feelings about love and death in a cathartic letter to Hungarian medical-psychoanalytic friends on June 11, 1923. His favorite grandson, Heinele Halberstadt (1918–1923), orphaned and in delicate health, had been taken from his aunt and uncle in Hamburg, and sent to Vienna to be cared for by Freud. He described the child's agonizing death:

> He was indeed an enchanting little fellow, and I myself was aware of never having loved a human being, certainly never a child, so much. . . . This child fell ill again two weeks ago, temperature between 102 and 104, headaches, no clear local symptoms, for a long time no diagnosis, and finally the slow but sure realisation that he has a miliary [widespread] tuberculosis, in fact that the child is lost. He is now lying in a coma with paresis [paralysis]. . . . I find this loss very hard to bear. I don't think I have ever experienced such grief; perhaps my own sickness contributes to the shock.

Schur added, "afterward he remarked repeatedly that this event had killed something in him, so that he was never able to form new attachments" for fear of suffering another devastating loss. Freud's emotional pain was intensified by the first symptoms of the cigar-induced cancer of the jaw that would kill him in September 1939. He thought he'd been punished for loving the boy too much, and felt guilty, as a grandfather and doctor, that he'd not been able to protect and save him. He must have bitterly reflected that an old and sick man like himself could live while the young and promising child had to die.

In *Civilization and Its Discontents* Freud wrote that "one day someone will venture to embark upon a pathology of cultural communities," and Mann did this in his allegory of Nazism in *Doctor Faustus* (1947). Freud's letter about the death of his grandson from tuberculosis in June 1923 has an extraordinary resemblance to Mann's description in that novel of Nepo's death from spinal meningitis five years later in June 1928. Mann fully dramatizes the episode that Freud briefly recounts. He portrays Nepo's appearance, speech and protracted death in ghastly clinical detail. As with Freud's favorite grandson, the enchanting and angelic five-year-old is sent to his relative, his Uncle Adrian Leverkühn, in order to improve his frail health, but instead suffers an agonizing death.

An "exceptionally beloved child," like the biblical Joseph, Nepo gives the impression of a fairy princeling, "of a guest from a finer, tinier sphere." Adrian is profoundly touched by "the sweet depths of that azure upturned smile" and by his delightful speech: "Well, you are glad I did come, yes?" Nepo's spinal meningitis resembles Adrian's cerebral meningitis, and Adrian's cold look glazes the clear blue eyes of Nepo, who cannot bear light and sound and retreats into a darkened room. These warning symptoms are followed by fever, vomiting, skull-splitting headaches, violent convulsions, paralysis of the eye muscles, rigidity of the neck and "twenty-two hours of shrieking, writhing torture"— then by a coma and a gnashing of teeth. Mann's narrator concludes, "that strangely seraphic little being was taken from this earth . . . in the harshest, the most incomprehensible cruelty I have ever witnessed" and mourns "the almost complete powerlessness of medical science in the face of this fatal onslaught."

Like Freud, Adrian has never loved anyone so much and never experienced such grief. Nepo's death has also killed a precious feeling inside him and he could never love anyone again. Adrian had agreed, in his Faustian pact with the devil which gave him twenty-four years of musical genius, that he would never form a human attachment or love any human being. So the devil punishes him for loving Nepo and he feels guilty about causing the child's death. It's unlikely that Mann ever read Freud's letter of June 1923. The character of Nepo was based on his own favorite grandson, Frido Mann, who did not suffer and die in real life, and the fictional description of his death horrified the boy's parents. Mann's genius as a writer enabled him—in one of the most powerful scenes he ever wrote—to dramatize the child's illness and death as if he himself, like Freud, had actually experienced them.

The meetings of Mann and Freud, during Mann's political exile and their personal danger, created one of the great intellectual and emotional friendships of the 1930s. Mann suppressed his doubts about Freud's fantastic speculations on Napoleon and Moses, abandoned his characteristic irony and remained extremely reverential to the older man. Freud graciously welcomed Mann's heartfelt tributes and admired the inherent nobility of the North German literary genius. Most significantly, Mann's adoption of Freud's concepts of sexual repression and instinctual triumphs enabled him to hide the fictional expression of his own homoerotic feelings. Mann's repressed homosexuality led not to neurosis and death, but to his greatest work: his portrayal of the secret emotions of Tonio and Hans Hansen in "Tonio Kröger," Aschenbach and Tadzio in *Death in Venice*, Castorp and Pribislav Hippe in *The Magic Mountain*, Cipolla and Mario in "Mario and the Magician," Adrian and Rudi Schwerdtfeger in *Doctor Faustus*.

3

ANNE FRANK

—— AND ——

AUDREY HEPBURN

I

The glamorous, famous and wealthy actress Audrey Hepburn, who died in her luxurious Swiss mansion in 1993, would seem to have nothing in common with Anne Frank, the Jewish teenager who died obscurely in a Nazi death camp in 1945. But they were born less than six weeks apart, in May and June 1929: Anne in Frankfurt, Audrey in Brussels. They spent their traumatic childhoods, separated by sixty miles between Amsterdam and Arnhem, in Nazi-occupied Holland. Unlike Anne, Audrey survived the war and went on to receive the adulation that Anne had dreamed of and only acquired after her death.

Anne's German father, Otto Frank, who'd been an officer in World War I, foresaw the Nazi threat to the Jews. In the fall of 1933, after Hitler took power, he left Frankfurt for Amsterdam where he had business interests. But he did not foresee the German invasion of Holland, which had been neutral in World War I and in 1918 had provided refuge for the deposed German Kaiser. Despite being trapped in Holland, Otto hoped to keep his family safe. He bought furnishings, clothing and food for the 100-square-foot Secret Annex. It was above his jam-producing business on the main floor, high over the street but psychologically underground. Otto took his family into hiding, along with three friends, when his older daughter Margot was suddenly ordered to work in a German labor camp. His company continued to operate during the war, run by gentile employees who kept the family supplied with news, books and food. The family stayed together but had no way to escape. If detected, they would all be arrested. Otto's desperate attempts to get life-saving visas had all been rejected. If Anne had escaped to America there would have been no *Diary*, but she was brilliantly talented and would certainly have written more mature work.

Anne and Audrey, who spent the war years in Holland from the age of ten to fifteen, had striking similarities in experience and character. If Audrey had been Jewish, she would have suffered the same fate as her soul sister. Anne wanted to be a great writer, Audrey trained for years to be a great ballerina. Eager for distractions in her crowded and claustrophobic space, Anne wrote: "I'm currently going through a dance and ballet craze and am diligently practicing my dance steps every evening. I've made an ultra-modern dance costume out of a lacy lavender slip. . . . I've tried to turn my tennis shoes into ballet slippers, but with no success." In the same makeshift way, Audrey's dance friend said, "we used to wear ballet shoes that were like wooden shoes—very heavy. Audrey was quite ingenious. She used to make tights from Ace bandages and dye them by soaking them in water with red crepe paper." Anne decorated the narrow walls of her bedroom with pin-ups of movie stars. If Audrey had been a star in the 1940s, her photo would have joined Anne's collection.

Both girls, extremely pretty and thin, nearly starved during the "hunger-winter" of 1944–45. Anne sometimes ate only boiled lettuce and rotted potatoes. Audrey subsisted on watery soup, green bread made from peas and cooked grass with nettles. They were terrified and in danger when the British, fighting toward Germany, bombed their cities in 1944. Anne hid with her family and friends, Audrey helped hide a downed British paratrooper; both were afraid they would be discovered and shot.

Anne recorded that the Nazis exacted retribution for resistance: "leading citizens—innocent people—are taken prisoner to await their execution. If the Gestapo can't find the saboteur, they simply grab five hostages and line them up against the wall." Audrey's Uncle Otto, one of five distinguished hostages, was actually shot on August 15, 1942, in retaliation for Dutch Underground attacks on Nazi soldiers. She once was forced to see a horrific incident that was very like the execution of her uncle: "I did once witness some men set against the wall and shot for some kind of reprisal. They used to make people stop." They couldn't walk on and had to watch the murder.

Anne and Audrey were extrovert, clever and resourceful, attractive, gifted and eager for fame. They worried about their poor food, tattered clothing and physical appearance. They hid from oppressive authority yet affirmed their independent existence. In the war years they began as precocious children, but developed rapidly and reached a new self-awareness. They felt hopeless passivity and psychological anguish, uncertainty and fear, and alternated uneasily between optimism and despair. Deprived of normal childhoods, they were forced into maturity by violent events. Their emotional and intellectual progress was closely connected to contemporary history and the long years of war.

Otto Frank, the first editor of Anne's *Diary of a Young Girl* (1947), sanitized the text and obscured Anne's adolescence and puberty by cutting out all her detailed sexual descriptions in the first, expurgated edition. Anne, who felt a surge of sexual awakening and physical desire, vividly recalls her developing breasts and strangely gratifying periods, discovering the truth (by reading and talking) about sexual organs and intercourse. She fell in love with the teenaged boy who was also in hiding in the Secret Annex and shared sexual secrets with him. Audrey, concentrating on ballet and survival, had no sex life in those years and later vicariously experienced those turbulent emotions when she read the *Diary*.

Anne hid in the Secret Annex from the age of thirteen to fifteen, July 1942 to August 4, 1944, when her family was betrayed by a Dutch informer. The main suspect was her father's warehouseman, the sinister thief Willem van Maaren. She was arrested by an Austrian SS sergeant and three Dutch Security policemen, and spent the next month in Westerbork, a holding camp in northeast Holland for Jews destined for extermination in Poland. In Auschwitz, Anne survived the initial selection for the gas chamber and was reprieved for slave labor. As the Russian army raced toward the camp, the Nazis tried to destroy all the evidence of extermination and blew up the gas chambers and crematoria. On October 28 Anne and Margot, separated from their parents, were moved west to Bergen-Belsen near Hannover, Germany, where the survivors of Auschwitz were killed.

Anne's *Diary* ended on August 1, 1944, three days before her arrest. Other sources provide the details of the horrific, almost unbearable extinction of her life. Emaciated and ragged, tormented by fleas and lice, ulcerated and febrile, the frail and sensitive child saw her sister die. Believing her parents were dead, though Otto was saved by a doctor, she lost her will to live. She died in March 1945 of typhus, an infectious disease carried by lice, a more prolonged and even more agonizing death than by cyanide gas.

It's amazing that the frail and starved Anne lived for as long as six months in two death camps. Had she been able to hide for only one month longer, Hitler's best-known victim might have survived the war. After hiding in Amsterdam for twenty-five months, she was arrested nine months before the liberation of Holland. On September 3 she was loaded on the very *last* train from Holland to Auschwitz. In November 1944 she was transferred from Poland to Bergen-Belsen, two months before the Russian liberation of Auschwitz. She died in March 1945 only *one month* before the British liberated Bergen-Belsen.

Edgar Allan Poe explained the poignant appeal of Anne's tragic fate in "The Philosophy of Composition," "The death of a beautiful woman is, unquestionably, the most poetical topic in the world." The Dutch have fully exploited Anne's tragedy, and the Anne Frank House, visited by millions of people, is now the second most popular tourist attraction (after the Rijksmuseum) in Amsterdam. But anti-Semitism was virulent in wartime Holland, whose government actively assisted the Nazis in killing the Jews. Anne was betrayed by a Dutchman and arrested by the Dutch police, who also loaded Jews into cattle cars. The Dutch Commandant at Westerbork was a sadist who tortured the Jews. Ian Buruma writes that 98,000 Dutch Jews, "75 per cent of Jews in the Netherlands, were taken away to be murdered, a higher percentage than anywhere else in Western Europe." In nearby Denmark by contrast, when the people and government actively resisted Nazi brutality, there were no mass arrests and deportations to extermination camps, and only 120 Danish Jews died. On May 4, 1944, Anne fiercely expressed the major theme of her *Diary*: "There's a destructive urge in people, the urge to rage, murder and kill."

II

Audrey's English father, Joseph Hepburn-Ruston, worked for Maclaine and Watson, tin merchants in Brussels, where she was born on May 14, 1929. Both girls adored their fathers. Otto, an ideal father, did all he could to save his wife and daughters, and was the only family member to survive the death camps. Joseph abandoned his family when Audrey was six and returned to England. She mourned his disappearance and called it "the most traumatic event in my life, a tragedy from which I don't think I've ever recovered. I worshiped him and missed him terribly from the day he disappeared." It's significant that many of her leading men in movies—Gregory Peck, Humphrey Bogart, Gary

Cooper, Cary Grant, Rex Harrison and, metaphorically, God the Father in *The Nun's Story*—were older father figures.

Audrey's parents were both fanatically pro-Nazi. Her mother, the Baroness Ella van Heemstra, whose family wealth came from trading in the Dutch East Indies, had two sons by her first marriage. She was honored by a personal interview with Hitler in Munich in May 1935. A poor judge of his character, she wrote about her ecstatic experience in the newspaper of the British Union of Fascists: "Hitler's deep blue eyes could have bored through me, such was their power. He was so pale, so composed, as he smiled that enigmatic smile, full of humility." Audrey's father, considered a traitor, was arrested in June 1940, and spent the rest of the war in London prisons and detention camps on the Isle of Man. He was released in April 1945 and moved to Ireland, which had been neutral in the war.

The slender, delicate Audrey was the complete physical opposite of the typical blond, blue-eyed and hefty Dutch woman. She was cared for by nannies and educated by private tutors on the cloistered family estate. An English citizen, she was sent to boarding school in England in 1934, but her mother, thinking that Arnhem would be safer than London, brought her home when the war broke out in September 1939. For the same reason, Otto Frank brought his family from Germany to Holland.

Audrey had taken dance lessons throughout her childhood. In July 1941, still influenced by her mother and mad to dance, the twelve-year-old began to perform publicly for German soldiers in Arnhem. In December she appeared onstage with her two older half-brothers for a Nazi-sponsored Mozart celebration. She later, quite understandably, deleted these episodes from her résumé.

But the young and impressionable Audrey had the courage to reject her parents' pro-Nazi beliefs and soon worked actively for the Dutch Underground. In 1942 Audrey shifted loyalty and began to give secret concerts to raise money for the Dutch Resistance. The innocent-looking girl, speaking perfect English and appearing like an Angel of Mercy, bravely risked her life by carrying hidden messages and food to British fliers who'd been shot down on bombing missions to Germany. Her family, now pro-Dutch, also hid a British paratrooper in the cellar of their house. Robert Matzen notes in *Dutch Girl: Audrey Hepburn and World War II*: "harboring an Englishman provided a direct, unbreakable connection between Audrey and Anne Frank. Audrey said that Anne's diary 'paralleled so much of what I had experienced.'" She also feared the paratrooper (like Anne in the Secret Annex) would be discovered and she would be shot. In March 1945—the month Anne died and two months before the liberation of Holland—Audrey was stopped by German soldiers rounding up young women to serve in their military kitchens. When they grabbed other women and were momentarily distracted, she managed to slip away.

Like Miranda in *The Tempest*, Audrey could say, "I have suffered with those I saw suffer." At the Arnhem railroad station, she recalled, "I saw families with little children, with babies, herded into meat wagons—trains of big wooden vans with just a little slat open at the top and all those faces peering out at you. And on the platform were soldiers herding more Jewish families with their poor little bundles and small children." This is exactly what happened to Anne after she was arrested, and Audrey might have seen her in the cattle car if she had lived in Amsterdam.

Worse came in the Battle of Arnhem from September 17 to 26, 1944, when most of the city was destroyed. General Bernard Montgomery dropped three airborne divisions behind enemy lines to secure the bridges on three rivers and prepare for the invasion of Germany. A military historian described the disaster. Strong German resistance barred the "Allied advance and bad weather prevented dropping reinforcements or supplies. Ringed by close-in artillery and mortar fire, with food and ammunition exhausted, and forced away from the Lek bridge, the defense collapsed. Some 2,200 survivors were evacuated across the river in assault boats during the night leaving 7,000 men behind them killed, wounded or captured."

Conditions were also terrible on May 4, 1945 when the Germans were finally driven out of Holland. Like Anne in the Secret Annex, Audrey and her mother "were in our cellar, where we'd been for weeks. Our area was being liberated practically house to house, and there was lots of shooting and shelling from over the river and constant bombing: explosions going on all night." After the agony of starvation and bombardment, fear of discovery and death during the war, Audrey finally felt the joy of seeing a free Holland. Anne died two months earlier and never experienced that happiness.

In October 1945 Audrey and her mother moved from Arnhem to Amsterdam. In another serendipitous connection, they lived below the apartment of the editor working on Anne's soon-to-be-released *Diary*. In 1947, when Audrey read the galleys in the original Dutch, they seemed to express her own deepest and most powerful emotions. She remembered "there were floods of tears. I became hysterical. . . . In this child's words I was reading about what was inside me and is still there. It was a catharsis for me. The child who was locked up in four walls had written a full report of everything I'd experienced and felt."

The *Diary* had a complex publishing history. After the Dutch police had ransacked the Annex, the manuscript was rescued by chance by one of Otto's employees who gave it to him when he returned from Auschwitz to Amsterdam in June 1945. He edited and typed the *Diary*, which was accepted by the Dutch publisher Contact and appeared in June 1947. It is ironic that Otto, who suppressed 35 percent of the original text, is listed as the leading coeditor of the "Definitive" edition in 1991, published eleven years after his death.

Like the original response to the manuscripts of Proust's *Swann's Way*, Orwell's *Animal Farm* and Lampedusa's *The Leopard*, publishers were blind to the merits of the *Diary*, which was rejected by sixteen English-language firms in Europe and America. The book that spoke for millions of child-victims had universal appeal and was finally published by Doubleday in New York in 1952 and by Valentine Mitchell in London in 1958. Since then it has been translated into seventy languages and sold more than thirty million copies. Anne left no grave, no physical remains of any kind—not even her death date. But aware of her extraordinary gift, she declared, "I want to go on living even after my death!" and was granted posthumous fame. Her late entry, "If God lets me live I'll make my voice heard, I'll go out into the world and work for mankind!" deeply affected and inspired Audrey. As goodwill ambassador to the United Nations Children's Fund from 1989 to 1992, she "worked for mankind," visiting, comforting and raising money for sick and starving children in Africa, South America and Southeast Asia.

Audrey was the only great star who had an aristocratic background and who suffered during the Nazi occupation of her country. In 1957, at the height of her fame and earning half a million dollars for each film, she was offered the part of Anne in the forthcoming movie, based on the sanitized and successful stage play, *The Diary of Anne Frank*. That year Otto Frank met her in Switzerland and urged her to accept the role of Anne. In their photograph Audrey, with slightly open mouth, dressed in a plain black sweater and scarf, looks amazingly like the handsome, smiling Otto, wearing a smart gray suit and tie. Audrey, who saw the concentration-camp number tattooed on his arm, wrote an idealized, self-reflective portrait: "He was a beautiful-looking man, very fine, a sort of transparent face, very sensitive. Incapable of talking about Anne without extreme feeling. He had a need to talk about her. He struck me as somebody who'd been purged by fire. There was something so spiritual about his face. He'd been there and back." In their emotional encounter, Otto found his long-dead daughter, Audrey found her long-lost father.

Despite Otto's pleas, Audrey refused the role for several persuasive reasons. She didn't want to personally benefit by exploiting Anne's life and death. She didn't think she could convincingly play a thirteen-year-old girl when she was twenty-eight. Most important, she didn't want to relive the horrors of the Nazi Occupation that would revive many agonizing memories. When she reread the *Diary*, she emphasized, "I was so destroyed by it again that I said I couldn't deal with it. It's as if this had happened to my sister. I couldn't play my sister's life. It's too close, and in a way, she was a soul sister."

Twenty years later Audrey was offered a role in the film about the Battle of Arnhem, *A Bridge Too Far*, but couldn't bear to revive the memories of hiding the British paratrooper and the destruction of her beloved city. In 1990, however, she gave a series of readings "From the Diary of Anne Frank," accompanied by the music of the Jewish composer Michael Tilson Thomas, in Philadelphia, Chicago and Houston.

Anne's *Diary* brilliantly describes the intellectual, emotional and sexual development of a young girl under extreme stress, what Ian Buruma calls "the pathos of innocence brutally defiled." Anne expresses a dominant theme in modern literature—*loss*—her lost childhood, lost literary genius and lost life. Audrey poignantly concluded:

> Anne's life was very much a parallel to mine. We were born the same year, lived in the same country, experienced the same war, except she was locked up and I was on the outside. Reading her diary was like reading my own experiences from her point of view. . . . It was in a different corner of Holland, but all the events I experienced were so incredibly accurately described by her—not just what was going on on

the outside, but what was going on on the inside of a young girl starting to be a woman.

Anne's acute perception of herself applies with equal force to Audrey: "I have an odd way of sometimes, as it were, being able to see myself through someone else's eyes."

4

ARTHUR RIMBAUD

—— AND ——

PAUL VERLAINE

I

In a notorious and influential letter of May 15, 1871, to his publisher-friend Paul Demeny, the sixteen-year-old provincial high-school dropout Arthur Rimbaud boldly defined his vision of poetic creativity:

> The Poet makes himself a *seer* by a long, gigantic and rational *derangement* of *all the senses*. All forms of love, suffering, and madness. He searches himself. He exhausts all poisons in himself and keeps only their quintessences. Unspeakable torture where he needs all his faith, all his superhuman strength, where he becomes among all men the great patient, the great criminal, the one accursed—and the supreme Scholar!—Because he reaches the *unknown*! Since he cultivated his soul, rich already, more than any man! He reaches the unknown, and when, bewildered, he ends by losing the intelligence of his visions, he has seen them. Let him die as he leaps through unheard of and unnamable things.

Like his prophetic soul mate William Blake, Rimbaud believed, "I must Create a System, or be enslav'd by another Man's." The same letter contained his most cryptic pronouncement: "*I* is someone else" ("*Je* est un autre"). Rimbaud not only advocated deliberate suffering and self-destruction, but also supposed the existence of two selves: a wild, creative self and an everyday self, cowardly, brutish and hemmed in by social restrictions.

Rimbaud's sophistication, poetic talent and extraordinary ideas exemplify the mystery of genius. A brilliant young scholar in an excellent *lycée*, one of the best in France, he was intellectually confident. But his childhood left him emotionally damaged and mentally troubled. He came from a severely deprived background in the bleak town of Charleville, in northeast France, near the Belgian border. His parents—a dashing army captain who'd fought in the Crimean War and a pious peasant who laboriously tilled the fields—were dramatically mismatched. The husband soon abandoned his family, but briefly returned every few years to impregnate his wife and burden her with another child. Rimbaud inherited wanderlust and courage from his father, bitterness and rage from his mother, who called herself a widow while her husband was still alive. Impoverished yet fiercely proud, she refused to allow her son to play with other children, bullied him mercilessly and never showed him the least affection.

Rimbaud survived by cultivating a spirit of revolt, and poured his anger and disgust into poetry. He not only instinctively hated the falsity and rottenness of family, school, politics and religion—all ruled, in his view, by fat-bellied dignitaries and stupefied by the constraints of bourgeois behavior—but also set out to undermine his own health, reason and reputation. He believed morality was a weakness of the brain, despised his birthplace and was revolted by its dullness. He thought "my hometown is the most idiotic of all provincial towns." He was stifled by his family and refused to finish high school, where he felt he had nothing more to learn. He made several attempts to run away from home, culminating in his third trip to Paris, where he began his torturous three-year relationship with Verlaine, poetic mentor, parent-substitute and lover. Rimbaud's adolescent precocity and rebellion coincided with the social revolution of the Paris Commune in 1870 and the avant-garde discoveries of the Impressionist artists. He has had more exegetes than the Talmud, more scholia than the works of Aristotle, and his ideas have had an enduring effect on twentieth-century literature.

Rimbaud's decision to derange the senses, including the most basic human emotions, seems willful and pathological, but was also rational and deliberate. He had a program: he would take drink, drugs, even poison; he would endure unspeakable tortures, commit acts of violence, become a criminal, risk losing his poetic insights, even risk death. During his years with Verlaine (1871–73), Rimbaud put his program into practice, experiencing exhaustion and starvation, filth and debauchery, degradation and disease, violence and destruction, while heightening his chaotic state with hashish and absinthe. After mastering the classics of literature and history, Rimbaud reversed centuries of cultural tradition. Instead of assuming that the artist's task is to create order out of experience, Rimbaud believed the disorder of the poet's mind was sacred. The visionary yet analytic poet, determined to grasp the unknown, tragically yet joyfully destroyed himself in order to escape from ordinary life, enter a higher reality and gain superhuman poetical power. This idea of the sacrifice of sanity to attain creative genius, familiar from the Faust legend, was not new. It originated in the *Phaedrus*, where Plato observed, "If a man comes to the door of poetry untouched by the madness of the Muses, believing that technique alone will make him a good poet, he and his sane compositions never reach perfection, but are utterly eclipsed by the performances of the inspired madman. . . . Madness, provided it comes as the gift of heaven, is the channel by which we receive the greatest blessings." But while Plato's poet passively waits to be touched and transformed by the *furor divinus*, "a gift of heaven," Rimbaud's seer actively induces his own state of madness, which is more closely related to hell.

Similarly, Rimbaud's division of the self—which W. H. Frohock called "the 'Je' who is 'autre' and the 'je' who is not"—contradicted a long literary tradition, in which writers create an artistic identity and take pride in their integrity and absolute self-mastery. The Hebrew Bible set the pattern. In Exodus 3:14, God rather solipsisticly told Moses, "I am that I am." In the early sixteenth century Sir Thomas Wyatt asserted his unchanging identity: "I am as I am and so will I be." In *Cinna* (1640), Pierre Corneille's Augustus followed Wyatt by forcefully confirming his own sense of himself: "I'm master of myself as of the world; / I am that, I choose to be that" ("*Je le suis, je veux l'être*").

Rimbaud's alienated and divided self, which allowed him to observe and describe his own disintegration, was inspired by all the doubled fictional characters in E. T. A. Hoffman and Edgar Poe, and foreshadowed all the divided souls from Fyodor Dostoyevsky, through Robert Louis Stevenson, to Antonin Artaud. In his bold but enigmatic pronouncement Rimbaud imagined himself both the pathetic invalid and the clinician diagnosing his own pathology. He twisted and extinguished the flamboyant, egotistical selfhood—dominant from Lord Byron to Oscar Wilde—that began in the Romantic era and ran through the nineteenth century. But Rimbaud's self-alienation, like Plato's *furor divinus*, also had a positive aspect. He now freed his other self to create or destroy. The "Je," inspired and transformed by the imagination, brought his poetry into being.

II

In 1871 Rimbaud had tried to escape Charleville by running away to various households, but quickly abused the hospitality he received and was sent packing. On his first visit to Paris he was sent home as a vagrant. In April he went to Paris again but, ragged and homeless in the chaos of the Commune, he was raped and humiliated by a gang of mocking soldiers. This most traumatic moment of Rimbaud's young life was the subject of his shocking poem, "The Stolen Heart":

> Under the jeering of the soldiers
> Who break out laughing
> My sad heart drools at the poop,
> My heart covered with tobacco-spit!

Like T. E. Lawrence, who suffered a similar homosexual assault when captured by Turks behind enemy lines during World War I, Rimbaud felt that his inner being had been polluted. As Lawrence wrote, "the passing days confirmed how in Deraa that night the citadel of my integrity had been irrevocably lost." At the same time, however, Rimbaud perversely gloried in his degradation.

But he was determined to get back to Paris, where he aimed to begin his career as a poet. Bored and penniless, Rimbaud wrote to Verlaine, enclosing some of his poems. Verlaine, instantly convinced of his genius, invited to him stay with him in Paris. Verlaine offered him exactly what he wanted: money, freedom, stimulating talk, useful contacts with poets and editors. Rimbaud and Verlaine, the first open and defiant gay couple in literary history, then began a tumultuous relationship that ended when Verlaine shot Rimbaud and went to prison.

Rimbaud was a thin, slight, scruffy and nondescript boy, but everyone noticed his intensely blue eyes, which looked like the bright sky when seen through the hollow orbs of a skull. In his pioneering chapter on Rimbaud in *The Cursed Poets* (1884), Verlaine described him in 1871 as "tall, well-built, almost athletic, with the perfectly oval face of an exiled angel, with tousled fair chestnut hair and unnervingly blue eyes." In his poem *"Crimen Amoris"* (the crime of love), written in prison two years later, Verlaine repeated the angelic imagery, substituted a crown of flowers for a crown of thorns and idealized his young lover:

Now the most beautiful of all the evil angels,
Sixteen years old under his crown of flowers.
His arms crossed above his necklaces and dangling fringe,
He dreams, his eyes full of flames and tears.

Verlaine's wife, Mathilde, was the same age as Rimbaud. She and Rimbaud were still in their teens, ten years younger than Verlaine and attracted to his poetry rather than his person. Mathilde's first impression of Rimbaud (retrospectively recorded) expressed disdain for her crude rival. She was not taken in by his *beaux yeux*: "He was a large sturdy lad with a reddish face: a peasant. He looked like a young schoolkid who had grown too fast. His trousers were too short for him, and you could see his blue cotton socks, clearly his mother's handiwork. His hair was tousled, his necktie stringy, his clothes untidy. His eyes were blue, rather beautiful, but they had a shifty look which, indulgently, we took for shyness."

Mathilde was pregnant, and just before the birth of his biological son Verlaine acquired a symbolic son who came to dominate him and wreck his life. Rimbaud's deliberately offensive behavior—he broke precious things, stole an ivory crucifix, defiled the house and insulted the hosts—made Baudelaire's famous dissipations seem almost genteel. His bizarre behavior, bordering on insanity, reminded one observer of "an orangutan escaped from the zoo." Rimbaud combined the manic malevolence of Dostoyevsky's Underground Man with the danger of Coleridge's demon lover in "Kubla Khan": "And all should cry, Beware! Beware! / his flashing eyes, his floating hair!"

Rimbaud's iconoclastic conversation fascinated and terrified Verlaine's bohemian poet-friends, and he repaid their interest by despising them. They tolerated Verlaine's homosexual relationship, but could not bear the outrageous behavior of this latter-day Villon. The critic W. H. Frohock called Rimbaud a boorish "juvenile delinquent with deviated tastes and possibly homicidal tendencies. . . . He was openly and aggressively offensive even to the associates who had befriended him. He lived parasitically on his friends, absorbed as much absinthe as he could, experimented with narcotics, tried to knife his companion, paraded his homosexuality, and broke up Verlaine's marriage." As Charles Doughty wrote of the Arabs, Rimbaud—a volatile mixture of shit (one of his favorite words) and striving for the heights of poetry—was like "a man sitting in a cloaca to the eyes, and whose brows touch heaven."

Verlaine didn't have to derange his senses to keep up with Rimbaud: he was already quite deranged when they first met. He also, like Rimbaud, had two very distinct selves: rational when sober, violent when drunk from absinthe. He was so completely deranged that he even beat up his beloved mother, who'd do anything for him—give him money, come running whenever she heard his pathetic pleas, rescue him from the clutches of Rimbaud, even forgive his unkind blows. His behavior was just as barbaric as Rimbaud's. As his wife's pregnancy advanced and she rejected his sexual advances, he followed the ancient French custom and tried to seduce their maid. When Mathilde reproved him, he pulled her out of bed and threw her onto the floor. Hopelessly drunk at three o'clock one morning, he threatened to set fire to some live cartridges and blow up the flat. His mother-in-law remonstrated with him and, weeping repentant tears, he proclaimed his eternal love for his wife. He usually ignored their infant son, Georges, but when Mathilde refused to give him more money, he threw the three-month-old baby against the wall and then tried to choke her. When he was drunk and his mother would not hand over more cash for more drink, Verlaine broke open the cupboard in which she carefully preserved the fetuses of her miscarriages. As the jars crashed and burst on the floor, he continued to smash his pickled siblings with his walking stick.

Rimbaud felt he had a great deal to offer Verlaine, that there was a rescue operation on both sides. This filthy, impudent teenager would liberate him from the fetters and confinement of boring bourgeois life with a vain and foolish wife and her oppressive parents, who lived in the same building and often broke up their fights. For the twenty-seven-year-old Verlaine, a far weaker character despite his seniority, Rimbaud provided the intense gratifications of companionable youth, adventure, drink, sex, poetry, freedom, travel and danger. In *Illuminations* he exclaimed: "In deepest sincerity, I had pledged to convert him back into his primitive state of a sun-child. . . . Poor brother! What terrible nights I owed him! 'I had no deep feeling for the affair. I played on his weakness. Through my fault, we would return to exile and slavery.' He believed

I had a very queer form of bad luck and innocence, and he added upsetting reasons." He repeatedly warned Verlaine to "remember what you were before you met me," cut him adrift from family and friends, encouraged his alcoholic excesses and turned him into a living version of Rimbaud's *bateau ivre*.

Both from the Ardennes region and sons of army officers, Rimbaud and Verlaine were even more uncongenial and tempestuous roommates than Van Gogh and Gauguin. (Both couples experienced a violent act, a sudden break in their friendship and a radical change in their lives.) Rimbaud brought all his opposing selves into his relations with Verlaine, and was at once chummy and caustic, flattering and sadistic, dominant and degraded, exalted and depraved, faithful and treacherous, angelic and demonic, radiant and disgusting, tender and violent, sexy and revolting, stimulating and cruel. Like their contemporaries, Monet and the French Impressionists—who moved from the northern suburbs of Paris, down the Seine to Rouen and the Normandy coast, and across the Channel to England—Rimbaud and Verlaine always headed north, returned to their roots in the Ardennes, fled into Belgium and crossed the sea to Dover. Turned on by exciting departures and sad farewells in railroad stations and harbors, they often indulged in dramatic scenes just before a train or boat left for a foreign country.

Verlaine, from the beginning besotted with Rimbaud, even suggested an absurd *ménage à trois* with his estranged wife. The poets flaunted their sexual connection, and a French newspaper reported that Verlaine had been seen in public "with a charming young thing, Mlle. Rimbaud, on his arm." Verlaine rashly told the guards at the Belgian frontier that "we make love like tigers" and showed them the knife wounds Rimbaud had made on his body. The Belgian police then recorded that "the two lovers have been seen in Brussels, openly practicing their love."

Their "love" was a struggle for domination, both physical and intellectual. Sadomasochistically boasting about his red badge of courage, Verlaine noted "the happiness of bleeding on the chest of a friend." Rimbaud described himself as "convulsed with wounds [and] racked by tortures," though he pronounced himself repelled by his notably unattractive lover. The author Alphonse Daudet heard Rimbaud, not known for his personal hygiene, exclaim that he preferred to remain the passive partner: "[Verlaine] can satisfy himself on me as much as he likes. But he wants *me* to practise on *him*! Not on your life! He's far too filthy. And he's got horrible skin!" But when Verlaine was arrested in July 1873 for shooting Rimbaud and continuing to threaten him with the gun, the Belgian police doctor who examined him concluded, "Verlaine bears on his person traces of habitual pederasty, both active and passive."

To get even for his sexual degradation Rimbaud repeatedly mocked Verlaine's ugliness, cowardice, toadyism, family connections and religious beliefs (which resurfaced in prison). Rimbaud called him despicable and weak and, just before the breaking point, goaded Verlaine by asking, as he returned with their meager provisions, "have you any idea how ridiculous you look with your bottle of [olive] oil in one hand and your [piece of] fish in the other?" After one of their explosive quarrels and separations, Rimbaud challenged him by asking, "Do you think life will be happier with others than it was with me? *Think about this!*—oh, certainly not! With me alone you can be free." Verlaine responded by pathetically crawling back to the harsh comfort of his savage messiah. "Love me, protect and trust me," he wrote. "Being very weak, I have a great need of kindness."

The shooting incident in Brussels was more operatic than tragic. One bullet hit Rimbaud in the wrist, the other went into the wall of their hotel room. On hearing the shots Verlaine's mother, anxiously on guard next door, clumsily tried to help Rimbaud, whose wrist was bleeding profusely. Dazed and out of control, Verlaine sobbed on the bed, recovered slightly, gave Rimbaud the revolver and told him to "unload it in my temple."

III

Amid all this stimulating *Sturm und Drang* the two poets produced an astonishing amount of impressive work. Nothing in Rimbaud's life, except his genius, explains his volcanic outburst of brilliant poetry from 1869 to 1874. Raymond Radiguet had a much shorter life, but was not as precocious as Rimbaud. The lives of other poets—Chatterton, Keats and Plath—were cut short by disease or suicide, but none of them reached Rimbaud's impressive achievement while still in his teens. Rimbaud also hurt Verlaine into poetry. A. E. Carter noted that "from the standpoint of poetry [Rimbaud] was not merely beneficial but starkly necessary. Verlaine would have been a minor poet had they never met. He forced Paul to choose: was he to be a worthy civil-servant, with a wife, children, and one or two pretty volumes to his credit, or a great poet whose work, at its best, touches the very summit of the art?" In one monstrous and miraculous year, from July 1872 to July 1873, Verlaine composed *Romances Without Words* and Rimbaud wrote *Illuminations* and *A Season in Hell*. In his account of his personal hell just before and after the shooting in Brussels, Rimbaud rejected the entire French literary tradition as well as all rational thought and, with psychedelic mania, reinvented the concept of poetry for the modern age.

A Season in Hell, especially the section called "Delirium" where Rimbaud portrays Verlaine as "The Foolish Virgin" and himself as "The Infernal Bridegroom," parodies their life together as an unreal and perverse form of marriage. And he misleadingly characterizes himself as the passive follower and Verlaine as his demon lover: "He was almost a child. . . . His mysteriously delicate feelings had seduced me. I forgot all my human duty to follow him. What a life! Real life is absent. We are not in the world. I go where he goes. I have to. And often he flies into a rage at *me, poor me*. The Demon! He is a demon, you know. *He is not a man.*"

Not all their poetry reached an exalted summit. In a shocking volume called *Defilements*, not printed until 1923, Rimbaud, spurred on by Verlaine, indulged his taste for the pornographic and the scatological. In "Our Backsides are not theirs," he declaimed:

> Oh! to be naked like that, and look for joy and rest,
> My head turned toward my companion's glorious part
> And both of us free murmuring sobs.

In the lubricious "Dark and Wrinkled" ("*Sonnet du trou du cul*"), Rimbaud and Verlaine, writing together, evoked a pastoral landscape and came up with an extraordinary subject—the celebration of an anus:

> Dark and wrinkled like a deep pink,
> It breathes, humbly nestled among the moss
> Still wet with love that follows the gentle
> Descent of the white buttocks to the edge of its border. . . .
> In my dream my mouth was often placed on its opening.

Two modern homosexual poets, W. H. Auden and Thom Gunn, both paid tribute to Rimbaud. Auden, writing in 1939, ignored his homosexuality and focused on his key concepts: derangement, irrationality and alienation:

Drinks bought him by his weak and lyric friend
His senses systematically deranged,
To all accustomed nonsense put an end;
Till he from lyre and weakness was estranged.

Gunn, writing sixty years later, wittily portrayed Verlaine's charming lyricism, their mutual masturbation and the phoniness of Verlaine's religious conversion:

The older poet, master of sweet sounds,
Couldn't keep up with all this penile strumming
Of the enthusiastic vagabond's.
He always felt religious after coming.

After the bullet wound and Verlaine's imprisonment (he was given the maximum sentence of two years, not only for the shooting but also for his officially recorded pederasty), Rimbaud rejected the now toxic package of Verlaine and homosexuality. Consistently perverse, he renounced poetry at the age of twenty and at the height of his powers. He rearranged his senses, unified his divided selves, decided to engage with the real world and set off to meet his fate in a quest for exotic travel. He went south to Italy and east to Java where, as a young recruit, he escaped through the jungle from the intolerable discipline of the Dutch army. He then traveled to Cyprus, Egypt, Arabia and Africa. No poet ever visited more countries, learned more languages or practiced more trades.

Few writers have had more disparate selves and varied lives than Rimbaud. He began as a passionate reader and outstanding scholar, mama's boy and adolescent rebel, frequent runaway and outrageous guest, homeless bum and chastened homebody, rape victim and homosexual seducer. He was a brilliant poet and renouncer of poetry, became an Alpine climber and desert wanderer, soldier and deserter, talented linguist and murderous foreman, risk taker and bold explorer, gunrunner and trafficker in the unknown, canny merchant and dupe of savage potentates, lover of African mistresses, would-be paterfamilias and syphilitic amputee. Blake observed, "Without Contraries is no progression. Attraction and Repulsion, Reason and Energy, Love and Hate, are necessary to Human existence," but Rimbaud's pursuit of contraries led him to an early and obscure grave.

Always sure of Rimbaud's genius, Verlaine gave him vital help at both the beginning and the end of his career. In addition to the chapter in *The Cursed Poets*, he brought out, with his own prefaces, the first editions of *Illuminations* in 1892 and Rimbaud's *Poésies complètes* in 1895. Rimbaud's daring and innovative poems soon eclipsed Verlaine's verse, and the older poet's reputation declined—as Rimbaud's soared—after 1900. Antoine Adam explained that "Mallarmé and Rimbaud, much more than [Verlaine], have dominated the sixty years that have passed since his death [in 1896]. Valéry extended the teaching of the former, the surrealists took over the legacy of the latter." Isolated in remotest Abyssinia, where he hated the boredom and treachery of commercial life, Rimbaud never knew that his poems had made him spectacularly famous.

Rimbaud's ideas were eagerly absorbed by innumerable modern writers. Three characteristic examples may represent the entire tradition. In *Thus Spake Zarathustra* (1883–92), Nietzsche—who, like Rimbaud, went beyond good and evil, and into a kind of pathological creativity—proclaimed "one must still have chaos in oneself to be able to give birth to a dancing star. . . . With my own blood I increased my own knowledge." In *The Magic Mountain* (1924), Thomas Mann has Nietzsche's diseased disciple Leo Naphta tell the intellectually innocent hero Hans Castorp that physical and mental suffering is the only true path to wisdom: "Men consciously and voluntarily descended into disease and madness, in search of knowledge which, acquired by fanaticism, would lead back to health after . . . that heroic and abnormal act of sacrifice." And the American poet Theodore Roethke actually put Rimbaud's ideas into practice by wandering naked in the snowy forests of Michigan in order to induce his own madness: "I played the Rimbaud business of really driving myself, seeing . . . [if] you could really derange the senses, and it can be done, and let me tell you, I did it. . . . I got in this real strange state. I got in the woods and started a circular kind of dance. . . . I kept going around and just shedding clothes. . . . I understood intuitively what the frenzy is." Both Nietzsche and Roethke paid for their insights with severe mental breakdowns. The fictional Naphta, instead of finding the path to health, kills himself, instead of his opponent, in a duel.

Rimbaud's fragmented self helped define the modern sensibility. He became the revered master not only of the Symbolists and Surrealists, the Beats and Bob Dylan, but also influenced many modern novelists. When asked what he had in common with his Jewish compatriots, Franz Kafka alluded to this fragmented self in a dry, satiric way and remarked, "I have hardly anything in common with myself and should stand very quietly in a corner, content that I can breathe." In Joseph Conrad's *Victory* (1915) the frightened and dependent Lena, stranded on a remote island with the enigmatic, self-enclosed Axel Heyst, surrenders her own identity and admits that she exists solely in his mind: "I can only be what you think I am." In *Remote People* (1931), Evelyn Waugh traced Rimbaud's footsteps in Abyssinia; the hero of *Scoop* (1938) has published a book on Rimbaud. In his Author's Note to *Brideshead Revisited* (1945) Waugh, dissociating himself from his own characters (extensions of himself), deliberately echoed Rimbaud by stating, "I am not I: thou art not he or she: they are not they." V. S. Naipaul related that his father, who seemed to have little in common with himself just before his mental breakdown, looked into the mirror and failed to see his own image. In this final stage, alienation becomes psychosis.

In his essay on "Verlaine in 1894," W. B. Yeats wrote that Verlaine (echoing Rimbaud's dangerous ideas) "had a great temperament, the servant of a great [poetic] daimon, and he fancied that, as one listened to his vehement sentences, that his temperament, his daimon, had been made uncontrollable that he might live the life needful for its perfect expression in art, and yet escape the bonfire." But Verlaine's uncontrollable daimon, like Rimbaud's derangement and alienation, did not allow him to escape the bonfire. Both men abandoned homosexuality and ended sadly—poor, lonely and sick. Verlaine, a chronic invalid, lived in and out of hospitals, depressingly sustained by a series of old whores. Rimbaud finished up with an Abyssinian mistress, a cancerous amputated leg and a prosthetic limb that didn't work. Yet, as Edmund Wilson observed, his poetry justified and even triumphed over his tragic life: "[Rimbaud's] career, with its violence, its moral interest and its tragic completeness, leaves us feeling that we have watched the human spirit, strained to its most resolute sincerity and in possession of its highest faculties, breaking itself in an effort to escape, first from humiliating compromise, and then from chaos equally humiliating."

5

T. E. LAWRENCE
—— AND ——
ANDRÉ MALRAUX

I

André Malraux admired intellectual men of action: Trotsky, Mao, De Gaulle, and believed "a man is what he does." The pattern and meaning of Malraux's complex life and work is illuminated by a comparison to T. E. Lawrence. He belonged to a vanished breed of mythomaniac adventurers (Burton, Doughty, Captain Shakespear), transformed his exploits into legend and was able to live out his private fantasies. Lawrence reached the peak of his career just as Malraux began his own brilliant trajectory through art, war and politics, and was an immediate and influential model for the literary man of action.

Throughout his life Malraux was obsessed by Lawrence, whom he saw as the archetypal scholar, soldier and writer as well as the Nietzschean precursor of his own fight against man's tragic destiny and attempt to transcend the limitations of his background and character. Both Lawrence and Malraux deliberately disguised their family background and the major events of their lives, and created their own exotic legends as an attractive alternative to reality. As Malraux wrote of the Lawrencean hero of his last novel, *The Walnut Trees of Altenburg* (1943): "He could perhaps have found some means of destroying the mythical person he was growing into, had he been compelled. But he had no wish to do so. His reputation was flattering. What was more important, he enjoyed it."

Both Lawrence and Malraux possessed a formidable erudition in their youth, despised academic pedantry, were attracted to remote civilizations and cultures, began their careers with archeological expeditions to the East and carried out explorations in the desert. Both flamboyantly led the underdog in a foreign war and became fascinated with flying. Both were heroes who shifted from a military to a political career at a crucial moment in history, and became the intellectual and ideological supporters of nationalistic leaders: Emir Feisal and De Gaulle. But Lawrence deliberately regressed from a lieutenant-colonel to a private in the Tank Corps, and Malraux, who adopted Lawrence's guerrilla tactics when he fought with the Resistance, began as a private in the Tank Corps and became a lieutenant-colonel. Malraux's capture of Strasbourg, the last French city in German hands, at the head of the Alsace-Lorraine Brigade, was the equivalent of Lawrence's capture of Damascus, the last Arab city in Turkish hands, at the head of the Bedouin legions. In *The Walnut Trees of Altenburg* Malraux observed: "Intellectuals are like women. . . . soldiers make them dreamy," and in his own life he attempted to turn his dream of Lawrence into reality.

Malraux planned to write the life of Lawrence as early as 1929. He wrote an essay intended for his book, "Lawrence and the Demon of the Absolute" (1946), in 1942. At the same time, he was working on *The Walnut Trees of Altenburg*, in which the hero's tribal warfare among the Senussi of the Libyan desert and his relation to Enver Pasha and the Pan-Turk movement are clearly based on Lawrence's achievements in the Arab Revolt. In the essay, Malraux remarks: "Whoever writes his memoirs (except to deceive) judges himself. There were in this book [*Seven Pillars of Wisdom*], as in all memoirs, two *personae*: the one who said *I* and the author." In his *Anti-Memoirs* (1967), Malraux imitated Lawrence's confessional mode and his use of two *personae*. Malraux's analysis and judgment of Lawrence in the essay synthesize his own dominant characteristics: "his pride: his appetite for glory and deceit, his scorn of his desire; his implacable will; his distrust of ideas; his need for relief from his intelligence; his anguished self-consciousness which led him to try to see himself through the eyes of others; his lack of all faith and his search for the limits of his strength."

In an interview with *L'Express* on March 22–28, 1971, Malraux claimed to have met Lawrence and discussed the English hero with a deferential reverence that he usually reserved for deities like De Gaulle:

> Lawrence, I've met him once. Once only, in a bar of a grand hotel, in Paris, I no longer know which one. We were not equals, you know. He had in his pocket the *Seven Pillars*, his collaboration with Churchill

during the Peace Conference, his rupture with the world and that halo of mystery that the Intelligence Service gave him.

Of course the true mystery was not there. I suspected it without being sure of it at the time. I was a young French writer with only the Prix Goncourt in my pocket. That was little enough. He was extraordinarily elegant. Of an elegance of today, not of his time. A pullover with a rolled neck, a kind of nonchalance and distance.

I don't remember the subjects we discussed. I remember simply that he was then passionate about motors, those of motorcycles and boats. It was a relatively short time before his death. Did he want to die? I have often asked myself that question without being able to answer it.

Unfortunately this statement, so appropriate to Malraux's mythomania, is patently false. It is significant that on this momentous occasion Malraux, who had a phenomenal memory, did not remember the name of the hotel or the subjects discussed. Apart from the fact that Lawrence never mentioned meeting Malraux, Lawrence did not drink nor frequent the bars of grand hotels; he did not collaborate with Churchill at the Paris Peace Conference of 1919, but at the Cairo Conference of 1921; he had never been in the Intelligence Service, though he did intelligence work for the Arab Bureau in Cairo during 1915–16; he was not at all elegant, but self-consciously shabby (the pullover with a rolled neck comes from the well-known photograph by Howard Coster that was taken at the end of Lawrence's life and reproduced as the frontispiece of the *Letters*); and though Malraux claimed to have met Lawrence in Paris after he had won the Prix Goncourt in 1933 (which he refers to with mock modesty), Lawrence did not leave England between 1933 and his death in 1935. For Malraux, the next best thing to actually meeting Lawrence was saying that he had met him. Toward the end of his career, when Malraux felt he had equaled Lawrence's achievement, he rather arrogantly appropriated his hero, transformed him into his own image and portrayed him as an elegant, nonchalant and mysterious Paris intellectual.

II

Malraux's rather abstract essay, "Lawrence and the Demon of the Absolute," like *The Walnut Trees of Altenburg*, reflects on Lawrence's experience in World

War I from the perspective of World War II. The defeat of the Loyalists in Spain and the German occupation of France had turned Malraux's thoughts towards the English hero of the last free ally in Western Europe. Malraux's description of Lawrence is obliquely but unmistakably autobiographical. He portrays Lawrence in the light of his own experience, considers how he can learn from and implement Lawrence's art of action, and reveals how Lawrence has inspired him to live his life and write his books. Malraux mentions Lawrence's "decisive struggle with the angel"—the original title of *The Walnut Trees of Altenburg*—and states that Lawrence's book had been lost (in the Reading train station in 1919) as Malraux's had been destroyed by the Gestapo; and he imitates in his novel the deliberately anticlimactic conclusion of *Seven Pillars of Wisdom*. Malraux's essay not only reveals the depth of his hero worship and close identification with Lawrence, but also provides an illuminating introduction to *The Walnut Trees of Altenburg*.

Malraux—writing in a transitional period of calm between his escape from a German prison camp and his enlistment in the Resistance (where he adopted the name of his fictional hero, Colonel Berger)—focuses on a crucial and depressing turning point in Lawrence's life. He quotes many passages from Lawrence's *Letters* and offers "not a critique of *Seven Pillars*, but an analysis of the feelings of the author in the presence of his book." In August 1922, Lawrence had resigned from the Colonial Office, was dissatisfied with the first three drafts of his book and was about to enlist as a private in the R.A.F. Malraux's "portrayal of the devastated and remorseful hero," writes Virginia Cunningham, attempts "to dramatize despair from inside Lawrence's mind" and "to justify what might otherwise seem to be a pointless abdication from the world of action and art."

Malraux believes that Lawrence wanted to sacrifice himself to help mankind and change the order of the world, and thinks art was Lawrence's ally against fate and against the absurd. Interpreting Lawrence's life in terms of the prevailing wartime philosophy, Malraux makes Lawrence into an Existential hero and declares: "Man is absurd because he is master of neither time, nor of anxiety, nor of Evil; the world is absurd because it involves Evil." Malraux justifies the use of power, not as an end in itself, but as a means to achieve great ambitions. Concentrating on the moment when Lawrence had rejected power in order to work on his literary epic, Malraux (prophesying his own future as minister under De Gaulle) writes of "the instinct which pushed a politician towards a ministry." Malraux also anticipates a major theme of *The Walnut Trees of Altenburg* by emphasizing Lawrence's idealistic motives and by observing that "every national movement is first of all brotherhood." The virile fraternity had also been portrayed in the masculine novels of Melville who had influenced Lawrence, and Conrad who had influenced Malraux.

Lawrence, opposing his historical narrative to the postwar legend created by Lowell Thomas, needed a transfiguring lyricism to convey the inspiration for the reconquest of Damascus and the nationalistic revival of the Arabs. Malraux, incited by Lawrence's example, had also participated in patriotic movements while fighting in Spain and France. He speaks of the failures as well as the triumphs of Lawrence's Nietzschean will; refers to his difficulties in portraying the minor characters in *Seven Pillars of Wisdom*; and comments on the dual and exemplary personae in Lawrence's great theme of solitude and inner defeat, and his (Existential) belief that "every human action is defiled by its very nature."

Focusing on the title of his essay in relation to the ironic subtitle of *Seven Pillars of Wisdom: A Triumph*, Malraux observes that "in the absolute, the triumph is a mockery" and (ignoring Lawrence's ironic self-deprecation) comments on the inevitable disparity between ambition and achievement: "Lawrence considered almost everything he had achieved to be negligible—or certainly less important than what he had dreamed of achieving." After noting the influence on Lawrence of Tolstoy and Nietzsche, Malraux defines two types of the great personality: the man who accomplishes great things and the man who expresses essential truths. Like Lawrence, Malraux believes that true greatness is achieved in art rather than in action.

Malraux defines Lawrence as a man profoundly at odds with himself and goaded into action by self-torment. He sees Lawrence as a secular saint or prophet without God, as "one of the most religious spirits of his time, if one defines a religious spirit as one who experiences the anguish of being a man to the depths of his being." Malraux concludes by acutely delineating the essence of Lawrence's character: pride, a taste for self-humiliation, a horror of respectability, a disgust for possessions, a charitable disinterestedness, a deep-rooted guilt, "a sense of evil, and of the nothingness of almost everything that men cling to; a need for the absolute, instinctive taste for asceticism." Malraux clarifies the title of his essay by quoting Lawrence's statement: "*There is an ideal standard* [an absolute] *somewhere and only that matters: and I cannot find it.*" He completes his essay with a definition of the absolute, which both inspires great action and destroys the hero who inevitably fails to achieve the ideal. It is "the last resort of the tragic man, the only solace, because it alone can consume—even if the whole man is consumed with it—the deepest feeling of dependence, remorse at being one's self." In "Lawrence and the Demon of the Absolute," as Denis Boak perceives, Lawrence is portrayed as a "forerunner of Malraux's own vision of the Tragic."

III

The characters in *The Walnut Trees of Altenburg*, like those in *Man's Fate* (1933) and *Man's Hope* (1937), live amidst the revolutions and wars that recur with each generation in Europe. The central character is Vincent Berger, but the novel portrays three generations of an Alsatian family. Dietrich Berger commits suicide in 1914; his son Vincent takes part in the Young Turk movement and fights in World War I. Vincent's son is wounded in 1940 and taken prisoner by the Germans. The introductory and concluding sections of the novel, both entitled "Chartres Camp," describe young Berger's imprisonment in Chartres Cathedral and the tank attack that led to his capture. The middle three sections take place shortly before and during World War I. The first describes his grandfather's funeral and his father's role in Turkey. The second concerns the intellectual debates at the priory of Altenburg, which are dominated by the ethnologist Möllberg. The abstract arguments in this section, placed in the center of the novel, comment on and interpret the action. The third describes a gas attack on the German-Russian front. The apparently loose structure is in fact carefully wrought. The novel considers the transcendent themes of the force of nature, the destiny of man, the significance of art and the meaning of civilization.

In *The Walnut Trees of Altenburg* Malraux alludes to and then quotes Pascal's *Pensées*, which portrays the human condition through the image of condemned prisoners—a central image and crucial contrast to the vital trees in the novel. (He also used this *pensée* for the title and epigraph of *Man's Fate*.) Later in the novel he writes that three books—*Robinson Crusoe, Don Quixote*, and *The Idiot*—can hold their own against prison life: "The first [hero] struggles through working, the second through dreams, the third through his saintliness." Like his novel about the Spanish struggle, which Malraux also wrote during (rather than after) the war it describes, it moves between action and contemplation, and combines reportage, propaganda and ideology with a fictional account of Malraux's experience in contemporary history. Like *Seven Pillars of Wisdom*, *The Walnut Trees of Altenburg* expands its traditional genre to include autobiography (Malraux's experience in prison and in the Tank Corps), military history, philosophy, ethnology and cultural criticism.

Malraux's original title, "The Struggle with the Angel," was, like Lawrence's, biblical. Genesis 32:24–30 narrates how Jacob wrestled with an angel of the Lord from night to daybreak. When the angel could not prevail, he threw Jacob's thigh out of joint. But Jacob would not release the angel until he had received his blessing. So the angel blessed him and called him Israel, for (like Lawrence and Malraux's Berger) he had power with God and with men, and had prevailed against a mighty adversary. Jacob believed he had had direct contact with the Lord—the Absolute—and would be exalted and protected by his blessing. Wrestling with the angel represents both Lawrence's experience in war and his struggle with artistic creation. The combat, the wound, the triumph and the blessing in Jacob's story are a perfect paradigm for Lawrence's career.

The Walnut Trees of Altenburg, like Conrad's *Heart of Darkness*, is narrated through a circular frame story. But Malraux's Berger, unlike Conrad's Marlow, is an omniscient narrator who tells his father's story as well as his own and reports specific details of conversations which he has never heard. The structure of the novel, which seems self-contained though Malraux asserts it is only the first part of his original conception, is extremely sophisticated. The five sections—a tripartite ABA song form (alternating: war, peace, war) enclosed within the framework of an introduction and a coda—imitates the musical structure of Wagner's Prelude to Act III of *The Meistersinger of Nuremburg*, whose title is closely echoed in the name of Malraux's novel.

The short introductory section, "Chartres Camp," takes place in June 1940. It is based on Malraux's imprisonment in Sens Cathedral and hints at Lawrence's imprisonment at Deraa, where he had been captured and tortured while on a reconnaissance behind enemy lines. The young intellectual, Berger, like Lawrence in Malraux's essay, had united "in one faith the two conflicting elements, religious and political." This scene introduces the theme of the virile fraternity and links the young Berger's fate in war with that of his father.

The German guards discuss Bamberg, "the Chartres of Germany," and both Gothic cathedrals anticipate the Gothic statues that Berger links with the walnut trees outside the priory during his moment of illumination at Altenburg. The conversation of the French prisoners (a small part of the two million soldiers captured by the victorious Germans) resembles the talk of the German soldiers before the gas attack in Part III and of the French soldiers during the tank attack in the concluding section on "Chartres Camp." All these scenes suggest the unity rather than the opposition of men at war. Their form-letters home, which are scattered in the wind and will never be delivered, foreshadow the fate of Möllberg's unfinished manuscript on African ethnology, which hangs "from the lower branches of various types of tree from the Sahara to Zanzibar" and will never be published. The presence of death and the fellowship of death in Chartres Cathedral recur in the war scenes in Libya, Turkey and Austrian Poland. Young Berger was wounded on June 14, 1940. His father, Vincent, had been gassed exactly twenty-five years earlier, on June 14, 1915.

Part I of *The Walnut Trees of Altenburg*, like the introductory and concluding sections on Chartres Camp, begins with a later point in time, includes a flashback and then returns to the present. It describes the character, suicide and funeral, in the Alsatian town of Reichbach, of Vincent Berger's father, Dietrich, who managed the family forestry business; and gives an account of Vincent's attempt during 1908–14 to create a new political order through the Young Turk movement and his subsequent disillusionment with the Pan-Turanian ideology.

Malraux's father killed himself in 1930. Lawrence's high-speed motorcycle rides on narrow country lanes were suicidal. Suicide, the freedom to choose life or death and to determine one's destiny, was one of the critical Existential issues in Camus' *The Myth of Sisyphus* (1942). Dietrich's baffling suicide "seemed to crown his life with a secret," but his rigidity of character, his extremist attitude and his streak of fanaticism help explain the reasons for his act.

After a dispute with the local priest about relaxations in the rules for Lent, Dietrich made a pilgrimage on foot to Rome—which anticipates Vincent's arduous journey from Constantinople to Afghanistan—and had an inconsequential interview with the Pope. When he returned to Alsace, he cut himself off from the Church, attended Mass outside the building and "ended up by spending twenty minutes on his knees in the nettles of summer or the mud of winter." Vincent respects a man who boldly kills himself, and Dietrich also sees his death as an expression of personal will. When asked what sort of life he would choose if he could choose another life, he replies: "*Whatever happens*, if I had to live another life again, I should want none other than Dietrich Berger's"—the life that will lead to suicide. Dietrich's statement, like Lawrence's spiritual suicide, when he renounced fame and power and enlisted in the ranks of the R.A.F. in 1922, suggests "it's possible for a man to go on caring deeply—fanatically—about himself, even when he has already detached himself from life."

Malraux introduces another Lawrencean theme through Dietrich's brother Walter, who organized the Altenburg Discussion Groups (based on Paul Desjardins' *Decades de Pontigny*) and had been a friend of Nietzsche. Like Franz Overbeck in real life, Walter had brought Nietzsche to Switzerland after his final mental breakdown in Turin; and he has preserved the Master's querulous letters, like sacred relics, in the archives of Altenburg. Malraux merely mentions Nietzsche's influence in his essay on Lawrence. But the philosopher's analysis of the Dionysian personality—morbid, masochistic, pathological; charismatic, passionate, possessed—had a powerful impact on Lawrence's character and career. Nietzsche's concept also influenced Malraux's brief but significant discussion of the shamanism—or magical power of leadership—of Vincent Berger, who lectures on Nietzsche's "Philosophy of Action" at the university in Constantinople. Nietzsche's ideas about the relation of suffering and knowledge, the value of creative agony, the need for self-overcoming and the supremacy of the will-to-power dominate and define the ideology of *Seven Pillars of Wisdom*.

The parallels between Lawrence and Berger are extensive and complex. Both men are fiercely anti-colonial but torn by divided loyalties: Lawrence between the English and Arabs; Berger, as advisor to Enver Pasha, between the Turks and Germans, and, as an Alsatian, between the French and Germans. (Vincent fights on the German side in World War I, his son fights on the French side in World War II.) As *éminence grise* to Enver Pasha and officer under General Limon von Sanders, Berger served with the enemies whom Lawrence had fought against in the Arab Revolt, which had been inspired by a common hatred of the Turks. Enver Pasha (1881–1922), a magnetic, charismatic and courageous character in the Lawrencean tradition, had organized the Young Turk Revolution against the Sultan in Macedonia in 1908, led the Ottoman resistance to Italy in the Libyan war of 1911, hoped to reunite the Ottoman Turks with the Turkic peoples of Russian Central Asia and had been killed in action against the Bolsheviks in Turkestan.

Like Lawrence with the Emir Feisal, Berger "had formed a close friendship with Enver [and] his proposals gave a shape to that young colonel's still confused [nationalistic] ideology." Berger did intelligence work, as Lawrence had done in wartime Cairo; and both men had a price put on their heads. Most significantly, Berger dedicated himself to the service of an alien people, helped Enver to impose discipline on the nomadic hordes, "mobilized the tribes of the Libyan Desert with the help of the Senussi, and [tried] to paralyse the Italians by modern guerrilla action without giving battle"—exactly as Lawrence, who invented a theory of guerrilla warfare that influenced Mao, Giap and Grivas, had done with the Bedouin tribes who fought against the regular Turkish army in Arabia, Palestine and Syria. Berger's belief that the austerity of the desert put the Arabs into more direct contact with the spiritual element, that "in the Senussi oases, the bareness of soul had been still more pronounced, but was in keeping with the blazing presence of God, with war, with the structure of united Islam," comes directly from Lawrence.

Enver's plans for a Pan-Turanian empire, which Berger hopes to implement, include the racial and religious "union of all Turks throughout Central Asia from Adrianople to the Chinese oases on the Silk Trade Route," and the creation of a capital in Muslim Samarkand. While attempting to forge links with the Kurds, the emirs of Bokhara and of Afghanistan, and the khans of Russian Turkestan, Berger undertakes a clandestine journey across the steppes of Asia to the Afghan city of Ghazni and becomes, among the primitive people, a romantic and legendary figure.

Berger, like Lawrence, is inspired by an overwhelming impulse to change the course of history and leave his mark on the world—by "the need to get away from Europe, the lure of history, the fanatical desire to leave some scar on the face of the earth, the attraction of a scheme to which he had contributed not a few of the finer points, the comradeship of war, friendship." But in Ghazni, Berger is attacked and beaten by a madman—as Lawrence had been attacked, beaten and left for dead by Kurds while walking alone through Syria in 1909—and suddenly realizes that Enver's concept of Ottomanism is an illusion.

In a similar fashion Lawrence, after witnessing the treachery in the Arab Revolt and the debacle after the capture of Damascus, became increasingly disillusioned with the Hashemite dynasty and with the concept of Arab nationalism. Both Berger and Lawrence—who "ceased to believe in his civilization or in any other"—long for the familiar scenery and the ordinary life of Europe, for "the smell of train-smoke, asphalt in the sun, cafés at night, chimneys under a grey sky, bathrooms!" Berger gratefully experiences the sensations of Europe when he disembarks at Marseilles and returns to Reichbach (following the circular structure of this section and of the novel) a few days before his father's suicide.

Lawrence and Berger are linked by a common impulse toward action and ambition, and by a deep-rooted belief that man is not what he hides (as Walter states), but what he achieves. (Dietrich's mysterious suicide subtly combines hidden motives and actual achievement.) As Jean Lacouture observes: "there is [in both men] the same attitude of mind, the same behavior, the same fanaticism, the same despair."

Part II of the novel, in which Möllberg denies that there is a unity in man or a continuity of civilization, seems to confirm Berger's disillusioning experiences with the Pan-Turanian ideology in Asia. But Berger's experiences on the Russian front in Part III, like his response to the symbolic walnut trees near the priory, refute Möllberg's brilliant but unsound arguments. *The Walnut Trees of Altenburg*, even more than Thomas Mann's *Doctor Faustus* (which also juxtaposes "direct experience of the Second World War and reflection on the First"), conveys the exciting cut and thrust of philosophical argument, and is the intellectual novel *par excellence*. The subject at Altenburg is "The Permanence and Metamorphosis of Man" and the central question is: "can one isolate a single permanent [not changing] factor which is valid throughout the world, valid throughout history, on which to build one's conception of man?"

Möllberg, like Lawrence at Carchemish in Syria, had undertaken archeological research in the eastern regions of the Turkish Empire. But his main work, like that of his model Leo Frobenius, had been done in African prehistory, archeology and ethnology. This antihero's quality of mind and his ruthlessly coherent but erroneous interpretation of man are revealed both in his physical appearance—in "his smooth skull and remarkably pointed ears that reminded one of a vampire"—and in the grotesque, sad and inhuman icons that he fashions from clay and bronze. His fetishistic figures and nostalgic gargoyles resemble Bosch's and "Goya's monsters which seem to remember they were once human."

Malraux's use of aesthetic analogies, influenced by Proust's technique (though Malraux does not allude to specific works of art), occurs most frequently in the Altenburg section and, like the parallels with Lawrence, illuminates the themes of the novel. Malraux's visual comparisons refer both to general periods and cultures (Peruvian, Egyptian, Greek and Gothic as well as Christian, Chinese and Japanese) and to particular artists (Cranach, Michelangelo, Brueghel, Rubens, Rembrandt and Goya). The archetypal works of art oppose Möllberg's theory and argument, and suggest a fundamental unity in diverse civilizations.

The antithesis of Möllberg's monstrous figures, the head of a young man in the Acropolis Museum (the first sculpture to have represented the human face), can withstand—rather than suggest—the concept of death. The two Gothic saints, carved in dark walnut wood (not in clay and bronze, like Möllberg's figures), which Berger contemplates while listening to a lecture, are an anonymous but individual expression of an artist of that time: "Gothic man is the author of Gothic art, in the same way that Rubens is the author of the pictures by Rubens." The boisterous behavior of the French prisoners in Chartres Camp has not changed since Brueghel.

Malraux's aesthetic analogies also evoke vivid visual images of tone and color, shape and form, appearance of landscapes and features or personalities of fictional characters. "Jews golden as Rembrandt's" suggest the harmony and tranquility of Reichbach before the war. The shrunken and collapsed prisoners at Chartres, writing futile letters on their knees, "crouched like Peruvian mummies." The tragic pathos of Germans carrying Russian soldiers after the gas attack is expressed in the image of their "arms hanging as in a 'Descent from the Cross.'" In this gas-filled landscape, the "jagged saw-tooth ridges stood out against the background of fog, as in the clear line of a Japanese print" (154), and the sunlit gap of a ravine in which Berger was tottering "gave a Chinese-ink precision to the rags of the lower branches, to the leaves falling in clouds like hanging capes, to the tentacles clinging to the tree-trunks, to this marsh-bottom world." Uncle Walter's features and character are suggested by gold-rimmed spectacles that "incongruously rested on his broken Michelangelo nose"; Möllberg's are suggested by a nose that is hooked like an Egyptian beak. Möllberg brings his own Cranach hunting scene (perhaps *The Stag Hunt of the Elector Frederick the Wise*, 1529) and hangs it near one of his chief monsters, as if to put himself back in touch with German culture.

Malraux quotes Pascal's affirmation that "in this prison [of our existence] we can *fashion images of ourselves* sufficiently powerful to deny our nothingness" (my emphasis), and Berger's belief in the transcendental power of art also refutes Möllberg's argument. As Jean Lacouture observes, in Malraux's art book *The Voices of Silence* he argues that "man exists as a coherent, permanent, universal concept. . . . A man creates the work—but the work becomes multiplied and proliferates, different from itself and from its creator, from one metamorphosis to another. This essay [on permanence *in* metamorphosis] was written specifically against [Oswald] Spengler and Möllberg."

The participants at Altenburg, as W. M. Frohock points out, expect Möllberg to state that there *is* a unity in man's development and a continuity in his civilization. But after considering primitive societies that are ignorant of the West's conception of fate, birth, exchange and death, and stating that "it is history's task to give a meaning to the human adventure," Möllberg arrives at a profoundly pessimistic conclusion that emphasizes, in a series of rhetorical parallels, the nothingness of man and the continual oblivion of metamorphosis: "If mental structures disappear forever like the plesiosaurus, if civilizations succeed one another only in order to cast man into the bottomless pit of nothingness, if the human adventure only subsists at the price of a merciless metamorphosis, it's of little consequence that men communicate their ideas and their methods to each other for a few centuries; for man is a chance element, and, fundamentally speaking, the world consists of oblivion."

Möllberg, the greatest authority on Africa, then explains to his astonished interlocutors—in a brilliant passage that echoes Conrad's *Heart of Darkness*—that the prehistoric void of the African earth and sky (which he had tried and failed to populate and reconstruct) had forced him to abandon his beliefs and his Malrauvian-titled manuscript, *Civilization, Conquest and Fate*, to the trees that stretched from the desert to the Indian Ocean. Möllberg's evocation of Africa recalls Berger's evocation of the steppes of Asia on his journey to Ghazni and of the Vieux Port of Marseilles on his return to Europe: "The endless succession of days [like the endless succession of civilizations] under

the dusty firmament of Libya [where Berger had fought the Italians] or the
heavy leaden sky of the Congo, the tracks of invisible animals converging on
the water points, the exodus of starving dogs under the empty sky, the time of
day when every thought becomes a blank, the giant trees gloomily soaring up
in the prehistoric void."

Though no one is able to defeat Möllberg's argument, Berger refuses to
accept his conclusions. He walks outside the priory, moves from the intellectual to the natural world, and finds an affirming truth by contemplating the
central symbol of the novel: the two strong, vital, old walnut trees, artifacts
of the earth, which provide a striking contrast to the gloomy African trees,
remind him of his father's forests, recall the two carved Gothic statues in the
library, and create a deep "impression of free will and of endless positive metamorphosis":

> Instead of supporting the weight of the world [like the statue of Atlas
> in the library], the tortured wood of these walnut trees flourished with
> life everlasting in their polished leaves under the sky and in their nuts
> that were almost ripe, in all their venerable bulk above the wide circle of
> young shoots and the dead nuts of winter. . . . Between the statues and
> the logs there were the trees, and their design which was as mysterious
> as that of life itself. And the Atlas, and St. Mark's face consumed with
> Gothic passion, were lost in it like the culture, like the intellect, like ev-
> erything my father had just been listening to—all buried in the shadow
> of this kindly statue which the strength of the earth carved for itself,
> and which the sun at the level of the hills spread across the sufferings
> of humanity as far as the horizon.

Lawrence would agree with Berger in his silent debate with Möllberg. According to Möllberg, intellectual constructs are pointless because all human
thought and action are destined for oblivion. Möllberg asserts that men are
"more thoroughly defined and classified by their form of fatalism than by anything else" and believes that all men must submit to fate. There is no ostensible
connection between Möllberg's destructive argument and the previous section
dealing with Vincent's activity in Turkey, though Vincent's disillusionment co-
incides with Möllberg's. But there is an implicit contrast between Möllberg's

pessimistic philosophy and the self-transcendent Nietzschean will of Lawrence and Berger, which opposes the traditional fatalism of the East. The gas attack in Part III represents an assertion of Western will (to defeat and conquer the enemy), which should lead to destruction and death and vindicate Möllberg's view. But the noble conduct of the German soldiers during the attack exemplifies the idea that there *is* a unity in man.

Part III takes place in June 1915 on the Vistula front, where the Germans are fighting the Russians. In Poland, Berger becomes conscious of the depth of the Slavic world extending across Siberia to the Pacific just as, in Turkey, he had been aware of the depth of the Turanian world extending from Constantinople to China. Like Lawrence, Berger admires the virile fraternity of war: "the masculine comradeship, the irrevocable commitments that courage imposes." But he feels ashamed when he is forced to participate in the humiliating interrogation—the antithesis of the virile fraternity—of a young woman suspected of spying for the Russians. His compassion for the innocent woman, his putative enemy, foreshadows his sympathy for the Russian victims of the German gas attack, who do not represent antithetical nationalities, but mankind in general.

In modern warfare, where intense propaganda arouses a hatred of the enemy, courageous self-sacrifice, comradeship with and commitment to the enemy are extremely rare. Just as Berger had fought for the Turks and Lawrence against them, so Malraux's moving scene is the exact antithesis of Lawrence's description of the Arab massacre of the Turks who had committed atrocities in the village of Tafas: "By my order we took no prisoners, for the only time in our war. . . . In a madness born of the horror of Tafas we killed and killed, even blowing in the heads of the fallen and of the animals; as though only their death and running blood could slake our agony."

The German soldiers' talk of suicide by hanging and of deadly gas escaping in a coal mine emphasizes Malraux's thrice-repeated statement that man is the only species that has learned it will die. Berger's doubts about the attack are first aroused by the inventor of the gas, Professor Hoffman, who watches the assault as if it were a scientific experiment. He icily notes the grisly symptoms of the gas—"the opaque cornea first goes blue, the breath starts to come in hisses, the pupil—it's really very odd—goes almost black"—yet speciously insists, as the wind blows loyally toward Russia, that gas is the most humane

method of warfare. There are two kinds of absurdity in the greatest scene in
the novel: Hoffman's is barbaric, the soldiers' is humane. For the victorious but
remorseful Germans, horrified into moral awareness by the petrified corpses
after the successful gas attack, wearily carry the suffering enemy, icons of a
"Descent from the Cross," back to the healing safety of their own lines.

The eerie description of the riderless horse that gallops straight into the
creeping advance of the poison gas and is swallowed up in the vast silence recalls Berger's ride to Ghazni, foreshadows the tank disappearing into the trap
in the concluding section and dramatizes, in the spectral landscape of *dead*
trees, the grim reality of war. Like his comrades, Berger, though asphyxiated by
gas, is overcome by pity and compelled by the vision of evil "to find a Russian,
any Russian, who had not been killed, put him on his shoulders and save him."
Impelled by pain and by brotherhood, he struggles desperately to carry back a
soldier, only to realize that the man he had hoped to save is already dead. Just
before he completely loses consciousness, Berger remembers the walnut trees
and realizes, amidst the carnage and devastation of war, that the main aim of
life is to achieve happiness. In a Note to the French edition of 1948, Malraux
explained that Berger's urge to happiness was not a simplistic answer to the
questions raised at Altenburg, but a psychological reaction to stress, pain, fear
and the threat of death.

The final section of the circular novel, also called "Chartres Camp," takes
place in the chaos of defeat in June 1940. It describes the other three members
of young Berger's tank crew and explains how he came to be a prisoner in the
opening section. The tank attack, a loud and violent equivalent of the quiet
and sinister gas attack, provides the blood that was strangely absent from the
earlier military episode. The principal enemy is not the Germans—who are
both good and evil, like all other men—but the broken track, the concealed
mine and the anti-tank ditch, which would lead the men either to death or to
prison. During the solemn "human sacrifice" of war, which resembles both
Dietrich's suicide and the primitive rituals witnessed by Möllberg in Africa, the
men panic as the surface of the earth slides suddenly away and the tank falls
into a deadly ditch. The four men in the tank, as trapped and damned as they
are in prison, await the fatal shell burst that they feel is bound to come. But
the driver is unexpectedly able to maneuver the tank out of the ditch, and the
machine moves forward at full speed, still fearful of the next trap.

After the tank safely reaches a condemned and abandoned village, Berger sees two old peasants outside a looted room. They are "propped against the cosmos" like two stones and are absorbing the healing sun that had also "spread across the sufferings of humanity" at Altenburg. They are the human equivalent of the walnut trees, and represent the hope of survival and the eternal order of nature that also appear in the great cyclical passage of Ecclesiastes 1:4–7: "One generation passeth away, and another generation cometh: but the earth abideth forever. The sun also ariseth, and the sun goeth down, and hasteth to his place where he arose. . . . All the rivers run into the sea, yet the sea is not full: unto the place from whence the rivers come, thither they return again." Möllberg's belief that there is no common unity in man (or even, as Berger discovered, in Turks), seems to be confirmed by the outbreak of war, which begins less than a year after his depressing peroration. But Malraux, arguing against Möllberg, suggests that the only alternative left to self-destructive man is our common humanity, symbolized by the rescue during the gas attack and by the old peasant couple.

IV

Malraux's *Anti-Memoirs* (1967), which include a long, revised section from *The Walnut Trees of Altenburg*, is structured by his description of a recuperative sea voyage to the Near East and Asia in 1965. This journey enables Malraux to trace retrospectively Lawrence's steps as well as his own. Malraux's autobiography contains scattered references to rather extensive discussions of Lawrence. At the end of his own distinguished career, he was no longer willing to worship the hero of his youth and wanted to minimize Lawrence's influence. As Malraux became increasingly aware of the disturbing aspects of Lawrence's personality, he began to stress the differences as well as the similarities between himself and his *alter ego*.

Malraux describes *Seven Pillars of Wisdom* as the account of a great enterprise and echoes Lawrence's belief that daydreaming gives rise to action. He recalls traveling through the Khyber Pass, not far from Miranshah, where Lawrence spent some isolated months in 1928. But here Lawrence's legend caught up with him; he was accused of spying and was repatriated to England. Malraux's ship stops at Jiddah, whence Lawrence left for the Arabian desert. And he compares Berger's "coming back to earth" in his own civilization to

Lawrence's return from Arabia, "though he said that he had never become English again." Malraux also mentions that Lawrence had carved in Greek "What does it matter?" above the door of his cottage, Clouds Hill. But when discussing the shocking death of the mother of his two sons, Josette Clotis, who fell under the wheels of a train, he contrasts his own feelings of grief to the stoicism of Lawrence, who "does not seem to have experienced the death of a beloved woman. It strikes . . . like lightning."

In Singapore, Malraux hears that Lawrence's colorful legend has eclipsed the reputation of the Asian adventurer, Marie-David de Mayrena: "The legend of Lawrence, especially as it was put about by Lowell Thomas at the beginning, is the dazzling legend of a Queen of Sheba army, with its Arab partisans deployed beneath flying banners among the jerboas of the desert, and imaginary battles in the defiles of rose-red Petra." The direct inspiration for one of Malraux's legendary feats—the flight over the Arabian desert in 1934 in order to discover the Queen of Sheba's lost city—came from Lawrence's penetration of the forbidden deserts of Arabia. Malraux, like Lawrence, frequently provided more than one version of the crucial events of his life; and his account of the flight over Sheba in *Anti-Memoirs* contradicts the substantial articles published in the newspaper, *L'Intransigeant*, between May 3 and May 13, 1934.

Having announced with considerable publicity and fanfare that he was able to undertake a flamboyant and heroic adventure, Malraux, who did not want to spoil the glorious opportunity by returning with a handful of dust, felt obliged to discover something spectacular. Given his predisposition to mythomania, his unwillingness to disappoint either his own expectations or those of his newspaper audience, and the impossibility of refuting or verifying the facts of his story, Malraux had virtually no choice but to invent an exciting and imaginative alternative to the dull reality of the empty desert. By the time of the *Anti-Memoirs* (not conventional, but selective and highly embellished memoirs), the search for Sheba, which had hardened into a legend that was impossible to deny, provided the ideal quest for the romantic adventurer. Malraux flew over Arabia, not to discover Sheba's city, but to realize his fantasies and create a legendary persona worthy of Lawrence.

Lawrence's leadership in the Arab Revolt and Malraux's in the Spanish Civil War confirm the courage and compassion portrayed in the Lawrence-inspired autobiographical hero of *The Walnut Trees of Altenburg*. Though *Seven*

Pillars of Wisdom has influenced authors as diverse as Ernest Hemingway and Wilfred Thesiger, Lawrence's epic has had the most profound impact on the life and works of Malraux. Throughout his life Malraux imitated, transformed and absorbed Lawrence. By the end of World War II their legends had merged and, in the French mind, "Andre Malraux and T. E. Lawrence became almost inseparable."

6

WYNDHAM LEWIS

—— AND ——

T. S. ELIOT

I

An impressive concentration of subtle minds took place when Wyndham Lewis first met T. S. Eliot, who became a lifelong friend, in Ezra Pound's little triangular sitting room at 6 Holland Park Chambers in Kensington, early in 1915. Eliot had made the acquaintance of Pound only a few days before, when Pound had proudly shown him Lewis' *Timon of Athens* drawings. The tall sibylline figure, "his features of clerical cut," greeted Lewis, the first artist he had ever encountered, with his characteristically prim manner and fastidious speech. The bombastic Pound, disappointed by the studied reserve of Eliot, who was less confident than his new friends, adopted his hillbilly dialect (perhaps to amuse Lewis and soften Eliot, for all three men had spent their childhood in America) and intimated to Lewis: "Yor ole uncle Ezz is wise to wot youse thinkin. Waaal Wynd damn I'se telling *yew*, he's a lot better'n he looks!"

Lewis, a vital and versatile painter, novelist, critic, poet, philosopher, traveler, and editor of *Blast*, had founded the Vorticist movement and was completing his first novel, *Tarr*. Eliot soon discovered that Lewis was a brilliantly amusing talker with a powerful critical intelligence and an astonishing visual imagination. In his 1918 review of *Tarr* in the *Egoist*, he called Lewis, in a phrase that has become famous: "The most fascinating personality of our time. . . . In the work of Mr. Lewis we recognize the thought of the modern and the energy of the cave-man." In *One-Way Song* (1933) Lewis portrayed Eliot's stern features, pessimistic poetic voice and lugubrious religious inclinations with affectionate irony:

I seem to note a Roman profile bland,
I hear the drone from out the cactus-land:
That must be the poet of the Hollow Men:
The lips seem bursting with a deep Amen.

"Appearing at one's front door, or arriving at a dinner rendezvous," Lewis recalled in his memoir of Eliot, "his face would be haggard, he would seem at his last gasp. (Did he know?) To ask *him* to lie down for a short while at once was what I always felt I ought to do. However, when he had taken his place at a table, given his face a dry wash with his hands, and having had a little refreshment, Mr. Eliot would rapidly shed all resemblance to the harassed and exhausted refugee, in flight from some Scourge of God."

Lewis published in the second (and final) *Blast* of July 1915 Eliot's "Preludes" and "Rhapsody on a Windy Night," which were his first poems to appear in England and contained the suggestive lines that Lewis especially admired:

I am moved by fancies that are curled,
Around these images, and cling:
The notion of some infinitely gentle,
Infinitely suffering thing.

But after the censorship of Pound's poem in *Blast I*, Lewis refused Eliot's "Bullshit" and "The Ballad for Big Louise." He called them "excellent bits of scholarly ribaldry" but stuck to his "naif determination to have no 'words ending in -Uck, -Unt, and -Ugger.'"

After World War I, Lewis replaced the friendship of the exuberant Pound with that of the cautious and circumspect Eliot, with whom he had more intellectual and less temperamental affinities. Eliot, whom Ottoline Morrell called "The Undertaker," would say at tea, "I daren't take cake, and jam's too much trouble," and showed a Puritan distaste for the sensual pleasures which Lewis so eagerly enjoyed. He resented being patronized by Lewis, who had greater vigor and vitality, and in a letter to John Quinn remarked on the temperamental difference between his friends, Pound and Lewis, and himself: "I consider that Pound and Lewis are the only writers in London whose work is worth

publishing. . . . I know that Pound's lack of tact has done him great harm."
Tactlessness was also one of Lewis' failings.

Just after he met Lewis in June 1915 Eliot, in "the awful daring of a moment's surrender," began his disastrous marriage with Vivien Haigh-Wood, the
daughter of a portrait painter, who suffered from poor health and "nerves"—
and who eventually went mad. After two unhappy years as a schoolmaster, he
became a bank clerk at Lloyds in the City and remained there from 1917 until
1925, when he joined Faber & Gwyer and soon became a prosperous publisher.
Eliot found the exuberant if volatile Lewis a welcome relief from his domestic
and commercial enslavement. Lewis' wife, Froanna, who liked Eliot best of all
their friends, said Lewis took Eliot to music halls and boxing matches.

Lewis frequently went to Paris to keep up with the latest developments in
modern art and to see the work of Picasso, Braque and Matisse. In the summer
of 1920 Lewis, who wanted to get away from his pregnant mistress, and Eliot,
who wished to escape from his wife, went on holiday together to Paris (where
they had an introduction from Pound to Joyce), to Saumur on the Loire, and
then down the river through Angers and Nantes, and north to Quiberon and
the Golfe de Vannes in Brittany, which Lewis had visited with his mother in
1908. Outside Saumur, Lewis, speeding along at a great pace, had a nasty bicycle accident: his handlebars snapped off, he was thrown violently on the road
and badly injured his knee. He returned to the town furious at the proprietor,
who brazenly tried to recover money for damage to the defective machine. The
travelers also visited a monastery in Saumur, which Eliot attempted to sketch
under the critical eye of Lewis: "The porter told us the hours, and suggested
that we fill in the time by visiting the church, a short way up the street. 'Ah you
should see that!' he boomed. 'It is very fine.—It is *very old—c'est très ancien!*'
Then detecting, as he thought, an expression of disappointment in our faces,
he added hurriedly—*C'est très moderne!*" At the end of each day, when they
drank their Armagnac in the café, Eliot maintained the habits of a bank clerk
and scrupulously entered the day's expenses in a small notebook.

Lewis and Eliot's first meeting with Joyce, which was engineered by Pound,
was brilliantly described in Lewis' autobiography. Though Joyce's work had
been praised by Pound, Lewis had read only a few pages of *A Portrait of the Artist*
when it appeared in the *Egoist* and found that it was too mannered, too literary and too sentimental-Irish for his austere taste. But Joyce (also primed by

Pound) was familiar with *Tarr* and Lewis' other works and gave a flattering start of recognition when Eliot introduced them. Both men seemed to be aware of the momentous occasion. Lewis found Joyce an oddity in patent-leather shoes and large powerful spectacles; and in his four drawings of Joyce he captured the extraordinary face, "hollowed-out, with a jutting brow and jaw, like some Pacific masks." Joyce played the Irishman in an amusing fashion and Lewis "took a great fancy to him for his wit, for the agreeable humanity of which he possessed such stores, for his unaffected love of alcohol, and all good things to eat and drink." He later called Joyce "a pleasing, delightful fellow, with all his scholarly egotism and Irish nonsense."

The ostensible object of the visit was to deliver a large brown parcel which Pound had entrusted to Eliot. When Joyce received their message and came to their hotel room with his tall son Giorgio: "Eliot rose to his feet. He approached the table, and with one eyebrow drawn up, and a finger pointing, announced to James Joyce that *this* was that parcel to which he had referred in his wire, and which had been given into his care, and he formally delivered it, thus acquitting himself of his commission. . . . James Joyce was by now attempting to untie the crafty housewifely knots of the cunning old Ezra. . . . At last the strings were cut. A little gingerly Joyce unrolled the slovenly swaddlings of damp British brown paper in which the good-hearted American had packed up what he had put inside. Thereupon, along some nondescript garments for the trunk—there were no trousers I believe—a fairly presentable pair of *old brown shoes* stood revealed, in the centre of the bourgeois French table."

The shoes and jacket were undoubtedly Pound's response to Joyce's letter of June 5, 1920: "I wear my son's boots (which are two sizes too large) and his castoff suit which is too narrow in the shoulders." Pound meant well by sending the cumbersome gift; but because of the unexpected arrival of a check (which may have paid for his patent-leather shoes), Joyce's circumstances had significantly improved before the literary messengers arrived with the footgear. Pound's unintentional revelation of his penury before (two equally impoverished) *confrères* aroused Joyce's Irish pride. Though he accepted their invitation to dinner, he insisted on paying for several days of lavish drinks, meals, taxis, and tips.

Eliot suffered a nervous breakdown at the end of 1921 and spent some time in a sanatorium in Lausanne. During the next three years (also an extremely difficult period for Lewis) he was sick, miserable, and acutely depressed: fearful of poverty and overcome by self-pity. In a 1923 letter Eliot wrote Lewis: "I am ill, harassed, impoverished, and am going to have 5 teeth out. I have managed to avoid seeing anyone for a very long time. I have several enemies."

II

In 1922 Lewis was present at the first reading of *The Waste Land* in London, when a friend of Mrs. Eliot, with splotches on his face, proudly identified himself as the "young man carbuncular." Eliot published the poem in October 1922 in the first number of the *Criterion*, when he was editing that magazine and encouraging Lewis to contribute to every issue. Despite—or perhaps because of—Eliot's good will and practical assistance, Lewis quarreled with him in January 1925, when Eliot advertised but did not print a long part of *The Dithyrambic Spectator*. The ever-suspicious Lewis had been publishing two Zagreus sections of *The Apes of God* in the *Criterion* (for which he received £43) and he warned Eliot, who was then friendly with Virginia Woolf and other members of the Bloomsbury set: "Should any of these fragments find their way into other hands than yours before they appear in book-form I shall regard it as treachery." Eliot explained that Lewis' 20,000-word essay was too long to print and that illness had prevented him from writing an explanation, and answered Lewis in a calm and disinterested manner: "Please do not think that I am pressing upon you . . . a reminder of supposed services. I consider that anything I do is equalised by any support you give to *The Criterion*. Furthermore I am not an individual but an instrument, and anything I do is in the interest of art and literature and civilisation, and it is not a matter for personal compensation. But in the circumstances I cannot help feeling that your letter expressed an unjustified suspiciousness."

But when Lewis continued his attacks in March—"Since before Christmas you have been guilty where I am concerned of a series of actions each of which, had I done the same to you, would have made you very indignant"—Eliot showed some exasperation and appealed to Lewis' faith in his integrity and their friendship: "I cannot work with you so long as you consider me either the tool or the operator of machinations against you. . . . Until you are convinced by your own senses or by the testimony of others that I am neither conducting nor supporting (either deliberately or blindly) any intrigue against you, I do not see that we can get any further."

Eliot, because of his sobriety and apparent equanimity, was a difficult man to quarrel with, and remained Lewis' loyal friend and staunch defender. He believed that Roger Fry and other critics had deliberately hurt Lewis' career, and placed him above Joyce as a prose stylist: "Lewis was independent, outspoken and difficult. Temperament and circumstances combined to make him a great satirist. . . . His work was persistently ignored or depreciated, throughout his life, by persons of influence in the world of art and letters who did not find him congenial. . . . [But he was] one of the few men of letters in my generation whom I should call, without qualification, men of genius. . . . Mr. Lewis is the greatest prose master of style of my generation."

It was highly ironic that the eminently respectable Eliot became involved in a stormy public controversy when Lewis painted his portrait in 1938, for the poet had changed a great deal since the *Waste Land* days of 1920. Eliot's association with Faber, beginning in 1925, rescued him from economic hardship and led to prosperity; his reception into the Church of England and acquisition of British citizenship in 1927 provided new strength and security; and his separation from his wife in 1933 finally freed him from the tragic bondage of her mental illness. Eliot had firmly established his literary reputation; he was widely admired as the successor to Yeats and acclaimed as the leading poet of his generation.

Eliot's respectability, religion, success, wealth, and fame impeded his friendship with Lewis, who had none of these qualities. Lewis emphasized the difference between Eliot and himself when he told Geoffrey Grigson that he once went to visit the poet and found Ottoline Morrell on her knees beseeching him: "Teach me how to pray!" Lewis may have felt residual resentment about his dispute with Eliot concerning the publication of his work in the *Criterion*, but both men remained fond of each other. Lewis spoke teasingly about Eliot, treated him with ironic affection, and (mistakenly) thought he had a better understanding of the world. He believed he had a superior intellect and never quite understood why he could not make the same artistic impression that Eliot did.

Lewis, who strongly projected his character in his own works and damaged his reputation with his vehement political tracts, criticized his friend's theory

of impersonality (which enhanced Eliot's magisterial image) in a chapter of
Men Without Art. He felt Eliot had made a virtue of becoming an "incarnate
echo" and ought to express rather than repress his personality: "If there is to
be an 'insincerity,' I prefer it should occur in the opposite sense—namely that
'the man, the personality' should exaggerate, a little artificially perhaps, his
beliefs—rather than leave a meaningless shell behind him, and go to hide in
a volatilized hypostatization of his personal feelings." When Eliot first saw a
review copy of Lewis' book he said: "Oh, I'm very interested in this," borrowed
the volume, and seemed to accept the validity of Lewis' criticism. Eliot found
Lewis rather difficult, for he disliked quarreling as much as Lewis enjoyed it.
But he thought Lewis was the liveliest and most original of his contemporaries
and always had the highest respect for his genius. Lewis was usually cautious
and discreet about Eliot with mutual friends, quietly agreed when the poet was
praised and tempered his criticism with admiration in writing about Eliot.

There was a great deal of conversation and laughter when Lewis was working on Eliot's portraits, for his remarks amused and entertained the poet.
Lewis expressed his favorable first impression of the handsome Eliot both
verbally and visually. He described Eliot as "A sleek, tall, attractive transat-
lantic apparition—with a sort of Gioconda smile . . . a Prufrock to whom the
mermaids would decidedly have sung, one would have said, at the tops of
their voices. . . . For this was a very attractive young Prufrock indeed, with an
alert and dancing eye . . . bashfully ironic, blushfully *taquineri* [teasing]. . . .
Though not feminine—besides being physically large his personality visibly
moved within the male pale—there *were* dimples in the warm dark skin; undoubtedly he used his eyes a little like a Leonardo."

Lewis actually did two portraits of Eliot in 1938. The first (now in Eliot
House, Harvard) is a study for the second and depicts the poet's head and
torso against a blank background. The second and much greater painting portrays Eliot, in waistcoat and lounge suit, slouched in an armchair with crossed
hands. He stares slightly downwards and to the left with great intensity, and
the planes of his face are more contrasted, his bold features more precisely
delineated than in the study. A shadow from his head appears on the pale green
panel behind the deeply etched parting of his sleek hair. The abstract designs
on both sides of the panel suggest the power of his imagination, while his
solemn composure and fixed concentration convincingly convey the strength

of his intellect. Eliot greatly admired this portrait, which captured the essence of his mind and art, and told Lewis he was quite willing for posterity to know him by that image. (A photograph of 1954, reproduced in Lewis' *Letters*, shows Eliot pointing to the portrait with smiling admiration.)

Lewis submitted the portrait to the judges of the Royal Academy exhibition in the spring of 1938. But *Blast* never got inside Burlington House, and the painting was rejected on April 21. The refusal of the portrait caused a furor in the British press, enabled Lewis to strike back at the citadel of artistic orthodoxy, gain some useful publicity and—ironically—attract the attention of a wider public. The refusal of the Eliot portrait came at the end of a long series of rejections suffered by Lewis in the 1930s. But the controversy aroused interest in the painting (which was refused·by the Trustees of the Tate) and in 1939 T. J. Honeyman of the Lefevre Gallery sold it for £250 to the Municipal Art Gallery in Durban, South Africa. This money enabled Lewis to escape from England and travel to North America.

III

During the late 1940s, the final phase of his artistic career, Lewis' painting seriously deteriorated because of his defective vision. The most important work of his late period was his second portrait of Eliot, who in 1948 had won the $40,000 Nobel Prize for Literature. Lewis dined frequently with Eliot, in Scott's on Mount Street or the Hyde Park Hotel Grill, where he ate oysters and dessert—and skipped the main course. Eliot used to send Lewis cases of champagne (he could drink nothing else at the end of his life), and Lewis meticulously noticed that it was not vintage. Still ignored and impoverished, he was inevitably jealous of Eliot's enormous success and resentful about the poet in his letters. He told Pound, who had been charged with treason, declared insane and confined to St. Elizabeth's Hospital in Washington: "You might almost have contrived this climax to your respective careers: yours so Villonesque and Eliot's super-Tennyson." And he wrote to his American friend, Felix Giovanelli: "Eliot is a solid mass of inherited slyness. . . . Eliot is no great favourite of mine in later years. Lesser poet than Pound, though not such an exasperating fool of a man. He *has* I agree kicked up a nasty stink around himself of *cult*."

When Lewis painted his second, much more bland and conventional portrait of Eliot (which lacks the sharp incisive planes of the earlier work) in

March and April 1949, he was obliged to scrutinize him very closely. As he wrote in "The Sea-Mists of the Winter": "When I started my second portrait of T. S. Eliot, which now hangs in Magdalene College, Cambridge, in the early summer of 1949, I had to draw up very close to the sitter to see exactly how the hair sprouted out of the forehead, and how the curl of the nostril wound up into the dark interior of the nose. There was no question of my not succeeding, my sight was still adequate. But I had to move too close to the forms I was studying. Some months later, when I started a portrait of Stella Newton, I had to draw still closer and even then I could not quite see. This was the turning-point, the date, December 1949." Another minor problem, as Lewis told a St. Louis friend, was that Eliot (whom he had described as "wriggling his lean bottom" in *The Apes of God*) became drowsy and his bottom "went to sleep" when he was immobilized in one position.

The portrait was completed in time for Lewis' exhibition at the Redfern Gallery in May, when both artist and subject were interviewed by *Time* magazine. Lewis' description recalled his earliest impression of the poet, haggard and apparently at his last gasp: "You will see in his mask, drained of too hearty blood, a gazing strain, patient contraction: the body is slightly tilted . . . in resigned anticipation of the worst." Eliot suggested that Lewis' intensity made him feel somewhat uneasy: "Wearing a look of slightly quizzical inscrutability behind which one suspects his mental muscles may be contracting for some unexpected pounce, he makes one feel that it would be undesirable, though not actually dangerous, to fall asleep in one's chair." When this portrait, like the earlier one of Eliot, was refused by the Tate, Lewis blamed the malign influence of Kenneth Clark. It was eventually acquired by Magdalene College for £300, and hangs on the narrow staircase of the dining hall, poorly lighted and difficult to see.

Lewis' last polemical book, *The Demon of Progress in the Arts* (1954), concluded his argument against abstract art and unleashed his final onslaught against Eliot's "melancholy exlieutenant," Herbert Read. If, for Lewis, Fry and Kenneth Clark were art dictators, Read was an ineffectual impresario and aesthetic buffoon. He led the dashing but dull rear guard of abstractionists, was besotted with theorizing, neglected the evidence of the eye and never really looked at a picture in his life. In *Wyndham Lewis the Artist*, (1939), he charged Read with willingness to provide any art movement with instant respectability and exposed his weaknesses with deadly accuracy: "Mr. Herbert Read has an unenviable knack of providing, at a week's notice, almost any movement, or submovement, in the visual arts, with a neatly-cut party suit—with which it can appear, appropriately caparisoned, at the cocktail party thrown by the capitalist who has made its birth possible, in celebration of the happy event. No poet laureate, with his ode for every court occasion, could enjoy a more unfailing inspiration with Mr. Read; prefaces and inaugural addresses follow each other in bewildering succession, and with a robust disregard for the slight inconsistencies attendant upon such invariable readiness to oblige."

The intensely independent Lewis (who had an integrated vision in art and literature and was consistent in his aesthetic theory and practice) stated the essential problem was that Read's rather tame and conventional literary work was exactly the opposite of what he daringly professed in the visual arts. Stephen Spender, who said that Read hated Lewis and thought he was evil, has explained that Read's conflicting duality was caused by the extinction of his imaginative powers: "The creative side of his talent has gradually been submerged, and the more this has happened the more depressed he feels about the arts in general. He has a line which is to support nearly everything that is experimental and he therefore gives his readers the impression of being in the vanguard, and someone in the vanguard is supposed of course to have burning faith and vitality: qualities which, in reality, H. R. lacks."

In *The Demon of Progress in the Arts*, which drew the reluctant Eliot into the controversy, Lewis repeated his accusations of 1939 and sardonically observed that Read's willingness to trim his sails to the prevailing aesthetic winds had finally earned him a knighthood in 1953: "In Sir Herbert Read we have a man who has been very recently knighted for being so 'contemporary'; for having been for years ready to plug to the hilt, to trumpet, to expound, any movement in painting or sculpture—sometimes of the most contradictory kind—which was obviously hurrying along a path as opposite as possible from what had appealed to civilized man through the ages."

Lewis' book finally stimulated Read's counterattack, which alluded to the title of Lewis' work and appeared in the *Sewanee Review* in 1955 as "The Lost Leader, or the Psychopathology of Reaction in the Arts." Read relegated Lewis to the ranks of the aesthetic rear guard and argued: "Reactionaryism is a negative doctrine. It vigorously denounces an existing trend—the historical present—and seeks to establish a contrary trend. It is revolution in reverse." In a note on the first page of his essay, Read mentioned that Lewis had provoked his response and made the unconvincing assertion that his own essay was impersonal: "It may be no accident that these thoughts came to me after reading *The Demon of Progress in the Arts*, an attack on the contemporary movement in art by Wyndham Lewis. It should be obvious, however, for reasons given in the course of my essay, that my observations have no application to Mr. Lewis himself."

When Eliot saw this article, he defended Lewis and criticized Read's "psychological" mode of argument. Read, embarrassed at Eliot's censure, became apologetic, maintained that he had always admired Lewis and claimed that Lewis' treacherous attack came as a complete surprise—though Lewis had been condemning Read, with considerable consistency, for thirty years: "The footnote in the *Sewanee* was inserted at the request of the editor, who felt that his American readers would not otherwise see the relevance of my article. . . . I find it difficult to explain why a man for whom I have always had friendly and loyal feelings should turn on me with such bitterness and resentment. . . . Lewis attacked me in a direct and extremely vituperative manner. I was surprised, and I could not reply in kind because I did not feel that way about Lewis—I had hitherto regarded him as a friend. . . . I now regret that I added the footnote—I remember that I added it with reluctance. . . . The harm is that I have shocked you, and there is no one in the world for whose good opinion I have more respect."

Though Read was chagrined by Eliot's displeasure, he continued to attack Lewis after his death in an abusive obituary, a negative review of the *Letters* which appeared under the appalling homiletic title: "A Good Artist But A Bad Friend," and in his 1966 memoir of Eliot. In the memoir Read asserted: "On one of the last occasions that I lunched with [Eliot] alone at the Garrick Club he confessed that in his life there had been few people whom he had found it impossible to like, but Lewis was one of them." It is significant that Read admitted there were no witnesses and did not publish his malicious story until after Eliot's death, for his account contradicted the entire tenor of the poet's forty-year relationship with Lewis. Lewis' April 1955 remark provided a convincing refutation of Read and a fitting conclusion to their longstanding controversy: "Not long ago Tom expressed to me his misgiving for having, in effect, given

Herbert Read his start, encouraging him to contribute to *The Criterion* and publishing some of his books, saying that there was no one whose ideas he considered more pernicious, and I agree with Tom."

IV

Just as Pound had helped Lewis at the beginning of his career, so Eliot sustained him at the end. Though grateful for the assistance, Lewis maintained his ironic attitude as the ecclesiastical Eliot hardened into a national monument: "Tom's always been timid, and afraid of what 'people' will say, 'people' these days for him being 'bishops.' . . . Oh, never mind *him*. [Tom's] like that with everybody. But he doesn't come *in here* disguised as Westminster Abbey." Lewis also continued his rivalry with Eliot. P. H. Newby, who discussed with Lewis the fee for a proposed BBC broadcast, has recorded: " 'I expect you give Tom Eliot much more than me,' Lewis said. 'No,' I replied. 'You would get the same. There are standard fees.' He was not disposed to believe that he would get the same fee as Eliot; I got the impression it was not the amount that mattered but the status it implied. . . . People were alarmed by him—but, in my experience, without justification."

Eliot lent Lewis £200 (which he repaid from his BBC commission) to go to Stockholm for X-ray diagnosis and therapy in June 1950. After Lewis became blind the following year, several friends (including Eliot and Naomi Mitchison) helped him get a Civil List Pension. Eliot encouraged Henry Regnery to publish American editions of Lewis' books in the early 1950s and in 1964 offered to write a preface to the paperback edition of *Self Condemned*, which he called "the best of Lewis's novels" and "a book of almost unbearable spiritual agony." Eliot read the typescript and proofs of *Monstre Gai* and *Malign Fiesta* (the last two parts of *The Human Age*), made suggestions about revising the novels, introduced the radio adaptations and published an essay on *Monstre Gai* in the 1955 issue of *Hudson Review*, which also contained a chapter of the novel. Eliot read the proofs of Lewis' last book, *The Red Priest*, and wrote a warm obituary in the *Sunday Times*: "The output was astounding. The views expressed were independent. . . . Wyndham Lewis was the only one among my contemporaries to create a new, an original, prose style. Most prose of my time, indeed, seems to me, when compared with that of Lewis, lifeless. A great intellect is gone, a great modern writer is dead."

The friendship of Lewis and Eliot was based on intellectual sympathy and mutual esteem. Lewis, who was six years older than Eliot and had a more forceful personality, tended to dominate. He used his failure and Eliot's success to his own moral advantage, for both men felt that Lewis had received much less recognition than he deserved. Eliot, somewhat embarrassed by his own fame, freely expressed his admiration for Lewis in a dozen books and essays published between 1918 and 1960. Once he was blind, Lewis became even more dependent on Eliot's friendship; and after his death in 1957, Eliot continued to praise his genius. Lewis sustained his long friendship with Eliot, as he did with Augustus John and Ezra Pound, because his respect for Eliot's artistic and intellectual powers restrained his caustic tongue and combative temperament. Lewis and Eliot, like Pound and Joyce, the other modernistic "Men of 1914," were all outsiders—three American and one Irish—whose artistic ideals and imaginative innovations transformed, during the early decades of the century, the cultural life of England.

7

EVELYN WAUGH

—— AND ——

ROBERT BYRON

I

Christopher Sykes was a close friend and touring companion of both Evelyn Waugh (1903–1966) and the intriguing but nearly forgotten travel writer Robert Byron (1905–1941). On a trip to Istanbul in 1951, Sykes and Waugh visited Santa Sophia, built as a Byzantine church and converted into an Ottoman mosque. In his biography of Waugh, Sykes recalled that Waugh, a self-styled connoisseur of architecture, "did what he could to make it impossible for me to enjoy and admire that defaced but splendid cathedral. He kept up a continual commentary of denigration."

Waugh also went on to denigrate the late Robert Byron, renewing his life-long conflict with a man who had once been a close friend. In his outburst Waugh insisted that Byron did not have a degree (though he took a Third) and maintained that his passion for Byzantine art was a merely a bogus perversion and fad: "he hadn't done his work and was sent down without a degree so he turned against the classics, and proclaimed post-classical Greek art as the ideal. He was so embarrassingly ignorant that he thought he'd discovered it. . . . Imagine [Sophia] a small building and it's nothing, whereas a small Baroque church can have all the beauty of the Gesù [1568] in Rome and more. [Sophia is] impressive because it's big, like a great big toad." When Sykes asked if he'd ever told Byron his opinion of this supreme Byzantine masterpiece, Waugh replied with astonishing rage: "I hated him! I hated him! I hated him."

Sykes (1975) and Waugh's other biographers—Martin Stannard (1986), Selina Hastings (1994), Douglas Patey (1998) and Philip Eade (2016)—follow each other with superficial accounts of Waugh's extraordinary hatred of Byron, but never provide a convincing explanation of the animus behind their emotional and professional rivalry. Both were close contemporaries, born in London with middle-class origins: Waugh's father was a publisher, Byron's father an engineer. But Byron's name was illustrious; though his connection to the poet was remote, it carried great prestige during his travels in Greece. Waugh's first name seemed effeminate and embarrassing and the risible Waugh seemed to rhyme with laugh. Both men were short, plump and physically unattractive. Waugh was not pleased when Byron teased him about his notable resemblance to Dylan Thomas—lower-class, obese and slovenly. Byron had been educated at Eton and Merton College, Oxford; Waugh at the far less prestigious Lancing and Hertford College.

At Oxford, Waugh and Byron were both homosexuals, and appeared wherever people cross-dressed and were drunk together. Both struck poses and pretended to admire Victorian bad taste. Byron bore a peculiar resemblance to Queen Victoria and did a star-turn imitating her costume and demeanor. They snobbishly sucked up to aristocrats, rejoiced in outrageous behavior and indulged in extreme rudeness. After Oxford they suffered mental breakdowns. Their similar temperaments were both the basis of their friendship and a principal reason for Waugh's reaction against his youthful companion. Waugh came to see Byron as an extreme embodiment of the characteristics he loathed in himself.

Anthony Powell described Byron's extraordinary looks. He was "stocky, very fair, his complexion of yellowish wax, popping pale blue eyes, a long sharp nose." Waugh, with ill-concealed revulsion, called him "short, fleshy and ugly in a painfully ignominious way. His complexion was yellow. . . . He dealt with his ill looks by making them grotesque" and dressing eccentrically to heighten the effect and attract attention.

Byron's ill-favored appearance did not restrict his sexual activity. After Oxford, and on his travels where he had more sexual freedom, Byron continued to exhibit his flamboyant manner, while Waugh concealed what he considered a shameful episode. Powell, the only close friend who discussed Byron's homosexuality, was told that on a train "in the Far East somewhere Robert was having an affair with the Japanese *wagon-lit* man." Powell also quoted Byron's most outrageous statement without explaining what he meant. Asked what he would like best in the world, Byron exclaimed, "To be an incredibly beautiful male prostitute with a sharp sting in my bottom." In his no-holes-barred fantasy Byron wanted to attract unlimited lovers while punishing them, like a sadistic wasp, for sodomizing him. Orwell famously condemned these "so-called artists who spend on sodomy what they have gained by sponging."

Despite his effeminate behavior Byron could be surprisingly strong and aggressive. Humphrey Carpenter wrote that, at Oxford, Byron once led the aesthetes in an attack that inflicted serious injuries on the hearties: "one heroic evening they fell like ninepins before a barrage of champagne bottles flung by Robert Byron from a strategic position at the head of the stairs with a force and precision that radically changed the pattern of Oxford rowing for the rest of the term."

Byron struck so many poses at Oxford that it was difficult to determine when he was serious. His homosexual friend Harold Acton recalled, he "believed that never had Britain been more resplendent than between 1846 and 1865. The vision of a 'large-limbed, high-coloured Victorian England, seated in honour and plenty' was constantly before him." But in his best book, *The Road to Oxiana* (1937), on travels through Persia and Afghanistan, Byron praises the anti-decorative and perfectly chaste Palladian style: "You cannot analyse it—nothing could be more lucid." His Victorianism, including imitations of the old queen, was actually a camp joke to oppose both his father's values and the deterioration of English taste in the nineteenth century.

Byron also expressed hostility to the superficial and derivative work of Bloomsbury artists by punning on the morbidity of Museum Street and recommending a much livelier but unfashionable district in west London: "Paddington is the symbol of all that Bloomsbury is not. In place of the refined peace of those mausoleum streets, here are public-houses, fun-fairs, buses, tubes and vulgar posters. Also here are small brick houses, Gothic mews, and great tapering tenements in which to live"—though he never chose to live there himself.

At Eton and Oxford, Byron emphasized his insularity and pretended to be horrified by going abroad and confronting foreigners, but actually spent most of his adult life making adventurous journeys. Like Waugh, Powell was a shrewd observer both fascinated and repelled by Byron. He wrote that Byron "was energetic, ambitious, violent, quarrelsome, with views in complete contrast with those of the typical precocious schoolboy of the period. Anti-Nineties, the very words 'intellectual' or 'good taste' threw him into paroxysms of rage. He was in any case habitually in a state of barely controlled exasperation about everything. . . . There was a great deal of toughness, mental and physical, both camouflaged by wild buffoonery and exotic behaviour." Powell called Byron, who adored his "artistic" mother and ignored his philistine father, "the Mum's Boy to end all Mum's Boys," but did not connect his maternal adoration to his homosexuality. All Byron's friends commented on his violent temperament and ferocious manners, his furious enthusiasms and tyrannical antagonisms. When an eminent bore droned on and on at dinner, Byron screamed at him with shocking rudeness, "Can't you shut up, you hideous old relic of the Victorian age?"

Byron's fierce opposition to the prevailing glorification of Classical Greece was the *basso ostinato* of his entire existence. He believed that the Byzantine Empire (330–1453) was the acme of Hellenic greatness. Acton, whom Byron visited in China in 1937, remarked that "Byzantium had captured his one-track imagination: it was the fount of all true art; so long as an object was Byzantine he saw a meaning in every line and curve. . . . Now every ray of his searchlight was directed towards El Greco, the culmination, for him, of the Byzantine ideal," which the Greek painter had introduced to Western art. Just as Waugh would later violently condemn Santa Sophia when traveling in Istanbul with Sykes, so Byron amused and irritated Acton, who recalled that he "inveighed against Chinese architecture, which he refused to accept as architecture. He exaggerated his contempt for my benefit. . . . 'These are tents, booths and summer-houses, pshaw!—contraptions for bazaars.'"

Sykes' description of Byron's egoistic blundering and comical performance when catching a boat in Cyprus exemplifies his assertion, when abroad, of superiority in act as well as in art: "I saw a round figure dressed in jodhpurs and a tweed jacket, and with a cigarette dangling from his lower lip, fairly charging along the jetty to a sound of clattering cameras, pencil-cases and folios which hung about him. A gigantic negro followed at a half-run with his bags. I watched from the deck. Arrived at the boat he showed his ticket, returned it to his pocket, and then made a sort of dive at the officials, swam through them on a breast-stroke and mounted the gangway. 'Hallo, I'm late.'"

What accounted for the confrontational behavior and pathological extremism of Roberto Furioso? Apart from an obscure organic disturbance, he always wanted to attract attention to himself, had a megalomaniacal belief in his own self-importance, was frustrated by the lack of wealth that many of his friends had inherited, and felt insufficiently respected and rewarded for his arduous travels and hard work.

Lacking unearned income and always short of funds to support his constant journeys, Byron was shamelessly greedy and unscrupulous when exploiting anyone who could help him. Yet Powell noted the self-defeating aspect of Byron's egoistic quest: "Not at all averse from going out of his way to make himself agreeable to rich or influential people likely to be of use . . . at the same time [he was] prepared to have a blood row at a moment's notice with anyone whomsoever, no matter how inconvenient to his own interests." Waugh was circumspect when cultivating the rich. But he shared Byron's anti-American streak, zest for foreign journeys and innovative travel writing. Sykes said Byron used "a typewriter as freely as a pen, with the cigarette never out of his mouth, and the wireless bellowing classical music at him."

II

Powell emphasized Byron's eccentricity and exoticism, and noted that he "was immensely competitive, which made him jealous of everybody, including Evelyn. . . . Evelyn certainly didn't care for Robert, while respecting him." Their competition heated up as early as 1929 when Waugh enviously wrote to Henry Green, "Robert Byron has beaten us all by going to India in an aeroplane which is the sort of success which I call tangible."

Byron's role in Waugh's first marriage the previous year (June 27, 1928) was a crucial turning point in their once amicable relations. In April 1927 Waugh recorded in his diary, "I have met such a nice girl named Evelyn Gardner and renewed my friendship with" Robert Byron. Three weeks before the wedding, Byron told his mother that they were all practically living together: "Evelyn Waugh has come to live opposite—Evelyn Gardner is living on the ground floor at Upper Montagu Street—so they both spend all their lives in here—as their own rooms are so disgusting." Two days before the wedding he mentioned his strong-armed ceremonial duty: "I have to *fetch* Evelyn Gardner to the church and I know she won't come."

Waugh liked to pretend that their marriage was an impulsive whim: "Evelyn and I began to go to Dulwich to see the pictures there but got bored waiting for the right bus so went instead to the Vicar General's [administrative] office and bought a marriage license." Acton described the hastily arranged and covert affair, at an unfashionable venue, with She-Evelyn's flat mate attending: "I found myself standing, in the guise of 'best man,' at a secret wedding in a Protestant church off Baker Street. Robert Byron gave the bride away. So overcome was she that she could scarcely bring herself to breathe the words 'I do.' Evelyn's brother Alec and Pansy Pakenham were the only others present, and I gave a 'wedding breakfast' at Boulestin's after the ceremony." Attended by two homosexuals, Gardner, whom Henry Green called "a very silly piece," was a boyish young woman, with a flat chest, short hair and long chin.

Following a disastrous honeymoon, Waugh's marriage ended abruptly after only thirteen months when She-Evelyn confessed her love affair with the caddish Irish baronet and journalist Sir John Heygate. Shocked and humiliated, Waugh sought sympathy from Byron, who seemed to feel *Schadenfreude* about the foolish marriage. In February 1930 he told his mother: "I had a letter from Evelyn poor creature about his divorce—he is still paying for the furniture in the flat now inhabited by the other Evelyn and Heygate. . . . They have both behaved abominably." Devastated by She-Evelyn's betrayal, Waugh sought refuge in religion and converted to Catholicism that year.

In 1936 Waugh pulled tassels to have his first marriage annulled and wed the homely "timid white mouse" Laura Herbert. She was a strict Catholic from an aristocratic family, and he engendered seven burdensome children to show he was a real (not queer) man. Waugh's friends would have been pleased to know that Heygate came to a bad end. He was divorced from She-Evelyn in 1936 and from his second wife in 1947, and became a widower when his third wife died. In 1976 he shot himself.

The most obvious reason for the rupture of Waugh's friendship was Byron's virulent anti-Catholic attacks, which shook the precarious foundation of Waugh's newly acquired faith. Byron's hostility, favoring Byzantine over Catholic art and architecture, was aesthetic as well as spiritual. Douglas Patey pointed out that "all Byron's books of the twenties pause to attack Rome, the papacy and Catholic art, favouring instead Byzantine and Islamic styles. . . . Waugh also meant to irritate Byron by consistently mocking 'the glamour of the East,' by running down the Orthodox churches he visited (always unfavourably compared to Catholic), and by his wholesale, deliberately Blimpish condemnation of Islamic art and culture."

Waugh shrewdly perceived that in *The Road to Oxiana* Byron had falsely attributed his own obsessive anti-Catholic ranting to an Orthodox priest. Sykes explained that Byron lived in great dread of a Vatican conspiracy—which he connected to Mussolini's fascism and Pope Pius XII's sympathy with Hitler: "He foolishly introduced this anti-Catholic mania into his book, and he did it in a way that Evelyn recognized as fraudulent. Robert was a very poor linguist. All the non-English conversations recorded in his book are invented. Among them is a supposed talk with a Greek priest in the Church of the Holy Sepulchre in Jerusalem. The Greek priest is represented as expressing his utter contempt of Roman Catholic pilgrims. Evelyn spotted that this was Robert up to his old tricks. . . . I was there and can positively affirm that even if the nice-mannered young priest had descended to vulgar abuse, Robert would have missed it through ignorance of Greek."

It was bad enough for Byron to inject venomous anti-Catholic propaganda into his books, but even worse when he was personally offensive. Sykes, a Catholic who often saw them together, was shocked when Byron became even "more violently and hysterically anti-Catholic than before. Whenever they met, Robert lost no opportunity of exasperating Evelyn by anti-Catholic tirades in which he often descended to the grossest blasphemy. After a while Evelyn . . . found it impossible to take this mixture of prejudice, ignorance, loutishness and sheer silliness with good humour. The friendship slowly terminated." Out of control as usual, jealous and envious when Waugh's career took off, Byron was either trying to test the limits of Waugh's tolerance or attempting to sever their relations forever. Rebecca West, infuriated by Waugh's convenient conversion, helped explain Byron's hostility: "Waugh made drunkenness cute and chic, and then took to religion, simply to have the most expensive carpet of all to be sick on. I DON'T LIKE IT."

Byron never wrote about Waugh, but Waugh alluded to Byron in two of his books, reviewed works by and about him, and wrote a caustic analysis of his character. Byron told Waugh he was "*very* cross" about the satiric portrait of him as a freakish, offensive and effeminate character in Waugh's first novel, *Decline and Fall* (1928). Lord Parakeet arrived late and drunk at Mrs. Beste-Chewynde's weekend party and "walked round birdlike and gay, pointing his thin white nose and making rude little jokes at everyone in turn in a shrill emasculate voice."

Byron's first book, *Europe in the Looking-Glass* (1926), whose title alludes to the fantasies of Lewis Carroll, describes his car trip from London to Constantinople. In his travel book *Labels* (1930) Waugh amusingly parodied—with a sting at the bottom—Byron's typically pretentious, chromatic and swooning description of the Sicilian island of Stromboli: "I do not think I shall ever forget the sight of Etna at sunset; the mountain almost invisible in a *blur of pastel grey, glowing on the top* and then repeating its shape, as though reflected, in a *wisp of grey smoke*, with the whole horizon behind *radiant with pink light*, fading gently into a *grey pastel sky*. Nothing I have ever seen in Art or Nature was quite so revolting" (my emphasis).

Waugh's review of *The Road to Oxiana* in the *Spectator* (July 2, 1937) revealed his own competitive streak but was generous, despite Byron's egregious faults, about his idiosyncratic opinions: "Mr. Byron is an inveterate and indefatigable professional; he began writing before most of his generation and will, I hope, long flourish when the rest of them have given up. . . . He admits no limits to his insatiable aesthetic curiosity and no standards of judgment but his personal reactions. It is a grave handicap, but Mr. Byron's gusto is so powerful that the reader can only applaud."

In the Catholic *Tablet* (December 7, 1946), five years after Byron's death, Waugh reviewed Sykes' *Four Studies in Loyalty*, which contained a long chapter of over-the-top adoration of Byron. Waugh respectfully held fire, paid homage to Byron and only hinted at his extreme hostility to his political views: "Sykes quotes extensively from Byron's published work. These extracts are pungent, bursting with life, exuberant, vehement in argument, rollicking in humour, like Byron himself." In contrast to "the earlier, carefree aesthete and traveller," Byron's dark mood in the last years of peace "arose from the sense of a personal, frustrated mission to arouse his fellow-countrymen to the imminence of war." Sykes admitted that Waugh, unwilling to offend Byron's memory or provoke his friends, did not mean a word of his praise. As Waugh told Nancy Mitford, who adored Byron, Christopher Sykes has written "a lot of balls about the late Robert Byron."

To balance Sykes' unseemly adulation, Waugh finally took revenge on Byron in two caustic pages of his late autobiography *A Little Learning* (1964). The title comes from Alexander Pope's couplet in his *Essay on Criticism*: "A little learning is a dangerous thing; / Drink deep, or taste not the Pierian spring." While

Waugh was modest about his own considerable erudition, he was outraged that the astonishingly ignorant Byron was treated as the learned authority of distinguished books. As Thomas Gray also wrote, "Where ignorance is bliss, 'tis folly to be wise." At Oxford, Waugh noted, Byron was a provincial, uneducated and awkward writer, who perversely thought *Hamlet* was an "emotional hoax":

> At the age of eighteen Robert gave no discernible promise of the adven-
> turous journeys and the frantic craving for knowledge which obsessed
> his later years. . . . Then he was as insular as I—"Down with abroad,"
> he used to shout when travel was mentioned. . . . He learned little at
> school or at the university and later was disposed to think that masters
> and dons had concealed from him for their own ends the information
> he subsequently acquired. Anything they had tried to teach him—the
> Classics and Shakespeare—he dismissed as an imposture. . . . He never
> learned to write elegant or perfectly correct English. His talent was for
> narrative, the sharply observed scene, the pungent anecdote, the fugi-
> tive absurdity. Later his aspirations grew vastly wider, but at Oxford he
> was purely a clown and a very good one.

Waugh thought Byron was deliberately provocative, specialized in bad behavior and was an ugly drunkard: "He leered and scowled, screamed and snarled, fell into rages that were sometimes real and sometimes a charade. . . . Wherever he went he created a disturbance, falling down in the street in simulated epilepsy, yelling to passers-by from the back of a motor-car that he was being kidnapped. . . . [He was determined] to force his way into the worlds of power and fashion; and he succeeded. Robert in his cups was pugnacious, destructive and sottish, lapsing before the evening was out into an unlovely sleep."

Though Waugh's travels extended from Guiana to Spitsbergen, he feared that Byron might surpass him. Waugh had initially forgiven his egregious faults and allowed that Byron "was much loved and, eventually, admired. I liked him and, until the fractious late 'thirties, when his violent opinions became, to me, intolerably repugnant, I greatly relished his company." When writing about Byron's extensive travels, physical appearance, outrageous behavior, offensive rudeness and frequent drunkenness Waugh was also writing about himself. But he does not mention Byron's homosexuality and attacks on religion, nor give the specific reasons for their political quarrel in the prewar years.

In an unusually sad and regretful comment about politics and the preservation of Georgian architecture in London, Byron said, "One spends one's life trying to save things—Jews, buildings, not to mention the world as a whole." He had seen the violent fascist demonstrations near Vienna in October 1928 and witnessed the rabid Nuremberg Rally in September 1938, when he and Diana Mosley sat close to Hitler. So he was one of the first British observers to recognize the fatal threat to European Jews. Acton reported that Byron "had no illusions about the Nazi menace: he could talk of little else. Tiresomely tactless, he scoffed at Chamberlain's supporters." When a dinner companion praised Chamberlain's disastrous appeasement of Hitler, Byron leaned across the table and provocatively asked, "Are you in German pay?" Not entirely satisfied with that public insult, he sadistically added: "I'd like very much to have you under a glass case with a pin struck through you. I'd have a label tied round your neck. I'd show you to people with strong stomachs. A perfect specimen of the British ruling class to-day."

Waugh was pro-Mussolini and anti-Semitic; Byron was anti-Hitler and pro-Zionist. Waugh hated him for his political views even more than for his anti-Catholic tirades. He mistakenly thought Byron was a Communist and, Sykes noted, regarded his politics "as no more than a violent expression of the fashionable Leftist silliness of Kingsley Martin's *New Statesman*. In short Evelyn saw in Robert a phenomenon which invariably roused his ire, a thoroughly overrated man."

Acton recalled that Waugh "was antagonized by the violence of Byron's opinions and talked as if he might become a public menace." He was even more furious in a letter to Acton of April 1948, when he exclaimed, "I greatly disliked Robert in his last years & think he was a dangerous lunatic better dead." After the war against Germany, when the anti-Nazi warnings of the "lunatic" proved all too accurate, Waugh still refused to recognize the value of Byron's prophecies. He could never accept the fact that Byron had been right and he'd been wrong.

Byron's mysterious death has been described in vague, misleading and even quite mistaken ways by several journalists and biographers. His sister's editorial note in Byron's *Letters Home* (1991) states that his ship was "torpedoed by the *Scharnhorst* off the north of Scotland," and Jeremy Treglown's biography of Henry Green (2000) repeats this error. In fact, the *Scharnhorst* was a battleship, not a submarine armed with torpedoes. It was not on the scene and was not involved in Byron's death.

On February 24, 1941, Byron, listed as a war correspondent, was a passenger on the cargo ship *Jonathan Holt*. It was sailing in a wintry sea from Liverpool to the coast of West Africa, and he planned to continue around the Cape of Good Hope to Egypt. Instead of heading directly south to Africa, the ship sailed northwest from Liverpool to rendezvous with a convoy of warships that would escort them to their destinations. But the *Jonathan Holt* was torpedoed and sunk by the German submarine U-97, in the north Atlantic Ocean between Scotland and Iceland. Six men were saved; Byron and fifty-one other men drowned. Trapped in the sinking ship, he gasped for air as his lungs filled with water. In "The Castaway" the eighteenth-century poet William Cowper vividly portrayed the terror of drowning at sea:

Obscurest night involved the sky,
  The Atlantic billows roared,
When such a destined wretch as I,
  Washed headlong from on board,
Of friends, of hope, of all bereft,
His floating home for ever left.

Four of the ten passengers were agents of the SOE (Special Operations Executive), who carried out espionage and sabotage in Axis-occupied Europe. Byron may have been a spy posing as a correspondent. His friends would have been glad to learn that in June 1943 the U-97 submarine, which had sunk sixteen ships, was itself sunk in the Mediterranean, west of Haifa, by a depth charge from an Australian plane.

Waugh's self-loathing and competitive spirit combined with Byron's tirades against Catholicism and vehement political views were the most obvious causes of Waugh's violent hatred. But there were also more subtle reasons. Byron had been an eyewitness and painful reminder of the two most discreditable and humiliating episodes in Waugh's life: his Oxford homosexuality and disastrous first marriage. The cuckolded Waugh wanted to suppress and forget them while the antagonistic Byron always remembered and ridiculed them.

After Waugh's marriage broke up, his competition with Byron continued with their emotional rivalry for the affection of the exceptionally beautiful Diana Mitford. Byron was chief usher at Diana's wedding to Bryan Guinness, heir to the brewery fortune, in 1929, the year She-Evelyn left Waugh. Diana later divorced Guinness and married Oswald Mosley, the leader of the British fascists. In March 1966, a month before his death, Waugh wrote a regretful letter to Diana explaining why, before she married Mosley and adopted his adoration of Hitler, their friendship petered out: "I was infatuated with you. Not of course that I aspired to your bed but I wanted you to myself as especial confidante and comrade. . . . I felt lower in your affections than Harold Acton and Robert Byron and I couldn't compete or take a humbler place. That is the sad and sordid truth." Waugh's feelings had become even more anguished when he learned that Diana's sister Jessica wanted to *marry* Robert Byron. But she misunderstood his kind of fashionable adult homosexuality, which confused and distressed her, and said "he was a total pederast. . . . This wretched pederasty falsifies all feelings & yet one is supposed to revere it" in sophisticated society.

Finally, Waugh felt guilty about the effect of the war on their lives and reputations. He had secured an army commission, had an undistinguished record during the British retreat from Crete and his military liaison with Tito in Yugoslavia. He survived the war and died straining himself on the toilet. Byron, whose violent temper prevented him from getting a commission, was Waugh's only close Oxford friend who died through enemy action. The dead Byron seemed to emerge from the war with more glory than the living Waugh. In venting his hatred, despite the great achievement of his novels, Waugh must have felt, as Gore Vidal sharply observed, "it was not enough to succeed, others [like Byron] must fail."

8

WAUGH

—— AND ——

RANDOLPH CHURCHILL

Evelyn Waugh and Randolph Churchill served on a military mission to Marshal Tito's Partisans in Yugoslavia from July 1944 to February 1945. Earlier in the war, Waugh had been insubordinate and unable to adjust to regimental life; Randolph, as always, had been notoriously drunk, belligerent and offensive. Like fierce ferrets confined in a cage, two of the most difficult and disagreeable officers in the British army acted out a disastrous vendetta. Their caustic clash alienated Tito and damaged the relations between Britain and its crucial ally during the German occupation of Yugoslavia.

One hundred and twenty pages of unpublished material from the National Archives and the Public Record Office in Kew, England, and from Churchill College, Cambridge University, cast new light on British policy in Yugoslavia, its military contacts with Tito, and the contrast between his communist Partisans and the pro-Nazi Ustashe; on Randolph's work, constant complaints and offensive behavior as well as his courage under fire; on Waugh and Randolph's near-fatal air crash, their English comrade Stephen Clissold, and Waugh's support of the Catholic Ustashe in opposition to official policy. This archival material explains why these tragicomic adventurers wound up in wartime Croatia, why they quarreled bitterly in an isolated village and why their important mission was doomed to failure.

Randolph (1911–1968) and Waugh (1903–1966), an odd couple and odd choice for this mission, were anti-communist, had no experience in Yugoslavia and no knowledge of Serbo-Croat. They had first met socially in the early 1930s, had many friends in common and maintained an intermittent, often

93

hostile friendship. Both men had made calamitous first marriages to unfaith-
ful wives. Randolph had all the qualities that the snobbish Waugh lacked and
craved. He was descended from John Churchill, Duke of Marlborough, one of
the greatest soldiers in English history, and was the son of Winston Churchill,
the all-powerful wartime Prime Minister. Tall, handsome, wealthy and influential, he was educated at Eton and Christchurch, Oxford, and was Member
of Parliament for Preston, Scotland, from 1940 to 1945. In April 1942 he joined
Major David Stirling's elite commandos in the Libyan Desert where he injured
his back in a serious road accident. Randolph and Brigadier Fitzroy Maclean
first parachuted into Drvar, Croatia, on January 19, 1944; Waugh arrived by
plane, six months later, on July 10. Though eight years younger than Captain
Waugh, Major Churchill outranked him and led the operation.

Christopher Sykes, a friend of both men and biographer of Waugh, described Randolph's habitual behavior. He recalled an outrageous 1939 luncheon
party at a local country house where "Randolph did everything he knew, and
he knew a lot, to distress, anger, exasperate and make miserable his host and
every one of his fellow guests!" After the war the unregenerate Randolph "still
insisted on laying down the law, still resented any show of opposition, still
bullied his audience into submission and was still incapable of controlling his
temper." Though more horrified than amused, friends continued to court the
well-connected and influential social lion.

The son of a middle-class publisher and critic, Waugh was short, baby-faced
and burdened with an effeminate name. He had gone to Lancing, a distinctly
less impressive public school, and to Hertford College, Oxford, where he was
frequently drunk, passed through an intense homosexual phase and left without taking a degree. He joined the Royal Marines in December 1939 at the age
of thirty-six, when he seemed too old to enlist yet fancied himself a military
man. But he was irritable and sarcastic with his men and lost his command
of a company. He participated in the failed raid on Dakar, in Vichy-controlled
French West Africa, in September 1940. He fought with Colonel Robert Lay-
cock's elite commando force during a failed mission to Libya in February 1941,
and took part in the evacuation of Crete after the Greek island was captured
by German paratroopers in May 1941.

Like the left-wing Loyalist factions who had fought each other as well as
their fascist enemy in the recent Spanish Civil War, Tito's communist Partisans,

Draza Mihailovic's Serbian Chetniks and Ante Pavelic's pro-Nazi Ustashe were fighting a savage ideological war during the German occupation for postwar control of their country. Michael Davie, editor of Waugh's *Diaries*, explained how early in 1944 Brigadier Fitzroy Maclean and Major William Deakin, serving behind enemy lines in Yugoslavia, effected a radical change in British policy: "Their reports on Tito's anti-German zeal, and the ruthlessness of his guerrillas, were enthusiastic. Mihailovic, by contrast, appeared to be less interested in fighting the Germans than in waiting his chance to restore the fortunes of Serbia [and the exiled King Peter II]. The British accordingly abandoned Mihailovic and put their full support behind Tito." Maclean's mission, whose headquarters were in the southern Adriatic city of Bari, Italy, was to assist Tito's irregular army with supplies and weapons in order to defeat the Germans.

Secret reports sent from English agents in Yugoslavia to Bari in July and September 1944, while Waugh and Randolph were serving in Croatia, revealed the complexity of Yugoslavian politics. Captain D. C. Owen thought the Partisans were more anti-Nazi than fanatically communist and emphasized their brutal warfare. Since the Partisans did not take prisoners, the Ustashe fought fiercely to avoid being captured:

> The majority of the Partisan forces, when asked, say "I am fighting for the Partisans now because I wish to help get rid of the Germans, but I have different political ideas after the war." This is the general trend and the general colour of the political instruction within the Corps is more "pink" than "red." . . . The USTASHI are determined fighters, as they know they will be killed anyway—no quarter given on either side. The Partisan leaders say that about 20% of the USTASHI have either been conscripted unwillingly or have no blood on their hands, and if captured would be given trial [i.e., summary execution], but front line troops difficult to persuade to take prisoners.

After Tito won the civil war Draza Mihailovic was executed. Ante Pavelic survived an assassination attempt in Argentina and died in Madrid.

Lieutenant J. H. Gibbs reported that the Yugoslavs—struggling for survival and aware of their ideological opposition to the British—both needed and exploited the ally who provided essential war materiel. They were naturally

suspicious and resentful of political and military interference by the country
that had recently backed their enemy Mihailovic. But distrust had subsided
and relations improved after the successful Allied landings in France on June 6,
1944, made victory in Europe seem likely:

> General impression, after 10 months with 6 Corps and 3 months
> with 10 Corps: we are of use to the Partisan movement for stores and
> propaganda—and last autumn, not even for stores. If they could get the
> same benefits without our presence they would not want us. They have
> no reasons for pinning us down (don't have after public professions of
> friendship), yet they are uneasy to set us free. Suspicious if we make
> friends. I know of one Partisan who was cross-questioned by the Corps
> Commandant as to what he talked about with the BLO [British Liaison
> Officer] and told to watch his step.
>
> One sometimes gets the feeling, when asking them for collaboration,
> that they have orders from a higher level to obstruct, but will not put
> their cards on the table and say so. This refers, of course, only to rela-
> tions with the higher officers, who incidentally are invariably correct
> and cordial and the above impression only slowly takes form. Outside
> that narrow circle, their relations are usually excellent. The BLO is
> welcomed and popular either as an individual or as an "Englishman"
> (very hard on the Scots)—both in peasant cottages and with ex-ZAGREB
> townspeople. Since the opening of the "Second Front" and the march
> through FRANCE, which has staggered the most hardened critics, pro-
> British and American feeling is very high.

Winston Churchill sent his only son to Yugoslavia to show his solidarity
with and personal commitment to Tito's Partisans. On June 28, 1944, before
leaving London, Randolph rampaged through the bar in White's club and
shouted: "Where the hell is Evelyn Waugh? I've tried everywhere! No one can
tell me! I need him immediately! . . . I've been commissioned to undertake a
subordinate mission under Fitzroy Maclean in Jugoslavia. . . . I told Fitz before I
left that I must have officers I can talk to and he agreed with me that Evelyn was
just the chap for me. It's all very secret," he added, his voice rising in volume.

Ignoring Waugh's contentious personality, Randolph thought the former commando had the right adventurous character and military experience to fortify the mission. Waugh's biographer Martin Stannard noted that "in civilian life Waugh often found Churchill stimulating, an eccentric eager for life, volatile, courageous, sentimental. In wartime this preposterous schoolboy seemed sadly diminished . . . unable to crawl from the weight of his father's fame." Stannard added that Waugh intensified their volatile mixture, "When drunk Waugh could be amusingly offensive; sober, he was caustic and melancholy."

Randolph also believed that Waugh, like a powerful medieval pope, would "be able to heal the Great Schism between the Catholic and the Orthodox churches." In fact, Waugh damaged relations with the Partisans by contacting the pro-Nazi Croatian Catholics, and was nearly expelled by the communists for interfering in their internal conflict. Brian Roberts, Randolph's biographer, expressed astonishment that he and Waugh had been recruited for such an important and sensitive task: "the choice of two such tactless, intolerant, quick-tempered and heavy-handed men for what was obviously a delicate diplomatic mission is incomprehensible. Neither of them had the slightest sympathy with Communism and they never attempted to pretend otherwise. Two more unlikely ambassadors to a peasant people is difficult to imagine." Both men felt they were entitled to special treatment: they ignored military regulations, disobeyed their superiors, and were hated by their fellow officers and men.

When Maclean met Randolph in Cairo in November 1943, he was recovering from his crash in the desert, was boorishly drunk, insulted generals and embarrassed his father. Nevertheless Maclean, who outranked Randolph and could control him, praised his social graces and wrote: "I began to realize what a marvelous companion Randolph could be. Maddening, of course, in a dozen different ways, but endlessly stimulating and entertaining." But Maclean was quite mistaken in thinking Waugh could control Randolph and was far off the mark in stating that Randolph could consider Waugh his social equal: "Here, at last, was someone well qualified to contain Randolph, someone whom, with major adjustments, he might even regard as his social and intellectual equal."

In his autobiography *Eastern Approaches*, published in 1949 when his poor judgment had become obvious, Maclean stubbornly and unconvincingly justified his choice:

Randolph would make a useful addition to my Mission. . . . For my present purposes he seemed just the man. On operations I knew him to be
thoroughly dependable, possessing both endurance and determination.
He was also gifted with an acute intelligence and a very considerable
background of general politics. . . . I felt, too—rightly, as it turned out—
that he would get on well with the Jugoslavs, for his enthusiastic and at
times explosive approach to life was not unlike their own. Lastly I knew
him to be a stimulating companion, an important consideration in the
circumstances under which we lived.

In fact, Randolph, who could be rather dim, did not get on with the Yugoslavs
or with Waugh, and his explosive approach to diplomacy created a tense atmosphere.

On May 25, 1944, two months before Waugh arrived, Randolph showed
the best side of his character. Though his mission did not include actual combat, he was awarded an MBE (Member of the British Empire) for outstanding
leadership and courage under fire:

Major CHURCHILL was with the British Military Mission in DRVAR when
the Germans made a sudden airborne attack on 25 May. After marching
for many hours throughout that day, he was sent off during the night to
a Partisan Corps some miles away. He successfully accomplished this
journey, which was through enemy occupied territory, and transmitted
some most important messages which had been entrusted to him. He
then took charge of the mission attached to this Corps and, in very
difficult circumstances, kept ITALY well informed of the progress of operations, so that the maximum Allied assistance could be given to the
Partisans. Later he was placed in charge of a British and Russian party
which was to be evacuated to BARI. Although continuously harried and
kept on the move by the enemy, he kept the party together until an
opportunity occurred for them to be evacuated by air. It was largely
due to his efforts that this evacuation was successfully accomplished.

Frank McLynn, Maclean's biographer, tried to explain the twisted motives
behind his choice: "[Waugh] was a character of some distinction, and Fitzroy

liked such people. . . . Fitzroy was dazzled by Waugh's reputation and thought it would add to the aura of the mission. . . . [He] had received an advance copy of *Put Out More Flags* [1942], liked it and thought it would be interesting to have a writer on the mission, especially one Randolph had requested." Waugh's novel included a flattering "Dedicatory Letter to Major Randolph Churchill" and was signed "Your affectionate friend, the Author." Maclean, choosing literary over military qualities, saw himself as a fictional Waugh hero and sought literary fame.

Though Maclean had chosen him, Waugh disliked his new commander at first sight and rather harshly described the Scotsman, dedicated to British interests, as "dour, unprincipled, ambitious, probably wicked; shaved head and devil's ears." Stannard called Waugh "a fake hard man"; real heroes, Maclean and Tito, "shocked him in their toughness." When Wilfred Thesiger, an equally tough explorer and soldier, met Waugh in Abyssinia in 1930, he immediately perceived Waugh's weakness and recalled, "he struck me as flaccid and petulant and I disliked him on sight." When Waugh asked if he could accompany him on a dangerous mission, Thesiger refused and fiercely remarked, "Had he come, I suspect only one of us would have returned."

Freddy Birkenhead, the son of the earl who was Winston's greatest friend, had been Randolph's superior at Eton. He was sent to Croatia as an emotional buffer when relations between Waugh and Randolph had reached the breaking point, and wrote that "the duties of the British missions in Yugoslavia were mainly to liaise with the Partisan military headquarters and the political commissars, and to spread with tact and care as much pro-British information as possible to counteract the . . . [influence of] Russia to whom they were attached by political and historical association." Soon after arriving Randolph confirmed, "I am now with Fitzroy Maclean. My job is to look after propaganda (a) about us to the Partisans and (b) to the outside world about the Partisans." But on January 27, 1944, the Minister of State's Office in Cairo had warned the Foreign Office in London to proceed with great caution: "We conceive that any overt attempt at propaganda penetration of Partisan movement would raise objections on the part of Tito and that this problem must be properly approached and with full information."

On July 10, 1944, Waugh and Randolph flew from Bari to meet Marshal Tito on the Adriatic island of Vis, which was protected by British planes based in Italy. As Britain's main ally in German-occupied Yugoslavia, Tito had to be treated with the greatest delicacy and tact, yet Waugh made him the target of a relentless joke. Stannard explained the origin of Waugh's amusing but provocative behavior: "In the early days of Maclean's mission, over a year before, no one had been certain whether Tito even existed, let alone whether this mythical figure were male or female. This tiny seed of gossip fueled years of Waugh's malice and, far from retracting the slander, he took every opportunity to embellish it." Waugh expressed his hostility to the communists by calling their leader a woman and even a lesbian, and tried to divert his colleagues by continuing to repeat that dangerous absurdity. Birkenhead recalled, "he never referred to the Yugoslav leader except as 'Auntie,' and claimed that the Marshal had been seen emerging from the sea off the island of Vis in a wet bathing dress and that there was no possible question about 'her' sex. . . . We became much concerned that the Yugoslav members of the staff would overhear him and that our work might be seriously imperilled." Warned by Birkenhead, Waugh cheekily replied, "Her face is pretty, but her legs are *very* thick." When Waugh was introduced to the unmistakably virile Tito, the heroic leader ignored the insult, stared at him and said, "Ask Captain Waugh why he thinks I am a woman." Waugh, for once, was reduced to silence. The Croats called Waugh Captain "Vo," which means "ox" in their language.

After the unfortunate meeting with Tito, Waugh and Randolph returned to Bari. On July 16, 1944, they flew at night to Partisan headquarters in Topusko, Croatia (about forty miles south of Zagreb), an important escape route for crews of downed Allied bombers and ex-prisoners of war. But their propeller-driven Dakota transport plane crashed from about four hundred feet and burst into flames in the remote village of Gajevi. Waugh recalled: "I was conscious by my ears that we were descending and circling the airfield, then we suddenly shot upwards and the next thing I knew was that I was walking in a cornfield by the light of the burning aeroplane talking to a strange British officer about the progress of the war in a detached fashion. . . . I had no recollection of the crash nor, at the time, any knowledge of where I was or why, but a confused idea that we had made a forced landing during some retreat." The pilot, who misjudged the length of the landing field, tried to gain altitude, lost speed, stalled and crashed. Nine passengers freed themselves from the rear of the plane; ten in the front were killed. On July17 Randolph cabled Winston, "asking him to inform Mrs. Joan Sowman that her husband Douglas Sowman [Randolph's batman] was killed in a plane crash in Yugoslavia and to send her his deepest sympathy and inform the wives of [the war correspondent] Philip Jordan and Evelyn Waugh that they are safe."

Randolph, escaping from his second near-fatal accident, had both legs crushed and could barely move. Waugh's head, arms and legs were burned but, anesthetized by the shock of the crash, he felt no pain. He recorded that when they returned, wrapped like mummies, to recover in the hospital in Bari, Randolph was "drinking, attacking the night nurse, wanting everyone's medicine and all treatment, dictating letters, plastering the hospital with American propaganda photographs with Serbo-Croat captions."

After a two-month convalescence in Bari, Waugh and Randolph flew to their base in Topusko, where enforced proximity with few duties set off their intense antagonism. They lived in a four-room, rat-infested farmhouse, the only cottage in town that had an indoor toilet, and were looked after by two local servants. Waugh, who had been granted unusual wartime leave to write *Brideshead Revisited* (1945), had a room to himself that allowed him to correct the proofs of the novel and afforded a temporary refuge. He loathed the fiery local *rakia* brandy that stank of sewage and glue and remained sober, which made Randolph's habitual inebriation all the more difficult for him to endure.

Topusko had been a spa before the war, and the machine that pumped water into the bathhouse was still in working order. Waugh recorded, "we go there daily & sit in the radio-active hot water which I find very enervating. The town has been laid out entirely for leisure, with neglected gardens and woodland promenades. It suits our leisured life well." In a photo taken in Topusko, Waugh—indoors, framed by the window and lit by the sun—looks shy, slim and boyish. The dissipated Randolph, standing outside in the shadow with his right arm on the windowsill and left hand on his hip, has a confident, devilish smile and looks older than Waugh.

By September 1944, however, Waugh minimized their mission's achievements: "We do very little & see little company except a partisan liaison officer, the secretary general of the communist party, the leader of the Peasant party & such people. We also arrange for the evacuation of distressed jews," an event that played an important part in his wartime *Sword of Honour* trilogy (1952–61). Fleeing the Ustashe genocide, the Jews felt unsafe in Europe and wanted to emigrate to Palestine. But the intricacies of Yugoslav politics were quite beyond Waugh's comprehension. A fanatical Catholic convert, Waugh defiantly sympathized with the pro-Nazi Catholic Ustashe and undermined the anti-German alliance between the godless communists and the Christian British. He completely misread the situation and recorded, "There is no gratitude to us among the Jugoslavs nor need there be, for we have no generosity to them. We pursue a policy of niggardly and near-sighted self-advantage and then whine when we fail to secure universal love and esteem." Britain certainly needed the military support of the Partisans, but did not expect to win their universal love.

Bored in Topusko, Waugh annoyed headquarters in Bari by sending trivial cables with a secret prefix that meant only senior officers could decode them. Famous for his wicked wit, Waugh was quick to retaliate when provoked. Randolph—a perfect target—gave him plenty of provocation and then complained about his satiric barbs. Neither was willing to change the habits of a lifetime to satisfy the whims of the other. When Randolph asked Waugh to agree that Winston's *Life of Marlborough* was a great work, Waugh, wounding his family pride, savagely replied: "As history it is beneath contempt, the special pleading of a defence lawyer. As literature it is worthless." Randolph retorted by asking, "Have you ever noticed that it is always the people who are most religious who are most mean and cruel?" To which Waugh, claiming that faith was the only thing that held him in check, said, "But my dear Randolph, you have no idea what I should be like if I wasn't [religious]."

Randolph's biography, written by his son (another Winston Churchill), minimized the conflict between his father and Waugh. He quoted Randolph's praise of Waugh's bravery and criticism of his self-destructive impulse, a judgment that applied with equal force to himself: "Waugh possesses both physical and moral courage in a very high degree. He has seen action in this war at Dakar, in Crete, and in Jugoslavia. His courage, coupled with his intellect, might have won him a distinguished military career. But he was usually more interested in driving his immediate superiors mad than in bringing about the defeat of the enemy. One of his superiors, an officer of high standing, had a nervous breakdown after only two months of having Waugh under his command."

In Croatia, Randolph was equally difficult, quarrelsome and inefficient. Tito's high-ranking comrade Milovan Djilas disdainfully wrote that Randolph "revealed through his drinking and lack of interest that he had inherited neither political imagination nor dynamism with his surname." No wonder the Partisans took what they could from the British and rejected them politically. After three months with Randolph, Waugh had wondered "how long I could bear his company, even he I think faintly conscious of strain. . . . [He made] it plain to me that he found the restraints of my company irksome." On February 5, 1944, the Resident Minister in Cairo had written to the Foreign Office in London suggesting that an expert join the mission: "We are all in agreement here that it is most important to have Clissold in Yugoslavia since we are not obtaining adequate political intelligence in the present circumstances." On October 13, 1944, the unexpected and fortunate arrival of Major Freddy Birkenhead and Major Stephen Clissold—a gentle former teacher from Zagreb, fluent in Serbo-Croat and political advisor to Maclean—prevented an outbreak of feral violence between Waugh and Randolph.

When Waugh first appeared Randolph publicly mocked him and incited another bitter confrontation. Birkenhead recalled, "'There he is!' roared [Randolph]—'there's the little fellow in his camel-hair dressing-gown! Look at him standing there!' Evelyn directed on him a stare cold and hostile as the Arctic Ocean, and remarked with poisonous restraint: 'You've got drunk very quickly tonight. Don't send any more signals.'" That same day Waugh wrote to his confidante Nancy Mitford (who was related to Randolph's mother) about Birkenhead's appearance: "It is a great joy having him not only for his own sour & meaty company but as a relief from perpetual watch with your cousin Randolph whose boisterous good nature, after weeks of solitary confinement with him, has begun to exhaust me." Birkenhead wrote favorably about Waugh in a 1973 volume of tributes but later, when he discovered that Waugh had portrayed him in his *Diaries* and *Letters* as drunk, boring and ineffective, he called Waugh "an odious, indeed a psychopathic character."

Waugh's personal writings, enlivened by the novelist's eye for telling details, contained a litany of comic complaints about his claustrophobic connection with Randolph, amusing to read but no doubt painful to endure. When talking to the Partisan liaison officer, Waugh noted, "Randolph got drunk in the early afternoon and had an endless argument with [Leo] Mates, going round in ponderous circles, contradicting himself, heavily humorous, patronizing, appalling."

Waugh lamented "how boring it was to be obliged to tell Randolph everything twice—once when he was drunk, once when he was sober. . . . His American slang, his coughing and farting make him a poor companion in wet weather."

The best time of Waugh's day was the first two hours of daylight when Randolph was still asleep. Once awake he became cantankerous and belligerent, then inebriated and comatose—and acted like a character in Waugh's satiric comedies. Waugh rejected Randolph's pleas for kinder treatment, condemned his cowardly abuse and tried to restrain his own short temper: "[He] left me unmoved for in these matters he is simply a flabby bully who rejoices in blustering and shouting down anyone weaker than himself and starts squealing as soon as he meets anyone as strong. . . . I must exercise self-control and give him the privileges of a commanding officer even though he shirks his responsibilities." He then cut to the core of their relations by confessing they were both unpopular officers and unemployable misfits: "No one else would have chosen me, nor would anyone else have accepted him."

Choosing hostility rather than restraint, Waugh wrote, "I have got to the stage of disliking Randolph which is really more convenient than thinking I liked him & constantly trying to reconcile myself to his enormities. Now I can regard him as one of the evils of war." He remarked that in an effort to control Randolph, who liked to gamble, rose to a challenge, and was fortified by brandy and cigars, "Freddy and I have bet him £10 each that he will not read the Bible straight through in a fortnight. He has set to work but not as quietly as we hoped. He sits bouncing about on his chair, chortling and saying, 'I say, did you know this came in the Bible "bring down my grey hairs with sorrow to the grave"?' Or simply, 'God, isn't God a shit?.' . . . Instead of purchasing a few hours silence for my £10 I now have to endure an endless campaign of interruption and banter."

When Randolph—sounding like a character in Beckett's *Waiting for Godot*—complained about Waugh's cruel treatment, Waugh hardened his heart, threatened to leave and mocked him: "[While] Freddy was talking gibberish to himself in the earth closet, Randolph broke into maudlin reproaches of my failure of friendship and cruelty to him. 'It can't go on. It can't go on.' 'All right then I'll go back to Bari.' 'I'm still fond of you. In spite of all your beastliness to me. I am wounded and grieved.'"

Randolph sent Bari a torrent of complaints about not receiving the supplies he had requested. But Robert Bruce Lockhart (who coordinated all British propaganda against the Axis powers) told Brendan Bracken (the Minister of Information) that "in point of fact Randolph has been getting all possible material for some time." Nevertheless, Randolph's most vituperative explosion, which almost led to fisticuffs, provoked a furious response from the journalist, radio broadcaster and diplomat Ralph Murray in Bari. He sent Lockhart a three-and-a-half-page, single-spaced typed letter, "MOST SECRET AND PERSONAL," about a disturbing episode when a Yugoslav major was present. Murray's letter revealed what Waugh had also been forced to tolerate. In unusually fierce and undiplomatic language, the deeply wounded Murray described Randolph's torrent of filthy abuse and horrible insults:

> I think it necessary to give you a short account of an incident with Randolph Churchill for your most confidential information. . . . It is difficult to write soberly of Churchill's behaviour. . . . He referred to our ignorance of his appointment, status and functions, and [forced us] to listen to a minor diatribe from him. . . .
> At the end of the meal, during which he had been rude to his American neighbours, he strove to pick a quarrel—I am being conservative in my expression—with me personally. He declared that . . . I had lied and obstructed him. . . . For nearly two hours we were treated to a violent and insulting diatribe of a degrading and shifty and horrible kind. . . . His insults to me in particular were of a character foul and deliberate. . . . I (who was, in sum, a filthy, scheming, obstructive little careerist) had intrigued against him, tried to get him out of Jugoslavia, to supplant him with Clissold, to hinder the war effort, the whole elaborated with degrading insults. . . . I understand that among his acquaintances such behaviour is treated lightly, and there is perhaps nothing else for them to do. [But] there can be no question of putting up with another such outburst of filth.

Though reprimanded by his angry superiors, Randolph repeated his abusive attack on Murray and offered a feeble but arrogant defense. Anyone else would have been immediately relieved of his command and sent home in disgrace but Randolph, the son of the Prime Minister, managed to survive. (Murray, 1908–1983, was later knighted and became ambassador to Greece.)

Not to be outdone by Randolph, Waugh was willing to risk his life to enrage and insult his adversary. During a German air attack on their farmhouse in Topusko on October 22, 1944, when the Heinkels dropped bombs and fired machine guns, Randolph thought the enemy had discovered his hideout and were trying to kill him in order to hurt his father. Birkenhead recalled:

> In the middle of this attack, the small figure of Evelyn, somehow over-looked, emerged from the Mission, clad in a white duffel-coat which might have been designed to attract fire, and which gleamed in leprous prominence in the dawn. At this sight, Randolph's face, empurpled with rage, appeared over the trench and in tones verging on hysteria he screamed: "You bloody little swine, take off that coat.! TAKE OFF THAT ***** COAT! It's an order! It's a military order!" Evelyn did not seem to regard even this dire threat as binding, and without removing the coat lowered himself with leisurely dignity into the trench among the bullets, pausing only on his way to remark to Randolph: "I'll tell you what I think of your repulsive manners when the bombardment is over." Evelyn's behaviour was difficult to forgive, and we shared Randolph's annoyance. It seemed to us that Evelyn had either chosen this extremely hazardous method of irritating his friend, or else been seized by some obscure death-wish. In either case, his action had endangered all of us.

After the attack Randolph, "drawing Evelyn aside, apologised if his manners had been abrupt . . . reminding him that as the Mission Commander he was responsible for the safety of all its members." Waugh, putting the knife in, replied: "My dear Randolph, it wasn't your manners I was complaining of: it was your cowardice."

On May 14, 1945—after the Partisans had conquered Zagreb, capital of Croatia—the British Mission reported to Bari that the political situation remained complex and uncertain, and there would be a lot of bloodshed before victory in the civil war was finally achieved: "It is difficult even to say whether the liberation of Zagreb is popular with the majority of citizens or not. In view of the number of them who must be aware that they have collaborated to some extent with the Ustashi Government it is probable that the proportion of people who are profoundly relieved that the Germans have gone is about equal to the number who feel uneasy that the Partisans have arrived."

The unpublished archival material reveals that Maclean mistakenly chose Randolph for the mission to Croatia, Randolph mistakenly chose Waugh, and both men did more harm than good. Randolph, a Member of Parliament, represented Winston and carried his tremendous prestige. But he behaved boorishly and obstructed the British mission, offended both the Partisans and the American allies, and stirred up a lot of unnecessary trouble at high levels in Bari and London. The pro-Catholic, anti-communist Waugh was supposed to entertain Randolph and support the Partisans, but constantly fought with him and made three disastrous mistakes. He openly courted the Ustashe fascists, publicly insulted Tito and endangered his comrades by flaunting his white coat during the air attack. Waugh was most amusing when filled with hate. In 1964, when Randolph had a tumor removed that turned out to be benign, Waugh remarked that the doctors had found "the only part of Randolph that was not malignant."

9

ROBERT FROST

—— AND ——

KAY MORRISON

I

The events that took place at the beginning of Robert Frost's love affair with Kay Morrison were tragic and turbulent. Elinor Frost's death in March 1938 changed the course of his life and the development of his poetry. His fierce quarrel with his daughter Lesley alienated him from the closest member of his family. He was also debilitated by illness and depression. He began to drink heavily and to use foul language and, by his own admission, was "crazy" for the next six months. In June he abruptly resigned from Amherst College and sold his house. No longer a husband, rejected as a father, he turned to Kay Morrison, when she appeared in his life in July, and became her lover. In August he resumed his long-term association with the Bread Loaf Writers' Conference, where her husband Ted Morrison was director. Scarcely recovered from the assault of grief and guilt, he proposed marriage to Kay. She refused but remained his manager, mistress and muse for the last twenty-five years of his life.

After forty years of a passionately monogamous marriage, Frost now had to endure the uncertainty of a love affair with a woman who could not always put him first. In the winter of 1938–39, on a tempestuous vacation in Florida with the Morrisons, Frost became bitterly jealous. In July 1939 the Frost scholar Robert Newdick suddenly died and Lawrance Thompson, who would also become sexually involved with Kay, became his official biographer. Frost entered the hospital for a hemorrhoid operation in January 1940 and in March went berserk from post-operative drugs and broke up the furniture in his flat. In October his son Carol killed himself. These deaths and his own emotional upheavals both challenged and strengthened Frost's character. His poetry was recharged and given new direction in the passionate love poems to Kay that he published in *A Witness Tree* (1942).

Kathleen Florence Johnston, the daughter of a Scottish Episcopal clergyman, was born on November 18, 1898, in Parrsboro, Nova Scotia, where her father had exchanged pulpits for a year. Soon after her birth, Robert Johnston accepted a church in Stirling, then in Edinburgh, and Kay, a British citizen, was raised in Scotland. The oldest of five children, she had two brothers and two sisters, and had to put up with the white mice they kept in the bathroom. Precocious and intellectual as a child, she accompanied her father when he visited parishioners in the slums of the city.

In 1910, when Kay was eleven, Robert was offered an attractive church in Philadelphia, where they lived on fashionable Chestnut Street and she attended Miss Hill's School. Their elegant house, which she helped to run, had fine antiques, old silver and Oriental rugs as well as several servants. Her father's private income enabled them to live in this grand style and to take summer holidays in Nova Scotia. Robert was liberal in church policy and in his Sunday sermons, but he went in for costly harebrained schemes. He suffered from "hysterical complaints" and would suddenly lose his power of speech. In the 1930s, while driving with his sister, Robert was killed in an automobile accident.

The attractive, capable and commonsensical Kay was a member of the literary society and editor of the *College News* at Bryn Mawr. She first met Frost at a lecture during her senior year. After graduating from college in 1921, she studied English at Oxford for a year. Kay wanted to come out as a debutante and blamed her mother for not offering her a glamorous social life. She met Ted Morrison, a young lecturer at Harvard, while they were both working on the *Atlantic Monthly* and married him on October 22, 1927. Their son Robert was born in December 1930, their daughter Anne in January 1937.

Frost's "devoted, astringent, and affectionate amanuensis" had a slight build and bright auburn hair. Well-dressed, elegant and *soigné*, she often mumbled her words and squinted her eyes. His friend Wade Van Dore said she was self-possessed in moments of crisis and that "outward calmness seemed to be hers by birthright." Daniel Aaron, her husband's colleague at Harvard, found her cold, distant, and officious. He thought she avoided intimacy with polite, wintry smiles and was amiable but not sexy. She was eager to maintain her husband's precarious dignity and was clearly more than a solicitous handmaiden to Frost.

Her daughter remarked that Kay was both proper and unconventional. She insisted on keeping up appearances and was content as long as things seemed all right on the surface. At the Vermont farmhouse the laundry, hung on the line with the intimate garments huddled in the middle, was snatched out of sight as soon as visitors appeared. Anne was allowed to smoke when she was ten, but no lady could ever smoke in the street. Frost, who contrasted Kay to Elinor's more straightforward ways, was bothered by her "society manners" and her academic approach to poetry. The poet Adrienne Rich, Ted's student at Harvard, noticed Kay's "repressed anger and bitterness." Kay's daughter believed this came from her frustrated social ambitions, her disappointment in Robert Johnston's failure to achieve eminence and become a bishop in the church, and her uneasiness about Ted's modest and ambiguous position at Harvard.

Ted Morrison (three years younger than Kay) was born in Concord, Massachusetts, in 1901, the youngest of four brothers. His father, an engineer, was head of the Lynn Gas and Electric Company. Two of his brothers, a pitcher-catcher team who had major-league baseball offers, went to M.I.T. and also became engineers. Ted, the literary member of the family, graduated from Harvard in 1923. He had been an editor at the *Atlantic Monthly* before joining the Harvard English Department. Since he had no doctorate, Ted could not be a professor; but as the effective and generous head of English A (which taught expository rather than creative writing), he eventually became a tenured lecturer. Kay, acutely aware that Ted's position was lower than his academic colleagues, resented the fact that her husband, like her father, had not fulfilled his promise and advanced his career.

The tall, handsome, tweedy, pipe-smoking Ted Morrison was a Roman Stoic and stiff-upper-lip New Englander who rarely revealed his feelings. He was also a kind and sensitive man who knew how to deal with Frost's moody and volatile temperament. Writing in September 1938 to Bernard De Voto, his close friend as well as Frost's, just after Frost had appeared at Bread Loaf, Ted criticized his public persona: "The colloquialism of Frost, his continually putting on the rustic tone and writing under his subjects and wearing homespun is also a limitation." Ted unfavorably compared Frost to Edward Arlington Robinson, completely missing the allusion to Robinson's "The Sheaves" in "Nothing Gold

Can Stay": "I doubt, honestly, whether Frost has ever had it in him to record the sudden vanishing from perception of the stacked-up corn sheaves in the autumn in an image as gorgeous" as Robinson's.

Ted had a puritan temperament and at Bread Loaf, despite his wife's liaisons, strongly disapproved of illicit sex (an outstanding feature of many writers' conferences). He spoke of such behavior with horror, and seductive poets were not invited back. (Louis Untermeyer, a great fornicator between and during his marriages, was protected by Frost and given special dispensation.) In September 1934, when De Voto sent his latest novel, *We Accept with Pleasure*, Ted (writing from Nova Scotia) minimized the importance of sexual relations, both illicit and marital. He opposed De Voto's idea that "some mystical and romantic value is to be attributed to illegal cohabitation" and declared: "The impression left by the book is that cohabitation out of wedlock is, if not the clue, at least a necessary ingredient in arriving at personal integrity. It ain't; not even in wedlock."

II

In the spring of 1936, when Elinor was ill and Frost gave the Norton lectures at Harvard, the Morrisons had a series of receptions for him at their Cambridge house. In July 1938, a few months after Elinor's death in March, Kay, who loved literature, sought Frost out at South Shaftsbury, Vermont. Realizing his desolation and loneliness, she invited him to join her family and friends at a nearby summer house. According to her daughter, Kay was a very unhappy woman who wanted a career rather than a family. "Incredibly romantic and passionate," she also craved more wildness in her life and more brilliance than Ted could offer. She wanted to help and rescue Frost, who was out of control after Elinor's death, and desperately needed both a new secretary and a new source of poetic inspiration. Frost—the same age and with the same first name as her recently deceased father—gave her what she had long been seeking. For the first time in her life, Kay could realize her ambition to achieve status, exert social and literary influence, and share the fame of a great man.

In the summer of 1938 Frost was a white-haired but handsome and vigorous man of sixty-four, Kay a refined and stylish woman of thirty-nine. Frost took a keen interest in the sexual life of his friends but had never slept with any woman but Elinor. Though Elinor's dowdy dress and chronic illness had made her seem much older than Frost, she had been his high school sweetheart, and he had remained faithful (despite many temptations) until her death. Just as Kay associated Frost with her father, so he was drawn to Kay by her similarity to his delicate, auburn-haired mother. Like Belle Frost, Kay had grown up in Scotland and come to America at the age of eleven. To Frost, who had discussed the significance of personal names in "Maple," her name had positive associations. Cathleen was the Celtic heroine of the Yeats play that Frost had put on at Pinkerton Academy; Morrison was the New Hampshire Superintendent of Public Instruction who had praised Frost's teaching and advanced his career.

A. B. Guthrie, who was loyal to Ted Morrison and observed Frost that summer at Bread Loaf, said he was "the captive of fierce and aberrant passions." John Ciardi also noted his powerful inner conflict: "Frost was intensely puritanical. I think he had also a very strong sexual impulse, and these two things set up a contest of forces"—in which passion won. His sexual urge, though always strong, had been restrained with Elinor, but he once admitted: "If I had a beautiful studio, I'd never paint. I'd have ladies visiting. . . . Might as well be candid." He dreaded the thought of trouble and a public scandal, and hated the dishonesty of Kay's double life, but frankly told Thompson: "I'm a perfectly normal animal; I can't always behave." He seemed to define his emotional and moral ambiguity in a prophetic letter of June 1937, when he said: "All our ingenuity is lavished on getting into danger legitimately so that we may be genuinely rescued." As Oscar Wilde remarked in *De Profundis*, illicit sex "was like feasting with panthers. The danger was half the excitement."

Frost openly discussed Kay with his close friends as well as with his biographers. He told the ponderous Robert Newdick that for the first time in his life he felt unconstrained, and Newdick wrote that he "needs, wants feminine companionship and friendship, and will have it. Is fearful of arrangement with K. Morrison—for her and Ted, rather than for himself. If he were Ted, he wouldn't permit it." But Kay aroused the old Adam in Frost and tempted him to fall. He was astonished that a woman who behaved so conventionally could be so wild sexually. When she suddenly, almost magically reappeared in his life, he felt: "Here's a lady who's willing, why not let go?" She would be good for him—and for his poetry.

In late July 1938 Frost accepted Kay's invitation, while Ted was away at Bread Loaf, to visit her in central Vermont. Troubled and excited by their long walks in the woods, he took along condoms (which he had been reluctant to use with Elinor). Kay had revered him as a poet for seventeen years and now realized how much he needed and wanted her. He talked brilliantly, describing his family tragedies, and he loved her that she did pity them. One day they came to a place Frost thought sufficiently secluded "for either rape or murder." They sat on the warm earth and talked some more. Then, according to Thompson's unpublished typescript, "Frost began making passionate love to her and found that she was willing. . . . All he had to do was to take off her drawers and consummate an urge that seemed mutual." Frost (to use one of his own favorite metaphors) rode on her own melting. The contrast between Elinor's virginal rejection of his first sexual overtures, which had made him feel bestial, and Kay's eager response, which revived and inspired him, was reflected in the placement of "The Subverted Flower" just after "Never Again Would Birds' Song Be the Same" in *A Witness Tree*. Their first, mutually gratifying encounter also provoked a comic quatrain on in-and-outdoor fooling. Frost wrote that no one could object to being legally wed when the marriage was consummated naked in bed. But it is an entirely different matter when you have sex out-of-doors with no clothes off but drawers.

Just after they became lovers, Frost proposed marriage and pressed Kay to divorce her husband. She firmly rejected this idea and told him that even if they were both twenty years younger and both free she would never agree to marry him. (Ted later wrote in his essay on the poet: "To marry Robert Frost was no light undertaking for any woman.") Kay felt that divorce was impossible: it would cause scandal and harm the children. She pleaded that their affair be kept secret. During the next few years, Frost strained their relations by forcefully pressing her to marry him. Although he agreed to behave with discretion, he distressed her by telling several close friends about the affair, hinting about it to others, and instructing his biographers to reveal the full story.

Frost confessed to Thompson that his love for Kay contained an element of sadism: "He punished her, and she (according to Frost) permitted him the somewhat brutal pleasure of having sexual intercourse with her. . . . Frost says that his initial love-making was motivated by resentments but that he suddenly found himself in love with Kay, and dependent on his love for her." Frost said he resented Kay for trying to help him, for making him depend on her, and for "mothering" him—as his mother Belle and Elinor had done. For many years he continued to punish her—quite irrationally—for sleeping with him, for taking Elinor's place, for refusing to marry him and for the guilt *he* felt about betraying Ted.

Frost was alternately invigorated, disturbed, grateful, jealous, vindictive and loving. At first his love for her revealed new and rather surprising aspects of his character, which seemed very different from his role as faithful husband and genial lecturer. Like Yeats after his late Steinach operation, Frost was passionate, wild, even mad. His old friend Margaret Bartlett (who did not yet know about Kay) saw a rejuvenated man and thought his liberation from Elinor explained his new energy and vigor. In letters to his friends (as in his poems) he struggled between concealment and revelation. Kay had agreed to handle his correspondence and arrange his readings. In early 1939 he jubilantly told Sidney Cox: "My secretary has taken me in hand to keep me lecturing and talking as of old. But I am very wild at heart sometimes. Not at all confused. Just wild—wild."

Just after the August session at Bread Loaf, Frost expressed his gratitude to Kay and contrasted her solicitude and Ted's with the callous behavior of President Stanley King of Amherst: "You two rescued me from a very dangerous self when you had the idea of keeping me for the whole season at Bread Loaf. I am still infinitely restless, but I came away from you as good as saved. . . . Stanley King's charge against me was ingratitude. It will be a sensitive subject with me the rest of my life. . . . Tears in my heart when I left you people." Tears in the writer would soon produce tears in the reader. Keenly aware of the difference between his daughter Lesley's cruelty and Kay's kindness, he tried to reassure his possessive and censorious daughter about the woman who had eased his loneliness. "You must be grateful to her for having helped me through my bad time," he wrote in November 1938. "I am best as I am, though the hours alone are sometimes pretty desolate."

In a revealing letter to Untermeyer that same month, Frost connected Kay's soothing voice to the music of his verse, explained that she had relieved his guilt about the treatment of his family and provided the absolution that Elinor had failed to give him. Although Kay was not an innocent girl, he idealized and saw her that way. She seemed perfect for him, and he called on the sympathetic Untermeyer to tell Kay how much he loved her:

My secretary has soothed my spirit like music in her attendance on me and my affairs. . . . I was thrust out into the desolateness of wondering about my past whether it had not been too cruel to those I had dragged with me and almost to cry out to heaven for a word of reassurance that was not given me in time. Then came this girl stepping innocently into my days to give me something to think of besides dark regrets. . . . You can figure it out for yourself how my status with a girl like her might be the perfect thing for me at my age in my position. I wish in some indirect way she could come to know how I feel toward her.

Frost told one friend that "there have been just two women in my life." But by May 1939, when he saw the poet Raymond Holden in Boston, Kay seemed to have supplanted Elinor. Unlike Kay, who adored Frost, was eager to please him and was attracted by his fame, Elinor had rejected his sexual overtures, disapproved of his public persona, criticized his self-promoting readings, did nothing to advance his career, condemned his egotism, complained of her sacrifice and resented his success. Frost considered women "sources of male gratification," but revealed that he was afraid of his powerful passion for Kay. He told Holden, "in his lightest, aphoristic manner that he had had many troublesome feelings about different women, but had loved only one. I do not know why I felt that he was meaning to imply that the one was not Elinor. . . . He once told me that he didn't dare let his emotions be aroused for fear that they would ruin him, so strong were they potentially."

Frost also poured out his heart to his bibliographer Louis Mertins, linking Kay to Belle and stressing her maternal role, crediting her for both saving and inspiring him, and revealing how profoundly his existence was now bound up with hers: "I owe everything in the world to her. She found me in the gutter, hopeless, sick, run down. She bundled me up and carted me to her home and cared for me like a child, sick child. Without her I would today be in my grave. If I have done anything since I came out of the hospital [in January 1940], it is all due to her."

When traveling and separated from Kay, Frost wrote about five hundred letters to her, but she destroyed most of them, cut and tore parts of many others, and only nineteen fragments have survived. He addressed her as Dearest and Milady (a dig at her social pretensions) as well as the classical Venusta,

Augusta, Egeria (a woman counselor) and consulatrix (a pun on consoler). The letters expressed his sentimental and romantic as well as his passionate and idealistic feelings. In one undated note he told Kay that the clock in his room had stopped ticking at the very moment she was boarding the train. Since she was the last one to wind it, he would let it remain silent as a token of their love. In a letter written at midnight in mid-October 1938, Frost includes a double entendre on lecturing and sex that sounds like Hemingway, a grateful acknowledgment of her inspiration, and a fervent but unfulfilled hope that she will keep his letters and eventually reveal their love:

> Egeria, You told me to do it well and so it is no brag. . . . I have a weakness *for* you but a strength *from* you. . . . Surely no one could object to love that courses in the inflection of my sentences like impassioned blood in the veins. You must find a place to keep the most earnest [love] words I ever wrote. They can only do you honor when the time comes to divulge them; and meanwhile they could in no way compromise you if discovered by chance. All this says I am yours in a very noble sense.

Four months later, while Frost was writing his love poems to Kay, he again assured her that her inspiration was vital to his work: "The poetry into which my heart would go for you aches at the threat of being denied birth." Ten years later he confirmed that he was still her faithful troubadour: "Ninety-nine per cent of the time I am yours and the Muses' only." Frost also expressed his love by buying rare and expensive first editions of his earliest books as presents for Kay, and by writing an amusing (and punning) poem, which contrasted her conventional wedding ring with the more exotic jewelry (of the sort pupils had noticed on his mother) that he had given her to symbolize their wildness and "sin." Her husband had given her a wedding ring to keep her virtuous. But Frost surpassed him by giving her an earring for erring and a necklace for being wickedly reckless.

But their honeymoon did not last very long, and during the early years their affair lurched from crisis to crisis. From December 1938 to January 1939 the Morrisons accompanied Frost on his annual trip to Florida. They spent a week at the Casa Marina Hotel in Key West and a week as guests of the novelist Hervey Allen near Miami. Their close proximity, the need to share Kay with Ted and even defer to her husband, caused constant anxiety and tension. Frost got into petty disputes with Ted, and Kay had trouble separating the antagonists. In February 1939 Frost told Untermeyer that "my chief signs of life are shown in any debate *with my rival*." Writing from Florida that same month he suggested, in a letter to Lesley, that they had come close to an explosion and that he was, as always, terribly lonely whenever Kay left him: "I came through the two weeks with the Morrisons pretty well considering all there was on all sides to dissemble. I am alone now in a rather desolated house. . . . My entanglement has had critical moments when it looked near openly declared trouble." After this anguished holiday, Frost would never allow Ted to come to Florida. Ted would remain at home, while Kay traveled south with Frost.

In early February 1939, to distract himself from Kay, Frost went to Cuba for five days with the poet Paul Engle. He told Lesley that he admired the tropical scenery and was thrilled by his first flight in an airplane, which "made a high sky" in one leap. Suddenly he found himself exiled on a strange island among loud but unintelligible speakers: "We went down to Camaguey, saw several cities besides Havana and plenty of sugar cane and royal palms. The land is rich; the people miserably poor. Everywhere beggars and beggar-vendors. We saw one great beach to beat the world . . . [with] the most transparent ocean water I have ever looked into. . . . I am not much on foreign parts. I favor that beach for you to resort to someday though. To me the best of the excursion was the flight both ways in the big Pan American plane and especially the swoop and mighty splash into the bays on arrival."

A second and more serious crisis erupted in the spring of 1939 when Frost and the Morrisons spent the night at Untermeyer's farm in Elizabethtown, New York. Frost had told Untermeyer that jealousy alone gave him the sense of being physically and emotionally held. Whenever he was locked into a triangle with Kay and Ted, he found it very difficult to maintain the pretense of innocence. At Untermeyer's house, Ted assumed the role of husband and slept with Kay in the only double guest bed. Frost felt rejected, became deranged and almost dared to force the moment to its crisis.

Frost continued to put pressure on Kay and thought she would eventually agree to marry him. When she remained loyal (after her fashion) to Ted and her children, the jealous Frost, driven to extremes of behavior by the confrontations in Florida and Elizabethtown, went dangerously out of control.

Thompson, accepting Lesley's view of her father and certainly exaggerating his condition (for Frost never lost touch with reality), recorded: "During the summer of 1939, in Ripton, and then during February 1940 in Key West, I saw Frost come very close to the verge of insanity. He was a wild man, he was frantic; he was deeply upset, he was just plain 'crazy' in some of his actions."

The situation became more tangled by Frost's illness in early 1940. "I have been very sick," he told Cox, "largely we now think from some very drastic medicine that doctors tried on me for cystitis. I went crazy with it one night alone and broke chairs ad lib till a friend [Dr. Merrill Moore] happened in to save me." Moore thought Frost's voice sounded strange on the telephone, rushed over to his apartment, found him almost unconscious and took him to the hospital.

Frost had had hemorrhoids for years but refused to see a doctor until his kidneys became inflamed and he was overcome by pain. The operation for "asteroids" took place in Boston on January 10. On February 1 Kay took him down to Key West and nursed him back to health. While there, she shrewdly wrote Thompson that whenever Frost was in a crisis he either bought land or took to his bed. In Florida he had used Kay "as a kind of safety valve" to release his frustration, anger and pain, and she had just been through the hardest two weeks of her life. Thompson suggested that Lesley visit Frost. But Kay, knowing the terrible effect the daughter had on the father, said that Lesley "would defeat anything the doctors could do" to help him. Thompson, rather than Lesley, finally took over as servant and nurse-companion. He told Kay that Frost was pathetically dependent on her letters and used his illness to exert power over his friends. In Florida he "ate his heart out . . . watching, between your many letters, for *more* letters. . . . He said, 'If I don't hear from her tomorrow, you're going to have your patient back in bed,' and he tried to smile while his eyes filled with tears and his lips quivered."

III

Despite frequent crises—when Frost became a possessive, jealous and demanding lover, and the unpleasant truth threatened to burst out—he and the Morrisons tried hard to preserve appearances. After a few years of distressing emotional upheavals, they eventually contrived a serviceable mode of existence and settled on a formula of transparent lies that seemed acceptable to all parties. In order to protect herself and preserve the status quo, Kay tried to placate and control Frost by telling him that she no longer had sexual relations with Ted. At the same time she assured Ted that her relations with Frost were purely secretarial. But Kay's insistent denials, to friends as well as to her husband, seemed to call Frost's manliness into question and he responded by indiscreetly boasting about his conquest. "Trying to prove himself 'a bad, bad man,'" Kay wrote, while trying to conceal the truth, "he laced his conversations with innuendoes of sexual exploits that were utterly foreign to his nature." But Frost's innuendoes were also a form of flirtation and seduction and tried to suggest, to Kay and to others, "what a devil I am!"

Torn between a wish to preserve secrecy and a desire to achieve eventual recognition for her crucial role in Frost's life, Kay boldly retaliated by declaring that he was merely a vain, boastful old man. In a characteristic letter to the wealthy businessman and Frost-collector Earle Bernheimer, Kay tried to quell the gossip by insisting that she was devoted to her family and was merely trying to be kind to Frost, who liked to indulge in sexual fantasies: "My friends know what I am doing for Robert and have backed me in my wish not to make him too unhappy and to give him care and affection while he lives. I am well settled with my husband and children and they know they are my first care. What I do for Robert is something different. He is devoted to me and sometimes is carried away in his talk beyond fact because he is emotionally upset and lonely and because he would have things different."

Kay gave the same story to Richard Wilbur, who accepted her account and later wrote: "No doubt Frost was enamored and possessive of her, and tried her good husband's patience; but she told me once that there had never been an 'affair' between her and Robert, and I believed her. When Frost 'let on' to the contrary, as he sometimes did, I think it was an old man's vanity talking."

According to Thompson (who knew the truth), Ted forced himself to believe everything Kay told him in order to preserve his sanity. But Frost found it more difficult to accept her transparent but necessary falsehoods. He "accused Kay of betraying their love, through the act of denying their love, and of pretending it never was [sexual love]. It's lucky for her that Frost has been willing to deceive himself by accepting as truths so many of Kay's deceptions."

Frost's relations with Kay were complicated by her contemporaneous involvement with at least three other men. Stafford Dragon (the name itself was irresistible) was Frost's lively and handsome hired man on the Vermont farm. Visiting writers familiar with the sexual situation at Bread Loaf (where Stafford's father sang ballads) joked about her social pretensions and knowingly referred to "Stafford-the-man-Kay-hires as 'Lady Chatterley's Lover.'" When Thompson urged Dragon to behave more discreetly, Dragon told him that he knew Thompson was also Kay's lover.

Kay had been sleeping with Ted's "best friend," the married writer Bernard De Voto. The short, porcine "Bennyvenuto" (as Frost called him) had thick glasses, thick lips and a broad flat Babe Ruth nose with tunnel-like nostrils. Born in Ogden, Utah, of Catholic-Mormon parents, a year before Kay, De Voto had graduated from Harvard in 1920 and returned to his home state to begin his career as a novelist. He came back to Harvard in 1930 but, not eligible for tenure without a doctorate, taught for six years on a temporary appointment. When he failed to get a permanent job, the embittered De Voto consulted Frost and then resigned to become editor of the *Saturday Review of Literature*. He had met Frost in Florida in 1936 and thought of writing his biography. He looked after Frost when he gave the Norton lectures and supported him when left-wing critics attacked *A Further Range*. In a vituperative but critically weak defense, De Voto exclaimed that R. P. Blackmur's "piece in the *Nation* may not quite be the most idiotic review our generation has produced, but in twenty years of reading criticism—oh, the hell with scholarly reservations, Mr. Blackmur's is the most idiotic of our time."

Thompson, an on-the-spot observer, noted the mutual recrimination and entangled moral issues: "Kay had described [De Voto's] innocence as impotence. Kay had been involved in his harem by Benny, very early. So when Frost moved into the picture, with Kay, Benny had become jealous. He had accused Frost of breaking up—not Benny's harem but the Morrison marriage." De Voto's frequently quoted but little understood condemnation of Frost at the Bread Loaf Conference in August 1938—"You're a good poet, Robert, but you're a bad man"—referred to Frost's relations with Kay. De Voto thought it was morally acceptable to sleep with Kay as long as he did not try to take her away from Ted. But when Frost proposed marriage to Kay, De Voto got on his moral high horse and expressed disapproval of Frost's attempt to break up Ted's marriage.

The third member of Kay's sexual ménage was the ubiquitous and "incredibly attractive" Lawrance Thompson. Eight years younger than Kay, he also maintained the necessary façade and helped her to look after Frost. Thompson's intimacy with Kay allowed him to participate in and even change the course of the life he was writing. During the Florida crisis of February–March 1940, which followed Frost's hemorrhoid operation, he secretly advised Kay to reject Frost's persistent proposals and even suggested a way to escape from his clutches. In another letter of March 3, he told Kay to protect herself from Frost's emotional onslaughts by being tough with him and by using (Elinor-like) silences to express her anger:

> (1) He has thrown the whole weight of his life on you, and has no freedom apart from you; (2) if, for his own sake, a substitution were made, the only substitute must be some woman whose unrestricted freedom to devote herself to him would or could attract him. . . .
>
> It takes your kind of commonsense plus a little ruthlessness (which you might borrow from Robert himself) to deal with Robert almost harshly. . . . Don't you worry too much about his *nerves*; worry more about your own. He has 'em plenty, but he isn't in danger of being killed by them—unless this present conflict becomes a "war of attrition." And don't let him bully or threaten; you bully and threaten with your silences instead.

Kay, who feared he knew too much, remained friendly to Thompson, but he finally became exasperated with her. Their relations became tense in January 1945 when he summoned her to New York. Her eight-year-old daughter Anne, who was also fond of Thompson, thought he might be getting married. Kay frowned at her suggestion, got upset and said, very stiffly, "No, it couldn't be!" When she discovered the truth, she became jealous of his wife. In his "Notes on Frost," Thompson complained that Kay treated his family (who also spent the summers near Frost's cabin in Vermont) like "poor relations." She never concealed her dislike and was "bitchy" to his wife, Janet, his children and himself.

Thompson often replaced Kay (both before and after his marriage) as Frost's companion, keeper and body servant, and he knew what she had to endure when Frost was in a bad mood. In September 1945 he criticized Frost's behavior, praised her forbearance and praised her for the way she handled him: "I admire you deeply for the long-suffering patience with which you've accepted his self-indulgence when it comes to asking more of your time and strength and life than he has a right to ask. . . . You've done a superb job under the most exasperating conditions, and I respect all your decisions and actions in all the difficult task of walking a tight-rope during all these emotional hurricanes and thunderstorms of his."

These dangerous, even treacherous, letters strengthened the bond between Thompson and Kay (since there was no one else she could turn to in this way), but they also gave her considerable power over him. If she had ever shown them to Frost, Thompson would have been cast into the outer darkness and his biography instantly terminated. The handsome Thompson also had an emotional hold over Kay, who was in love with him and helped him because they were lovers. He had to remain on good terms with her through all the *Sturm und Drang*. If she became Frost's literary executor and disliked what Thompson wrote (and wrote about her) in his biography, she could withhold permission to quote from Frost's works. If Thompson wanted Kay to remain a vital ally, he would not only have to take her side, rather than Frost's, during the recurrent emotional crises, but would also have to conceal her relations with Frost.

Frost agreed to maintain the deception during his lifetime, but he created another tense conflict by insisting the truth be told after his death. He believed the full story of his relations with Kay was essential to an understanding of his life and work, and hated to have his passion for her belittled or demeaned. He believed, as he had written in "Birches," that "Earth's the right place for love," and warned Thompson: "Don't let it be confused with anything so pale as platonic." Frost realized that Kay would be opposed to any revelations about their affair (and for this reason did not appoint her his literary executor). But he believed that she should not be allowed to conceal the importance of their sexual relationship—even if the revelation hurt her: "He thought there were certain penalties which Kay had to pay for intimacy, and one of them was to have the story told." When he asked how widely the story was known, Thompson replied that many of the writers at Bread Loaf (Ted, De Voto, Guthrie and Ciardi) suspected they were having an affair and others (Untermeyer, Hervey Allen, Bernheimer and Thompson) knew because Frost had told them about it. Frost felt so strongly about this matter that he threatened to leave the beloved farm at Ripton to Lesley if Kay did not permit Thompson to tell the whole story.

But Thompson (unlike most biographers, who struggle with the family to reveal rather than conceal the truth) did not agree and was bound by Kay's rather than by Frost's wishes after his death. He twisted Frost's desire for revelation into a supposed wish "to glamorize and dramatize the story, so that he and Kay Morrison as lovers would seem noble and dignified in their ways of pretending that Ted Morrison blocked them off from fulfilling their romance." Thompson died in 1973, and when the third volume was completed by R. H. Winnick three years later, Kay and Ted (who were very much alive) gutted the volume before publication by excising all traces of her intimacy with Frost.

Kay and her four lovers followed their instincts and their passions, pursuing their own interests and behaving in a selfish but understandable manner. Ted's situation was more difficult, his response more enigmatic. He could not get away from Frost, either in Cambridge or Vermont, and visitors sometimes confused him with Frost—even in his own house. During meals at the Ripton farm, Thompson noted, "Kay always sits farthest from the kitchen, which means that Ted, nearest the kitchen, always does the hopping and fetching." Though Ted *seemed* to accept the situation, several close friends—De Voto, Ciardi and Guthrie—expressed anger on his behalf and intensified his pain.

Friends never saw the tight-lipped, courtly Ted show any rage or resentment. He found it hard to reach his own emotions and tried to deny the reality of the situation. He did not express physical affection, even with his children, but he too had human feelings and was furious underneath. His daughter Anne still remembers terrible fights at home when she was a little girl. Ted, who was usually so gentle, terrified Anne by radiating anger, storming out of the house and slamming the door. After drinking a great deal at a party, Ted once admitted to Richard Wilbur: "I hate the position I'm in. I never want Robert to be in my house." The year after Frost's death, Ted, almost apologetically, told Thompson: "Well, let's face it: I didn't like him."

Ted was willing to put up with anything as long as his marriage *seemed* to be happy. Despite Kay's affair with Frost, Ted still loved her, continued to sleep with her and felt he was achieving a higher good by his personal sacrifice. A somewhat bloodless character, he had a low sex drive, was used to his wife's infidelities, and would have done anything to avoid publicly accusing Kay of adultery and going through a scandalous divorce. Though his acceptance of

Kay's lovers was personally humiliating, Ted thought it was worth the sacrifice not only to preserve his marriage, but also to sustain Frost and enable *Frost* (if not himself) to write great poems. Ted also endured the situation and went to great lengths to protect Kay. His tolerance enabled him to be the "better" person and do the noble thing.

All these New England puritans had been brought up to maintain superficial propriety—no matter what passions thrashed beneath the surface. The suppression of emotions, the preservation of decorum, the denial of intolerable reality, were all intensely Jamesian. The lies hurt everyone concerned, but all the players gained something valuable by accepting them. Family, friends and lovers all learned the Lesson of the Master and realized that they had to be sacrificed for Art.

Frost's, Thompson's and Anne Morrison Smyth's view of the poet's relations with Kay were inevitably quite different. Frost thought his love was paramount and that he and Kay had made the greatest sacrifice by not marrying. He felt Kay was torn apart and suffered greatly, believed they were "caught in an awkward situation, and acted as honorably and as nobly as love would permit them to act. . . . The cost to both of them had been heavy, [and] had even been injurious to Kay's emotional and spiritual and physical health." Thompson disliked Frost intensely and saw the affair in a negative light. Though in no position to judge others, he declared: "The more evidence I find on the story, the more unpleasant and shameful the 'romance' becomes."

Anne, remembering all the quarrels and lies, did not think that Kay had made a noble choice. By attracting men and forming several attachments, she used marriage for her own convenience and was both disloyal to Frost and "rotten about Ted." Entering middle age but filled with romantic longing, Kay (I believe) felt great power by manipulating a number of distinguished men while assuring her place in literary history. The great irony, according to Anne, was that Kay told her she had never experienced sexual satisfaction with anyone. Sexually unfulfilled, she lived vicariously through Frost (Anne thought) and caused great pain to everyone connected to her.

IV

Kay became Frost's secretary and manager in September 1938. He paid her an annual salary (which reached $2,000 in 1954 and rose to $3,000 in the early 1960s), and she was supposed to work at his home—first in Beacon Hill and then in Cambridge—from 9:30 to 4:00 on weekdays. Kay typed, edited, read proofs, answered the mail, kept files, scheduled the readings, made the travel arrangements, managed the money, paid the bills, furnished his flats and houses, drove him around, advised him about family problems, entertained guests, protected him from unannounced visitors and often from himself. She fussed over Frost, was solicitous about his food and made sure he did not get too tired. She even cleaned up when his puppy soiled the rug. But he demanded even more from her, and she had to be entirely at his disposal. "I could be summoned after hours," Kay wrote, "on Saturdays and Sundays, on holidays, sometimes finding real problems but more often emotional upsets." This, of course, put an additional strain on her family. As Kay told Thompson in February 1940: "He cannot be alone any more and it is impossible to promise steady companionship."

Frost soon became completely dependent on Kay and resented the power she exerted. Their intimacy allowed Kay to nag him and Frost to vent his anger. She could be as stern and exasperated as a schoolmarm, and many friends were irritated by the way she guarded him. Though he admitted that women—such as his mother and Elinor—had always run his life, he called Kay a very severe disciplinarian. She would ask, "What's wrong with you?" whenever she wanted to bring him "out into the open for a hunt." Since she took dictation, he called himself her "Easy Dictator," but he could also be a temperamental and difficult tyrant. Kay complained to Thompson about Frost's unremitting demands and his desire to dictate every aspect of her life. Frost wants "complete control of a person," she wrote in 1940. "More and more he tells me what to think and say."

For emotional and practical reasons, the lonely and jealous Frost wanted to be with her all the time. When she left him after their annual trip to Florida, he called her his "chronic deserter" and (in a passage deleted from the published letter) hinted to Earle Bernheimer of his conquest and desire to pursue her. After three weeks of the most perfect bliss, he said, Kay had deserted him to return to Cambridge. The weather (though not his emotional life) was still perfect, and he had great difficulty controlling his impulse to follow her north. When Frost could not have his way, he sometimes regressed to infantile behavior. In December 1946, when Kay made plans to spend New Year's Eve with friends, Frost retaliated by pretending he had invited some cronies for a party of his own. He upset the furniture, filled the room with cigar smoke, spilled whiskey on the table, broke glasses on the carpet, and scattered the remains of crackers and cheese. After discovering the mess the next morning, Kay immediately saw through his ruse but could not summon up much pity for the lonely celebrator.

Frost's possessiveness lasted until the very end of his life. In 1962 Kay again complained to Thompson that "Frost had been so jealous, during the past year, that he had made it impossible for her to go on any trips with Ted" during his sabbatical. The only way she could ever escape from Frost was by refusing, despite his urgent pleas, to accompany him on foreign trips. She desperately needed a rest from him and did not want to assume an even greater burden by becoming his traveling companion, so she let the eager Thompson take her place. Daily proximity had cooled their passion and led to frequent quarrels. She once got so exasperated that she threw a bucket of cold water over Frost. When the strain became too great she would explode, resign her job and take to her bed. But there would always be a tender reconciliation.

The ferocious Lesley, whose very appearance was enough to send Frost straight to bed, and who was as jealous of Kay as she had been of her mother and sisters, intensified the turmoil. Of the two, Lesley (a year younger) was more lively and attractive, Kay more intelligent and sophisticated. Each had two children. But Kay had graduated from Bryn Mawr and was married to a teacher at Harvard, while Lesley had dropped out of college and was divorced.

Lesley's hatred of Kay was fueled by her profound resentment of her father. She was grateful that she did not have to do Kay's job and take care of Frost, but she also looked for things "to get Kay on." Lesley saw Kay as an "intruder" who had taken her place in Frost's life and was severely moralistic about her sexual infidelity. She feared that Kay might get her share of Frost's increasingly valuable estate and condemned her, Thompson wrote, as "a scheming, money-grubbing crook." Lesley was especially enraged by Frost's love poem to Kay, "The Silken Tent." Though it was written in August–September 1938, soon after Frost met Kay, Lesley insisted he had composed it "way back in her mother's day" and wanted to engrave the opening line, "She is as in a field a silken tent," on Elinor's gravestone. Frost tried to mollify Lesley in December 1938 by gently encouraging her "to be grateful to Kathleen for her ministrations. The closest criticism will discover no flaw in her kindness to me." But Lesley remained adamantly bitter and even referred to Kay as "the whore."

Donald Hall, Frost's friend and protégé, took (like most others) a benign view of Kay and admired her devotion as well as her defiance: "Kay Morrison was devoted and worked hard and was tolerant although I think she had much reason for impatience. Robert came first. She was concerned for Frost: to protect him, to please him. One did not feel that anybody else in the room had the importance that Frost did, and certainly Frost wanted it that way. . . . Many people were frightened of him. Day in, day out, Kay may have done more standing up to him than anybody else." Thompson saw only base, even mercenary motives. Ignoring her devotion, he emphasized her high salary, gifts of money and property, and the Morgan horses Frost bought for Kay and her daughter. Although he himself had greatly benefited from his association with Frost, Thompson also declared that Frost "satisfied Kay's grotesque fondness for lion-hunting and for name-dropping." John Ciardi, who disapproved of Frost's liaison with Kay, resented both Kay's power over Frost and her malign influence on Frost's friendships:

> It was almost impossible to spend time with Frost apart from the Morrisons. . . . Kay had a mind that naturally spun intricate webs. It is quite possible that I came to see Frost in considerable part through her machinations. They were more intricate than evil . . . but they may have influenced me more than I know in my views of Robert.
>
> I was already aware that he was a literary politician in ways I found personally distasteful. . . . If I have been swayed to look for something like evil in Robert, it may have been Kay's hissing that I heard. I do believe he was self-centered—enough so, I believe, to have been a disastrous father. . . . I believe she might have stewed [my innocent remark] in witches' brew for a year before letting me know she had taken the hex off it.

As Kay's children grew older, Frost became an avuncular figure in their household. Since Kay was, in any case, "not a very maternal type," the children did not mind all the attention she paid to him and came to adore the benign old gentleman. Frost, for his part, was fond of Bobby and Anne, who were the same age as his grandchildren. He wrote them charming letters, taught them to memorize poems, gave them money and presents, encouraged them to be rebellious and took a keen interest in their schoolwork.

When Anne's horse got sick and she had to inject it every four hours throughout the night, she told Frost that she had to get some sleep between the treatments and could not stay up to talk to him. Nevertheless, he appeared at the farmhouse at ten at night and talked away, as usual, until two in the morning. Still fearing the dark in old age, he thought Anne would also be afraid to walk to the barn alone in the middle of the night. His impulse was both selfish and kind: he would not let her sleep, but he stayed up to accompany her to the barn.

Tragedy struck the Morrisons in December 1954 when the twenty-four-year-old, recently married Bobby, like his grandfather before him, was killed in an automobile accident. During a skiing trip at Stowe, while taking chains off a tire at the edge of the road, he was hit by a car driven by a sixteen-year-old French-Canadian boy. Since the weather was exceptionally beautiful, Frost said, in a Hemingway-like phrase: "It's a bad day to be dead." But he was so upset that Kay had to calm *him* down. Anne, the first to hear the tragic news, had to break it to her parents and always felt she had "not done it properly." To comfort her, Frost talked about the deaths in his family and assured her that one somehow survives every tragedy. Although his therapeutic comfort helped Anne while she was still in a state of shock, she also—like Kay—felt overwhelmed by *his* grief.

Anne, who grew up idolizing Ted and hating Kay, saw enough affectionate gestures between Frost and Kay (there was no public display between Ted and Kay) to know the truth. When Ted drove them up to Vermont, she would ride in the back with his dog Gillie and watch Frost, seated next to Kay, with his arm around her. Anne knew what was happening but, unwilling to choose between Frost and Ted, or to hurt either of them, she followed the repressive Jamesian rules and "crafted denial." They never talked about the real situation or expressed their true feelings.

When Kay's book was published in 1974, she and Ted were apprehensive that reviewers might allude to Kay's real relationship with Frost. They sat down with the thirty-seven-year-old Anne and assured her that Kay and Frost had never had a love affair. She knew they were lying. They wanted to protect her, but they also wanted her to continue to keep the secret. Frost's oft-quoted but little understood couplet in *A Witness Tree* opposes speculation against knowledge and suggests how the truth remained hidden: "We dance round in a ring and suppose, / But the Secret sits in the middle and knows."

Anne, still bitter about some aspects of her childhood, feels that Kay hurt other people because she had been hurt by her father. She hurt Ted by her affairs with Frost and other men; she hurt Frost by refusing to leave Ted and by making him jealous of his rivals; she hurt her children (Bobby even more than Anne, for he was older and "saw the craziness more clearly") by her betrayal and her lies.

But Kay's behavior also had some positive aspects. She rescued Frost from emotional chaos, enabled him to write and inspired some of his finest poems. She greatly enhanced the children's lives by making Frost a member of their household. Ted cooperated in her effort to keep the family together. They preserved appearances and convinced almost everyone that they had a happy life. Kay managed, somehow, to hold things together when they constantly threatened to break apart.

V

The full story of Frost's relations with Kay finally reveals—as he intended—the real meaning of *A Witness Tree*. The book, published on April 23, 1942 (four months after America entered the war), was dedicated, not to Kay and Ted, but "to K. M. for her part in it." Though rejected by the Literary Guild and the Book-of-the-Month Club, it sold 10,000 copies in the first eight weeks and won Frost's fourth Pulitzer Prize. Since few readers knew about Kay or expected to find sexual passion in Frost's poetry, the revelation of his love went unnoticed. In a typically obtuse review, the *Booklist* spoke of "characteristically quiet poems with little emotional stress," and the innocent *Catholic World* exclaimed: "Here again are some honestly beautiful nature poems."

Though the sexual imagery in these love poems is as powerful as Dylan Thomas's "force that through the green fuse drives the flower," the poetry gains in strength by its more subtle expression of emotion. With characteristic elusiveness, Frost declared that metaphor is the divinely appointed way of writing one thing when you mean another, instead of clearly stating what you mean. As the poet James Dickey observed: "He's able to say the most amazing things without seeming to raise his voice."

In May 1943, Frost acknowledged Kay's inspiration in a letter to his editor William Sloane: "you can find internal evidence in the book itself that but for her there would have been no seventh book. . . . [I] couldn't have been induced to do anything except with something far better than tact. . . . The dedication of the book is no ordinary acknowledgment." A witness tree, which is called "deeply wounded" in the opening poem, "Beech," is a tree trunk and iron stake that mark the boundary of a piece of country property. The signature at the bottom of "Beech," "The Moodie Forester," refers to Frost's temperament as well as to his mother's maiden name. It links Kay to both mother and son, and testifies (or witnesses) that he will respect the boundaries of their love. The first section of the book, "One or Two," takes up the question of whether Frost will be alone or joined with Kay. It includes the fourteen best poems in the book—from "The Silken Tent" to "The Discovery of the Madeiras"—all of which express, directly or indirectly, his love for Kay. Frost also makes several affectionate but subtle allusions to Kay in *A Masque of Reason* (1945), the book that followed *A Witness Tree*. In this work the enchanting Kay appears as Job's wife, Thyatira, and is named for a city famous for its witches. Thyatira is beautiful, she does not try to be platonic and she has a past that won't bear looking into. She also, like Kay with Frost, falls asleep whenever Job tries to read to her and always claims she hasn't been asleep.

"The Silken Tent," which opens the love sequence in *A Witness Tree*, is a perfect example of Plato's concept of the horse and charioteer, of passion restrained by art. The original title of this intensely personal poem was "In Praise of Your Poise." Reuben Brower points out that "as the first poem of his eightieth birthday selection, *Aforesaid*, Frost printed 'The Silken Tent,' where it takes the place of 'The Pasture,' the dedicatory poem [to Elinor] of several earlier volumes." This sonnet, written in a single sentence and dominated by a single metaphor, was inspired by the sensual imagery of the Song of Solomon— "I am . . . comely . . . as the tents of Kedar" (1:5)—an exotic contrast to the stony harshness of rural New England, and by the seductive invitation in John Donne's "The Baite":

Come live with mee and bee my love,
And we will some new pleasures prove
Of golden sands, and christall brookes,
With *silken lines*, and silver hookes.

In Frost's poem the beloved woman is compared to a silken tent in a field when the summer breeze—an allusion to the "correspondent breeze" of the Romantic poets, which represents inspiration and creative power—has dried the dew on its ropes so that it sways gently in "guys" (a triple pun on ropes, mockery, and men). Its masculine cedar pole (a hint of the aromatic cedars of Lebanon) shoots upward toward heaven, symbolizing the sureness of the soul. Though not strictly held by any single cord, the feminine tent, supported by the masculine pole, is loosely bound by countless silken ties of love. Only when the ropes become taut as the summer air becomes capricious (another pun on the lady's whimsy and the man's goatish lust) is the tent made aware of the slightest bondage.

This love poem describes, with the greatest possible delicacy, the conflict between Kay's bondage and freedom as she is pulled, loosely by Ted in marriage or tightly by Frost in love, but remains "strictly held by none." The "silken ties" refer to her lovemaking, not to her marriage, and suggest (as Frost wrote in "Not Quite Social"): "You have me there, but loosely, as I would be held." Her daughter said Kay was "ecstatic" about this tribute and agreed that the poem described the two men and two ties of love that pulled Kay in different directions.

"All Revelation," which follows "The Silken Tent," refers back to "the agitated heart" in Frost's early poem "Revelation." "All Revelation" describes sexual intercourse and the revelation or insight that comes from that experience. This act is repeated metaphorically (and rather awkwardly) in the third stanza as the male cathode ray enters the concave geode. Eyes gazing at eyes, as the man and woman make love, seem to bring out the stars and the flowers, concentrate the earth and the sky, and make them feel, through their union, a part of both earthly nature and the heavenly cosmos.

"The Most of It," in "One or Two," which describes Frost's longing for and response to Kay, harks back to "Two Look at Two," in which the tame buck and doe encounter the lovers (based on Frost and Elinor). In the later poem the man seems alone and finds nothing but a mocking echo in answer to his call for companionship. When he calls out to life, he wants an "original" (that is, a novel and also elemental, primitive and even godlike) response. His cry is answered by an embodiment of sexual power when a great buck suddenly appears on the opposite cliff and swims across the lake. He walks with horny tread, penetrates the brush and creates an orgasmic waterfall so that his mate can make The Most of It. Frost had identified with a buck as early as July 1921 when he told Raymond Holden that he would soon be crashing through the woods in his direction.

"Never Again Would Birds' Song Be the Same," which appears between "The Most of It" and "The Subverted Flower," is (Frost said) an "old-fashioned praise poem about a lady's voice" that his audience would "have to like whether you like it or not." In this sonnet the birds in Eden recognize Eve's sound of sense and grasp her tone of meaning without understanding her actual words. Her soft eloquence influences the birds so profoundly that their song permanently changes and will never again be the same: "And to do that to birds was why she came." Emphasizing the bold sexual pun on the final word, Frost suggests that, just as the lady's voice intensified the birds' song, so Kay's sexual passion inspired the words that made this poem.

The long narrative poem in couplets that concludes this section, partly based on a story in Richard Hakluyt's *Voyages* (1600), is so puzzling and uncharacteristic that Brower, Richard Poirier and William Pritchard, who have all written well about Frost, do not even mention it. The narrative describes two contrasting women. One is a weak, silent and unresponsive lady, stolen and brought aboard ship by her lover and then left with him on the Atlantic island of Madeira, where she dies of a weak heart. The other is a passionate Black slave who kisses her lover, "drinks" his breath and is overwhelmed by sexual desire. When she becomes infected by her lover's dangerous fever, they are bound naked, face to face, and thrown overboard in a funereal wedding. One woman shrinks from life; the other sacrifices herself for love.

In February 1938, the month before Elinor died, Frost alluded to the metaphysical image in "Two Tramps in Mudtime" and took a characteristically antiplatonic stance. He told a poet friend that he was philosophically opposed to having one "Iseult" for his vocation (poetry) and another for his avocation (sexual love). His aim was to write—as he did with Kay—about the real and the ideal in one woman. In "The Discovery of the Madeiras," the "stolen lady" symbolizes Tristan's theft of Iseult; the feverish bound slave girl represents Iseult's fatal passion. The pale, thoughtful lady was based on Elinor; the dark lady was based on Kay. In this poem Frost revealed how Kay had supplanted Elinor.

IO

EDMUND WILSON
—— AND ——
SCOTT FITZGERALD

Edmund Wilson has usually been perceived as a "father figure," a staunch friend and an enthusiastic supporter of Scott Fitzgerald. In the only essay on their friendship, William Goldhurst in *F. Scott Fitzgerald and His Contemporaries* writes, "From the beginning [Wilson] offered Fitzgerald guidance and encouragement, and did much to infuse into the fledgling a feeling of self-confidence and assurance." This view is primarily based on Wilson's fine editorial work on Fitzgerald's posthumous books, *The Last Tycoon* and *The Crack-Up*, published when Fitzgerald was no longer a rival and a threat.

During Fitzgerald's lifetime, however, before Wilson became the magisterial old man of letters, his private and public criticism of Fitzgerald's character and work was often very harsh. Far from encouraging Fitzgerald's talent, Wilson's criticism sometimes seemed intent on destroying it. The supportive-destructive nature of Wilson's criticism had its source in their tense and ambivalent friendship, which began at Princeton and continued until Fitzgerald's death in 1940. During that time, Wilson assumed the role of stern tutor to a brilliant but wayward disciple.

In 1940 Vladimir Nabokov arrived in America and (in many respects) replaced Fitzgerald in Wilson's emotional and intellectual life. Wilson helped Nabokov publish his work at the beginning of his American career. But when the pupil no longer needed the lesson of the master, the talented beneficiary once again aroused Wilson's jealousy and became his rival and adversary. During the 1960s Wilson repeated the pattern he had established with his

Princeton disciple, turning against Nabokov and quarreling with him as he had done with Fitzgerald.

Fitzgerald's overpraised early novels brought him extraordinary fame and wealth at a time when Wilson, his senior, was still trying to establish himself as a journalist and critic. Fitzgerald's popular and financial success gallingly underscored the contrast between their characters and talents. To Wilson the critic, Fitzgerald's early work provided an exhilarating challenge, an opportunity to participate in his friend's creative work. At the same time, Fitzgerald's fiction revealed to Wilson, an aspiring novelist, the relative paucity of his own fictional gifts. Wilson's competitiveness and confidence in his critical astuteness were fed by Fitzgerald's habit of self-abasement before those he considered his moral and intellectual superiors. Although Wilson met Fitzgerald's requests for advice about his work with intelligent insight, such requests created a fund of animosity and resentment that Wilson often revealed in an ugly public way. Reluctant, like most men, to recognize the genius of a slightly younger contemporary, Wilson subtly and perhaps unconsciously tried to pull him down. As Max Perkins shrewdly observed, "Edmund Wilson would give his eyeteeth to have half the reputation as a novelist that Scott Fitzgerald has."

Wilson was often prickly, ungracious and contemptuous toward Fitzgerald. Though he sometimes inflated Fitzgerald's worst work, his remarks tended to range from qualified praise to brutally frank, even malicious criticism. Fitzgerald, content to remain a disciple and always eager to learn, listened patiently to this often salutary but sometimes merciless commentary. As Leon Edel wrote introducing Wilson's *The Twenties*, "He respected Edmund too much to want to be seriously hurt." But Fitzgerald exacted revenge in his fiction. It was no coincidence that the head of the appalling bond firm in *The Beautiful and Damned* and the man who killed Jay Gatsby were both named Wilson.

Hemingway, who would write his own subtly denigrating portrait of Fitzgerald in *A Moveable Feast*, was also well acquainted with the destructive side of Wilson's criticism. Still angry about Wilson's essay in *The Wound and the Bow*, which had argued that Hemingway's creative work originated in some hidden psychological weakness, in 1950 Hemingway warned Arthur Mizener, Fitzgerald's first biographer, about the baneful influence of Wilson's egoistic and self-serving criticism. He noted in a letter of May 12, 1950, that Wilson was

"an excellent critic about many things but he has strange leaks in his integrity."
To Hemingway, Wilson's shrewdness as a critic was counterbalanced by his
disloyalty and destructiveness. Wilson's negative criticism of Fitzgerald showed
that he failed to recognize his greatness until after he was dead. Wilson's response was always tempered by his lack of respect for Fitzgerald's character,
his envy of his charm and worldly success, his dismay that true creativity could
be manifested in so unworthy a person.

Born in New Jersey in 1895, the son of a Princetonian who was a brilliant
trial lawyer and a sometime attorney general of the state, Wilson was a solid
member of the eastern gentry. Haughty and aloof, Wilson attended the Hill
School, graduated from Princeton with an outstanding record in 1916 and
served overseas with the ambulance corps in World War I. Fitzgerald, impulsive
and open, was born in St. Paul a year later, the son of a genteel failure and the
embarrassingly eccentric daughter of a self-made Irish immigrant. He attended
an obscure Catholic prep school, flunked out of Princeton (without even learning to spell) and spent the war years in American army camps. Plain in appearance, the stocky, auburn-haired Wilson was intellectual and sternly rational,
stiff and self-conscious. The dazzlingly handsome Fitzgerald had an imaginative and intuitive mind, a spontaneous and impetuous approach to experience.

At Princeton, Wilson had all the advantages. A year ahead of Fitzgerald and
editor of the *Nassau Lit.*, he heavily edited Fitzgerald's one-act play "Shadow
Laurels" and his story "The Ordeal" and published them in the college magazine in 1915. They collaborated that year on a musical comedy for the Triangle
Club, Wilson writing the book and Fitzgerald the lyrics for *The Evil Eye*. It was
understood between them that Fitzgerald was the brash, superficial upstart,
destined to make a splash but perhaps also doomed to fail, while Wilson was
the solid intellectual who would set him straight.

In 1916 Wilson and his classmate John Peale Bishop published a satiric
poem that put the popular but cheeky Fitzgerald, who had failed out of college,
in his proper place. They contrasted his shallowness to their own substantial
intellects, and deflated his flashy cleverness, superficial reading, derivative
cynicism and unworthy ambition by having Fitzgerald exclaim:

I was always clever enough
To make the clever upperclassmen notice me;

I could make one poem by Browning,
One play by Shaw,
And part of a novel by Meredith
Go further than most people
Could do with the reading of years;
And I could always be cynically amusing at the expense
Of those who were cleverer than I
And from whom I borrowed freely,
But whose cleverness
Was not of the kind that is effective
In the February of sophomore year. . . .
No doubt by senior year
I would have been on every committee in college
But I made one slip:
I flunked out in the middle of junior year.

After college and military service, both young men embarked on literary careers in which they contrived to act out their familiar roles with each other. Wilson was the first to move to New York, where he shared an apartment in Greenwich Village and worked for the *New York Evening Sun*. When Fitzgerald visited him in 1919 Wilson seemed to embody the ideal literary life. He had been transformed from "the shy little scholar of Holder Court" into a promising symbol of cosmopolitan life. "That night, in Bunny's apartment," Fitzgerald recalled in *The Crack-Up*, "life was mellow and safe, a finer distillation of all that I had come to love at Princeton . . . and I began wondering about the rent of such apartments."

Thereafter, Wilson became Fitzgerald's literary mentor. He discussed the art of the novel with Fitzgerald, urging him to pay more attention to form. He commented on Fitzgerald's work before publication, and wrote reviews that helped him to define his art. Fitzgerald regularly deferred to Wilson's literary judgment, appeared to surrender his intellectual conscience to his mentor (he called Hemingway his "artistic conscience"), and yet, in Wilson's view, sacrificed his integrity by publishing trashy stories in popular magazines. Wilson's uneasy role was exacerbated by their common belief that the novel was a higher and more valuable form of endeavor than literary criticism. Wilson longed to be a creative writer, but his great knowledge and appreciation of the literature of the past inhibited his creative urge. He made his living as a literary journalist. In April 1919 Fitzgerald sharply defined the difference in their talents and careers by presciently warning Wilson, who would become an accomplished anthologist: "For God's sake, Bunny, write a novel and don't waste your time editing collections [of war stories]. It'll get to be a habit."

Soon after they left college, Wilson recalled, Fitzgerald had presumptuously declared: "I want to be one of the greatest writers who ever lived, don't you?" Assuming his familiar Johnsonian persona with the Boswellian Fitzgerald, Wilson in "Thoughts on Being Bibliographed" contrasted (as he had done in his undergraduate poem) his own high intellectual standards with those of his bumbling disciple, who took a long time to mature: "I had not myself quite entertained this [great writer] fantasy because I had been reading Plato and Dante, Scott had been reading [the Princetonian] Booth Tarkington, Compton Mackenzie, H. G. Wells [both of whom influenced his early novels] and [the intoxicating rhythm of] Swinburne; but when he later got to better writers, his standards and his achievement went sharply up, and he would always have pitted himself against the very best in his own line that he knew." Wilson failed to acknowledge that Fitzgerald, despite his naiveté, had actually achieved his fantasy by learning from his older contemporaries instead of pitting himself (as Wilson had done) against impossible standards.

After Fitzgerald's death, Wilson sought to explain his dual role as supporter and attacker by asserting that this part had been forced upon him by Fitzgerald. In "A Weekend at Ellerslie," Wilson wrote that Fitzgerald "had come to regard himself as somehow accountable to me for his literary career. . . . It was his own artistic conscience that accused him, but this was beginning to make our meetings uncomfortable." Wilson thus echoed Fitzgerald's own admission in *The Crack-Up* (1936) that "for twenty years a certain man had been my intellectual conscience. That was Edmund Wilson." Despite Wilson's fundamental hostility, he always remained Fitzgerald's ideal reader. As Wilson told John Peale Bishop in a letter of January 2, 1941, two weeks after Fitzgerald's death: "Men who start out writing together write for one another more than they realize till somebody dies."

Wilson helped Fitzgerald get started in New York by introducing him to George Jean Nathan, who, in the fall of 1919 published his first stories (written as an undergraduate) in the *Smart Set*. When Fitzgerald completed the first draft of *This Side of Paradise*, he naturally sought Wilson's opinion. Wilson responded, as usual, with friendly derision, backhanded compliments and discouraging faint praise. He compared Fitzgerald's novel to the trivial bestseller by the adolescent Daisy Ashford, spotted the influence of the hero of Mackenzie's *Sinister Street*, mocked Fitzgerald's intellectual pretensions, offered sound criticism and warned him in a letter of November 21, 1919, about preferring popularity to serious art:

> I have just read your novel with more delight than I can well tell you. It ought to be a classic in a class with *The Young Visiters*. . . . Your hero is an unreal imitation of Michael Fane, who was himself unreal. . . . As an intellectual [Amory] is a fake of the first water and I read his views on art, politics, religion and society with more riotous mirth than I should care to have you know. . . .
>
> It would all be better if you would tighten up your artistic conscience and pay a little more attention to form. . . . I feel called upon to give you this advice because I believe you might become a very popular trashy novelist without much difficulty!

In 1922, Wilson opened his review of the novel with his usual put-down: Fitzgerald "has been given imagination without intellectual control of it; he has been given a desire for beauty without an aesthetic ideal; and he has been given a gift for expression without any idea to express." Though Wilson clearly had the intellectual control, aesthetic ideals and abundant ideas, it was Fitzgerald who had somehow blundered into the creation of a phenomenally popular novel. Trying to account for this surprising critical success, Wilson praised the book's vitality: "I have said that *This Side of Paradise* commits almost every sin that a novel can possibly commit: but it does not commit the unpardonable sin: it does not fail to live. The whole preposterous farrago is animated with life."

Evaluating the work of Thomas Wolfe, another Scribner author, in the late 1930s, Fitzgerald echoed Wilson by telling his Hollywood secretary: it "doesn't commit the cardinal sin; it doesn't fail to live." But Wilson himself had probably been echoing the tinge of patronage in Ford Madox Ford's judgment of D. H. Lawrence's first novel, *The White Peacock*: "It's got every fault that the

English novel can have. . . . But, you've got GENIUS." Later on, in *The Crack-Up*, Fitzgerald expressed his irritation and resentment of Wilson's severe criticism of his youthful work. He admitted that there was an element of intellectual pretentiousness in the novel, but defended its essential truth and integrity: "A lot of people thought it was a fake, and perhaps it was, and a lot of others thought it was a lie, which it was not."

In 1920 Fitzgerald was riding high on his newfound wealth and fame as spokesman for the postwar generation, and had fulfilled Wilson's prediction that his shallowness would make him a popular success. Wilson, still toiling as an obscure journalist, found other ways to attack him. He now became as critical of Fitzgerald's personal faults as he was of his literary failings. Burton Rascoe, writing in the *New York Tribune*, quoted Wilson's gratuitous remark that Fitzgerald mispronounced more words than any other educated person that Wilson had ever known. Wilson and John Peale Bishop, whose creative work was also eclipsed by Fitzgerald's, drew up a satiric catalog for a "Proposed exhibit of Fitzgeraldiana for Chas. Scribner's Sons." These items—which reflected Fitzgerald's immaturity, vanity, shallowness, narcissism and undistinguished military career (Bishop, like Wilson, had served in Europe)—consisted of three double-malted milks, a bottle of hair tonic, a yellow silk shirt, a mirror, his entire seven-book library (including a notebook and two scrapbooks) and an "overseas cap never worn overseas." The yellow silk shirt anticipated Gatsby's exhibition of his wardrobe; the overseas cap was cunningly adopted by Fitzgerald in *The Crack-Up*. Though emotionally vulnerable, Fitzgerald usually tolerated Wilson's sharp criticism with good-natured resignation.

Fitzgerald had good reason to put up with Wilson's attacks. He was being well paid for his work and perhaps understood Wilson's envy. He also knew that he was not an intellectual novelist and, though his popular stories were hastily composed, that his style and subject matter were his own. He must have instinctively known that his work derived from his personal faults and emotional crises. His role as passive target was, moreover, fundamental to his relationship with Wilson. Had he become angry and broken with him, he would have lost access to Wilson's harsh but stimulating criticism. Fitzgerald undoubtedly acquiesced in Wilson's most spiteful remarks.

Fitzgerald submitted his second novel, *The Beautiful and Damned*, for Wilson's comments in 1921 just as he had done with *This Side of Paradise* in 1919. In

February of that year Wilson told his friend Stanley Dell that he was impressed by Fitzgerald's ability to describe the seeds of destruction in his marriage: "I am editing the MS of Fitz's new novel and, though I thought it was rather silly at first, I find it developing a genuine emotional power which he has scarcely displayed before. . . . It is all about him and Zelda." Fitzgerald would finally and fully portray their mutual destruction, after his alcoholism and her insanity, in *Tender Is the Night.*

Wilson must also have been pleased by his brief but flattering appearance in Fitzgerald's second novel, *The Beautiful and Damned,* as Eugene Bronson, "whose articles in The New Democracy [i.e., *The New Republic*] were stamping him as a man with ideas transcending both vulgar timeliness and popular hysteria." Continuing his practice of commenting negatively on Fitzgerald's personal as well as literary life, Wilson also reported in a March 25 letter to Stanley Dell that Zelda (whom he liked) was "offended by the [assumed] cynical indifference of Fitzgerald to the baby," and that alcohol had aged his handsome profile as experience had tempered his mind: "He looks like John Barrymore on the brink of the grave . . . but also, somehow, more intelligent than he used to."

Fitzgerald had by now learned to absorb Wilson's criticisms without flinching. After reading Wilson's review of his first two novels in March 1922, Fitzgerald told George Jean Nathan that he had actually enjoyed the cruel dissection. Wilson had shown him the typescript before publication, and Fitzgerald, appreciating the serious analysis, modestly accepted the criticism. Though he asked Wilson to delete references to his drinking and his criticism of the war, which would have offended Zelda's parents, he told him: "It is, of course, the only intelligible and intelligent thing of any length which has been written about me and my stuff—and like everything you write it seems to me pretty generally true. I am guilty of its every stricture and I take an extraordinary delight in its considered approbation. I don't see how I could possibly be offended at anything in it"—though Wilson clearly feared he well might be. Less confident and resilient authors might have been seriously discouraged by the review, but Fitzgerald, mining the scrap of praise, was particularly pleased by Wilson's conclusion in "Literary Spotlight: F. Scott Fitzgerald" that "*The Beautiful and Damned,* imperfect though it is, marks an advance over *This Side of Paradise*: "the style is more nearly mature and the subject more solidly unified, and there are scenes that are more convincing than any in his previous fiction."

Fitzgerald brought out collections of stories soon after the publication of his novels to capitalize on the success of his more ambitious works. In *Vanity Fair* of November 1922 Wilson, reviewing *Tales of the Jazz Age*, concluded that Fitzgerald had advanced in his short fiction, as he had in his novels: "Scott Fitzgerald's new book of short stories . . . is very much better than his first [*Flappers and Philosophers*]. In it he lets his fancy, his humor and his taste for nonsense run wild . . . though he still suffers from the weakness of not focusing his material sufficiently."

Despite his previous strictures about shallow, formless works, Wilson actually enjoyed and encouraged Fitzgerald's stories about silly, vain young people, perhaps still appreciating the undergraduate jokes they had written together. Wilson's misplaced delight in this kind of writing led him to inflate the merits of Fitzgerald's worst full-length work, *The Vegetable, or From President to Postman: A Comedy in Three Acts*. Fitzgerald once told Wilson that "he had looked into Emily Post and had been inspired with the idea of a play in which all the motivations should consist of trying to do the right thing." In this play, a drunken railroad clerk suddenly becomes president of the United States and, after a predictable series of disasters, finally finds his true calling as a postman. Wilson, who had admired Fitzgerald's fantasy when they collaborated on a musical comedy, showed for the first time real enthusiasm for his work. He told Fitzgerald that *The Vegetable* was "one of the best things you ever wrote" and "the best American comedy ever written." Unwittingly encouraging the weakest aspect of Fitzgerald's talent, Wilson urged Fitzgerald "to go on writing plays."

Wilson, then married to the actress Mary Blair, also tried to help place the play in New York. When it was published in 1923, after a dismal theatrical failure in Atlantic City the previous year, Wilson stuck to his earlier judgment, calling it in his *Vanity Fair* review "A Selection of Bric-a-Brac," "a fantastic and satiric comedy carried off with exhilarating humor. . . . I do not know of any dialogue by an American which is lighter, more graceful or more witty." In gratitude for Wilson's support, Fitzgerald dedicated the play to his childhood friend Katherine Tighe and to "Edmund Wilson, Jr. / Who deleted many absurdities / From my first two novels I recommend / The absurdities set down here."

The following year, Wilson cast the critical debate between himself and Fitzgerald into the form of an imaginary conversation, after the style of Walter Savage Landor, between the critic Van Wyck Brooks and Scott Fitzgerald. In

"Imaginary Conversations," Wilson portrayed himself as the careful, thorough, learned and scholarly Brooks, who "knows far more about American literature than anybody else in the world," and gave Brooks all the best lines. The critic freely censured Fitzgerald for haste, superficiality and commercialism; for writing too much and too fast; and for allowing himself to be corrupted by such high-paying magazines as the *Saturday Evening Post*. This influential and frequently reprinted essay contained some useful admonitions, but it made Fitzgerald look foolish and shallow, outclassed by the heavyweight critic.

In 1924 Wilson also reviewed Hemingway's Three Mountains Press pamphlet *in our time*. He told Fitzgerald about Hemingway and inspired their meeting in Paris, just after the publication of *The Great Gatsby* in April 1925. Wilson's recognition of Hemingway coincided with his perception that Fitzgerald had produced his first fully realized work. He was gratified to discover that Fitzgerald had followed his advice and moved from a loose, subjective novel to a unified, impersonal one. Though he did not review the novel, whose significance at that time was not generally recognized, Wilson told him in a letter of April 11, 1925, with his usual qualifications, "It is undoubtedly in some ways the best thing you have done—the best planned, the best sustained, the best written."

Four years later, in a crucial letter to the novelist Hamilton Basso, Wilson, with uncommon modesty, unfavorably contrasted his own recently published novel, *I Thought of Daisy* (their fictional heroines had the same name), to Fitzgerald's best work of fiction. For the first time, but privately, he acknowledged Fitzgerald's superiority and placed his achievement on a national rather than on a merely personal level. In Wilson's May 9, 1929, letter to Basso, he wrote: "[I've been] thinking with depression how much better Scott Fitzgerald's prose and dramatic sense were than mine. If only I'd been able to give my book the vividness and excitement, the technical accuracy, of his! Have you ever read *Gatsby*? I think it's one of the best novels that any American of his age has done." Five years later Fitzgerald included Wilson's minor novel among "Good Books That Almost Nobody Has Read."

Wilson continued to be obsessed with Fitzgerald's charming but narcissistic personality. His attitude toward him—a mixture of condescension and envy, admiration and dislike—remained as ambivalent as it had been in college. In Wilson's "The Crime in the Whistler Room" (1924), which appeared in the same volume as the imaginary conversation between Fitzgerald and Brooks, Fitzgerald appears as a handsome, dissolute, and rather uneasy fellow (like "Barrymore on the brink of the grave") who has the same transparent self-centeredness that Wilson had satirized in his Princeton poem. He is "an attractive young man with a good profile, who wears a clean soft shirt and a gay summer tie, but looks haggard and dissipated. . . . His manner . . . alternates between too much and too little assurance, but there is something disarmingly childlike about his egoism."

Between 1924 and 1931, when Fitzgerald lived mostly in Europe and Wilson inevitably saw less of him, Wilson became more tolerant of his personal behavior. Later on, he even defended Fitzgerald's drunken prank with the wealthy and pretentious wife of John Peale Bishop. "I know that he wrote on Margaret Bishop's dress with a lipstick," he told Dos Passos. "But did he do this more than once?" Though Fitzgerald could be boorish, he gradually came to embody the glamor and romanticism that Wilson merely dreamed of. In a March 3, 1950, letter to Arthur Mizener, Wilson nostalgically recalled the vitality of the handsome young man and his beautiful wife, "The remarkable thing about the Fitzgeralds was their capacity for carrying things off and carrying people away by their spontaneity, charm, and good looks."

Wilson's tolerance was stretched to the breaking point in February 1928 during his weekend at Fitzgerald's magnificent house, Ellerslie, outside Wilmington. Fitzgerald wanted to revive their friendship, which had suffered a certain chill when he began to need appreciation much more than advice. "The aftermath of a Fitzgerald evening was notoriously a painful experience," Wilson remarked in his lively memoir "A Weekend at Ellerslie." "Nonsense and inspiration, reckless idealism and childish irresponsibility," he wrote, "were mingled in so queer a way." The weekend—like most of their meetings—was chaotic, disappointing and intensely irritating.

Their relations remained cool for the next five years, while Zelda had her first breakdowns and Fitzgerald struggled to complete *Tender Is the Night*. After the tensions between them had almost led to a rupture, Wilson attempted to escape the pontificating role that Fitzgerald's behavior demanded. In January 1933, after Hemingway had achieved great success with *A Farewell to Arms* and Fitzgerald's career was stagnant, he turned up drunk for a dinner with Hemingway and Wilson in New York. In a review of Morley Callaghan's *That*

Summer in Paris, Wilson recalled how Fitzgerald had humiliated himself with Hemingway—as he had done on previous occasions with Dreiser, Conrad, Joyce and Edith Wharton.

Fitzgerald's behavior shocked Hemingway and Wilson, the two notorious drinkers, who would never have used their drunkenness as an excuse to degrade themselves. In his review, Wilson mentioned the incident to illustrate Fitzgerald's self-humiliation, which enabled him to excuse his own failings and attack others without provoking retaliation. "The last time I ever saw [Hemingway]," Wilson wrote in "That Summer in Paris," "I had dinner with him and Scott Fitzgerald. Hemingway was now a great man and Scott was so much overcome by his greatness that he embarrassed me by his self-abasement, and he finally lay down on the restaurant floor, pretending to be unconscious but actually listening in on the conversation and from time to time needling his hero, whose weaknesses he had studied intently, with malicious little interpolations."

Fitzgerald belatedly apologized in a letter to Wilson of February 1933. He completely agreed with Wilson's interpretation of his behavior, and tried to explain his uneasy relationship with Hemingway: "I came to New York to get drunk and swinish and I shouldn't have looked up you and Ernest in such a humor of impotent desperation. I assume all responsibility for all unpleasantness—with Ernest I seem to have reached a state where when we drink together I half bait, half truckle to him."

In a letter of December 4 of that year, Wilson protested to Fitzgerald about the similar falsity in *their* friendship. Weary of perpetuating the roles they had adopted in college, Wilson acknowledged his share of responsibility: "What I object to is precisely the 'scholar and vulgarian,' 'you helped me more than I helped you' business. I know that this isn't entirely a role you've foisted on me: I've partly created it myself."

Just as Wilson chafed against Fitzgerald's obsequious persona, so Fitzgerald finally tried to assert his independence by rejecting Wilson's critical pronouncements. The previous October, Fitzgerald had written, for Wilson's *New Republic*, an unusually sensitive and poignant obituary of his cynical friend Ring Lardner. Jealous of Fitzgerald's friendship with and admiration of Lardner, Wilson criticized the rather rhetorical conclusion of the piece: "I thought the phrase 'great and good American' sounded like a political speech. Lardner . . .

wasn't exactly great, was he?" Though Fitzgerald did not answer this comment directly, he no longer accepted Wilson's infallibility. He had perceived Wilson's hostile attitude and defended the title he had provided for Lardner's collection, *How to Write Short Stories*, by defiantly stating: "You are wrong about Ring's book. My title was the best possible. You are always wrong—but always with the most correct possible reasons." Though Wilson had the inevitable reservations about *Tender Is the Night*, which was published in 1934, he thought Fitzgerald had "got something real out of the marriage relationship" of Dick and Nicole Diver.

Fitzgerald saw Wilson (then married to Mary McCarthy) for the last time in the fall of 1938, when he took Sheilah Graham to visit his old friends on the East Coast. Struck once again by the great and sudden change in Fitzgerald, Wilson attributed his new normality and tameness to Sheilah, who had encouraged him to give up alcohol. At the same time (and retrospectively) Wilson held Zelda responsible for Fitzgerald's crazy behavior. But, as he told his old Princeton teacher Christian Gauss in a letter of October 27, 1938, Fitzgerald, though now calm, had also lost a good deal of his old vitality: "He doesn't drink, works hard in Hollywood, and has a new girl, who, though less interesting, tends to keep him in better order than Zelda. . . . He seems mild, rather unsure of himself, and at moments almost banal." After this meeting, Fitzgerald, who had lost his self-confidence after a series of personal tragedies and disastrous experiences in Hollywood, resumed his youthful role as Wilson's disciple. "Believe me, Bunny," he wrote on May 16, 1939, stressing as always Wilson's superior intellect, "it meant more to me than it could possibly have meant to you to see you that evening. It seemed to renew old times learning about Franz Kafka and latter things that are going on in the world of poetry, because I am still the ignoramus that you and John Bishop wrote about [in the poem] at Princeton."

Wilson's intellectual influence continued until the end of Fitzgerald's life. When working with Budd Schulberg on the screenplay for *Winter Carnival* in February 1939, he frequently and respectfully referred to Wilson in their conversations. While trying to develop his political awareness in the troubled 1930s, Fitzgerald would sit in the California sunshine reading Marx's *The Eighteenth Brumaire* "like an eager sociology student bucking for an A in Bunny

Wilson's class in social consciousness." Despite his apparent political naiveté, Fitzgerald resisted the Zeitgeist. He never swallowed, as did the more sophisticated Wilson, the illusory bait of Communism. As he shrewdly told Perkins, while attempting to explain Wilson's gloom: "A decision to adopt Communism definitely, no matter how good for the soul, must of necessity be a saddening process for anyone who has ever tasted the intellectual pleasures of the world we live in."

Just after hearing about Fitzgerald's death in December 1940, Wilson stressed, in a December 27 letter to Zelda, his closeness to Fitzgerald, who seemed to represent an aspect of his own character that had somehow failed to develop: "I feel myself as if I had suddenly been robbed of some part of my own personality." Deeply moved by Fitzgerald's death and perhaps remorseful that he had not fully reciprocated his friendship and appreciated his genius, Wilson attempted to make amends for his blindness and occasional cruelty by becoming the guardian of Fitzgerald's posthumous reputation. In February and March 1941, Wilson commissioned for the *New Republic* critical essays on Fitzgerald by Dos Passos and Glenway Wescott and an elegy by John Peale Bishop. By editing and supplying the title for Fitzgerald's unfinished Hollywood novel, *The Last Tycoon* (1941), and compiling his uncollected essays, notebooks, and letters (more than half of them to Wilson) in *The Crack-Up* (1945), Wilson was primarily responsible for the remarkable revival of Fitzgerald's languishing reputation.

Writing to Perkins on February 16, 1941, Wilson ignored the portrayal of psychiatry in *Tender Is the Night* and rather grudgingly conceded that *The Last Tycoon* was "the only one of Scott's books that shows any knowledge of any field of human activity outside of dissipation." Wilson's two-page foreword called it "Fitzgerald's most mature work" and "the best novel we have had about Hollywood." Though his criticism was cursory, Wilson's reconstruction of Fitzgerald's notes, which suggested how the fragmentary novel would develop and conclude, was absolutely brilliant.

Wilson's editorial work on *The Crack-Up* was also extensive and important. He told Perkins that he had hated Fitzgerald's confessional essays (as he had disliked *The Beautiful and Damned*) when they first appeared in *Esquire* in 1936. They must have reminded him, in a menacing way, of his own alcoholism and nervous breakdown. But he admitted in his February 16 letter to Perkins, after Fitzgerald's death, that "there was more truth and sincerity in it, I suppose, than we realized at the time." Perkins did not agree with Wilson, however, and the valuable and influential book was eventually brought out by New Directions. This volume included, in addition to Fitzgerald's work, admiring letters to him from Gertrude Stein, Edith Wharton, T. S. Eliot, Thomas Wolfe and John Dos Passos; essays by Dos Passos, Paul Rosenfeld and Glenway Wescott; and poems by Bishop and Wilson. (Hemingway was conspicuously absent.)

Wilson's elegy in heroic couplets, written in Wellfleet on Cape Cod in February 1942, was influenced by the description of the Atlantic gale in Yeats' "A Prayer for My Daughter." At the start of the poem Wilson mentions that he had edited his friend's works from the very beginning until the very end of Fitzgerald's literary career. His life's work, it seemed, was to correct that errant genius. Even in this memorial poem, however, which served as the "Dedication" to The Crack-Up, Wilson portrays him in a narcissistic and degrading moment. At Princeton, Wilson had once found him with

> Pale skin, hard green eyes, and yellow hair—
> Intently pinching out before a glass
> Some pimples left by parties at the Nass;
> Nor did [he] stop abashed, thus pocked and blotched,
> But kept on peering while I stood and watched.

The poem concludes more sympathetically by returning to the once emerald and now dead eyes of his lost friend:

> Those eyes struck dark, dissolving in a wrecked
> And darkened world, that gleam of intellect
> That spilled into the spectrum of tune, taste
> Scent, color, living speech, is gone, is lost.

After Fitzgerald's death his imperfect work had, for Wilson, almost the look of a classic. His final judgment, in a paragraph added in 1945 to his foreword to The Last Tycoon, was that "Fitzgerald will be found to stand out as one of the first-rate figures in the American writing of the period." While preparing

The Crack-Up, Wilson, referring to Fitzgerald and Bishop, honestly told Christian Gauss in a letter of May 15, 1944, "I was more fortunate than either of them, not in gifts, but in the opportunity to survive." But Wilson, who outlived Fitzgerald by thirty-two years, survived as a critic. Fitzgerald, with Wilson's ambivalent help, survived as an artist.

II

WILSON

—— AND ——

ALLEN TATE

The ideological conflicts of two literary titans, Edmund Wilson and Allen Tate, represent a crucial division in modern American thought and culture. They clashed between social context and New Criticism in literature, between North and South in history, between progressive and reactionary in politics, between atheist and Catholic in religion. Wilson was slightly older than Tate and helped launch his career, but he had an insider's advantage in New York when the two intensely ambitious men competed for literary power and fame. They reviewed each other's books, but carefully undercut their praise with incisive criticism. In the 1920s they had similar literary values and became friends, but the prevailing left-wing politics of the post-Depression 1930s brought their personal and cultural conflicts into sharp focus. They finally quarreled, insulted each other and drew apart, as longtime friends often do in contentious old age.

These long-lived contemporaries, Wilson (1895–1972) and Tate (1899–1979), had a great deal in common. They were well educated in the classics, and close friends of the Princeton graduate and poet John Peale Bishop. Prolific men of letters in many genres, they wrote poems, plays and novels as well as criticism, history, biography, memoirs and polemics. They were influential editors, generous to other writers and well placed to help attractive young women succeed.

Both men, wobbling between being heavy drinkers and certified alcoholics, had serious financial problems and bitter fights with the Internal Revenue Service. Though often short of cash, Wilson had four marriages, Tate had three and divorced his first wife twice. Tate married two poets and a nun, Wilson trumped him with an actress, socialite, novelist and aristocrat. Wilson had three children, Tate topped him with four. Wilson's second wife and Tate's twin son died in freak accidents. Margaret Canby fell down a staircase, the infant Michael Tate choked on a toy telephone. Both included prominent writers in their impressive seraglios. Wilson had liaisons with the poets Edna St. Vincent Millay, Léonie Adams and Louise Bogan as well as the diarist Anaïs Nin and the film critic Penelope Gilliatt. Tate had affairs with the poets Laura Riding and Jean Garrigue, the novelists Katherine Ann Porter and Elizabeth Hardwick, and the concert pianist Natasha Spender.

Their differences were even more significant and turned the old friends into intellectual enemies. Wilson, descended from the New England Puritans and the seventeenth-century minister and author Cotton Mather, was the son of the attorney general of New Jersey and friend of President Woodrow Wilson. Tate, descended from Kentucky plantation owners, was the son of a heavy drinker, pouncing philanderer and active racist, who repeatedly failed as a small businessman. Wilson was educated at Princeton; Tate was educated under John Crowe Ransom at Vanderbilt in Nashville. "Bunny," who kept his childhood name, was plump; Tate, a dandy with mustache, bowtie and cane, was cadaverously thin.

Tate studied violin in a conservatory; Wilson had no interest in music, though he liked popular culture and was an amateur magician. After caring for wounded and mutilated soldiers in a military hospital in France in World War I, Wilson strongly opposed all wars, even the one against the Nazis. Tate had been too young to serve. Wilson, a fluent and independent professional writer who poured out his work with full-throated ease, disliked teaching. Tate, a college professor at Sewanee and the University of Minnesota, sometimes suffered from writer's block. He couldn't finish the planned sequel to his only novel, *The Fathers* (1938), and dried up for long stretches without writing poems.

Wilson was interested in the biographical and cultural background of the writers he analyzed; Tate was an apostle of the fashionable New Criticism, which taught critics to ignore the cultural context and focus exclusively on the text. They had antithetical attitudes about the Civil War, slavery and racial equality. Wilson, a Northern liberal, made strenuous efforts to break away from the values and prejudices of his class, and identified with the underdog. Tate clung desperately to his conservative Southern values throughout his life. He was an antebellum reactionary who dreamed of a Southern victory in the War Between the States and a return to the genteel traditions of the Old Plantation, including the estate that had been owned by his family.

Wilson, a more profound thinker than Tate, had a wider range of interests and greater knowledge of languages, including Latin, Greek, French, Italian, German, Cyrillic Russian, Semitic Hebrew and Finno-Ugric Hungarian. Beginning with Paul Valéry and Marcel Proust, Wilson wrote about many foreign authors. Tate wrote mainly about American and English poets. In 1935 Wilson traveled for five disillusioned months in Russia, studied communist doctrine and spent six weeks recovering from scarlet fever in a primitive Odessa hospital. He then wrote *To the Finland Station* (1940), a study of socialism and communism, with portraits of Lenin and Trotsky. Tate despised Soviet life and ideology. Wilson traveled to Haiti and Israel, and sympathized with the Jews. He wrote about the biblical Dead Sea Scrolls, the Zuni Indians in New Mexico and the Iroquois in New York, and the culture and politics of Canada. Tate, except for his lover Laura Riding, had no interest in Jews or minority cultures.

Wilson disapproved of Tate's vain display when he wore three-piece suits with his Phi Beta Kappa key strung across his vest. Wilson lived on Cape Cod and his ancestral home in upstate New York. Tate, obsessed with the bluegrass and bourbon of Kentucky, wound up in the frozen wasteland of Minnesota. Wilson's fourth wife was devoted to him and his last marriage ended happily. Tate's third wife, an ex-nun, hated him and treated him harshly during his long last illness. Both men were keenly interested in literary news and gossip, and asked (like King Lear) "Who loses and who wins; who's in, who's out." In Nashville, two days before he died, Tate asked Stephen Spender about the current reputation of his fellow-poet Louis MacNeice.

Wilson could be combative, but Tate was more waspish, vituperative and manipulative. The poet John Berryman, noting Tate's ambivalent personality, called him "a very generous and corrupt man, open-hearted, wily, spiteful." In the fall of 1949 Berryman's wife Eileen Simpson heard that Tate was "an operator, who in recent years (a time when he had not been able to write poetry) had become divisive and jealous over the success of others." Tate's colleague Walter Sullivan emphasized his destructive streak: "Not even his own self-interest could deter Allen's characteristic impulse toward confrontation and dispute." His poetic disciple Randall Jarrell defined Tate's greatest fault, which intensified his clash with the more flexible Wilson, as "a defect of sympathy in the strictest sense of the word, a lack of ability to identify himself with anything that is fundamentally non-Allen."

Tate was the editor of the highbrow, small-circulation, Southern-oriented *Fugitive* journal in provincial Nashville, and when he came to New York in 1924 the serial seducer worked for the appropriately named Climax publishers. Wilson, still in his twenties, was a well-respected and influential editor at *Vanity Fair*, the *Dial* and the *New Republic*. Though both men were quite short, about five feet, six inches, Tate's biographer Thomas Underwood writes that he "was a bit intimidated by Wilson, who seemed both physically striking and intellectually threatening." The struggling Tate had recently married the poet Caroline Gordon, and Wilson arranged for the young couple to get an emergency grant of $250 from a writers' relief fund.

In 1923 Tate had sent poems to Wilson at *Vanity Fair*. Wilson rejected them, but encouraged Tate by saying: "I look forward to something extraordinary from you. But do try to get out of the artistic clutches of T. S. Eliot." Two years later he told Tate that "Mr. Pope" and "Death of Little Boys" are your best poems: "You have a very curious quality, not only a gift of imagery but a beauty and a 'strangeness' which makes me willing to bet on your future." Tate, a better poet than Wilson, could afford to flatter his competitor. In 1929 he returned the compliment by puffing Wilson's rather commonplace verse: "Edmund Wilson has written some of the most accomplished poetry of our time."

The first strains of discord appeared in December 1926 when Tate and the critic Malcolm Cowley got angry about Wilson's essay "Poe at Home and Abroad." They felt it was based on their conversations with Wilson, who had appropriated their thoughts. Tate angrily told Cowley that "Wilson's shameless exploitation of the economic value of an idea was really humiliating." But Wilson had his own thoughts about everything, and it's unlikely that he took his ideas from Tate, who believed that he owned Poe.

Four years later Tate attacked Wilson's review of T. S. Eliot's major poem: "Edmund Wilson's review of 'Ash Wednesday' seems to me to be very unsound; it ends up with some very disconcerting speculation on Eliot's private life which has no significance at all." In fact, Wilson was right to oppose Tate's narrow-minded critical dogma. He was one of the first to see that Eliot's poems, despite his high-minded disclaimers, were intensely personal and that the autobiographical elements had great significance. *The Waste Land* included the speech of his deranged wife Vivien and alluded to his own nervous breakdown.

Tate thought Wilson was an "excellent man and critic" when he praised Tate's work, but was not so good when he criticized it. Wilson's March 1928 review of "The Tennessee Poets" irritated Tate by alluding to Eliot's influence, and by undermining his praise with serious qualifications and degrading comparisons. Tate's great skill, it seemed, was merely decorative: "even where Mr. Tate is imitative he possesses a strange originality, a special vein of macabre imagination. . . . Though, line for line, these poems are amazing, they seem, in some way, as wholes, to lack emphasis, to fail of cumulative effect. . . . [They] are like elaborate oriental ornaments which have been produced at an immense expense of materials, patience and cunning skill." Still, in October 1928, Wilson told their mutual friend John Peale Bishop that Tate "has become a great friend of mine." Despite their quarrels, the men were always eager to meet for literary gossip and stimulating talk.

Wilson was a brilliant and generous critic. He introduced America to Hemingway in 1924 and to Yeats, Joyce, Eliot and Gertrude Stein as well as Valéry and Proust in *Axel's Castle* (1931). He encouraged his third wife, Mary McCarthy, to write fiction, revived Scott Fitzgerald's reputation in the 1940s and launched Vladimir Nabokov's career in America. In 1947 he sent Nabokov's novel *Bend Sinister* to Tate, who published it at Henry Holt.

Tate, the mentor of Robert Lowell and Randall Jarrell, moved easily from Lowell's *Lord Weary's Castle* to Wilson's *Axel's Castle*. Before he became testy with Wilson, he perceived the major theme in Wilson's masterpiece: the alienation of the modern writer. In his July 1931 review in *Hound and Horn*, he observed: "Mr. Wilson is the first American critic to formulate a comprehensive philosophy of French Symbolism as it has affected writers in English." He praised "Wilson's sensitive and finely modulated prose style, the emotional subtlety of his insight into the sensibility of his six writers," and called the book "a brilliant history of the increasing cross-purposes of the artist and his industrialized society." Speaking of both Wilson and himself, Tate predicted their impending conflicts, "though being of the same generation in time, we are of such remote spiritual generations that we shall seem very obscure to each other."

Wilson agreed that he and his friend and contemporary were intellectually opposed, and told Bishop, their mutual go-between and Father Confessor, "Tate

is falling foul of everybody of his own generation, charging them with romanticism, impressionism, Bohemianism, and all the stock crimes . . . of people
who produced literature to be guilty of. He has buried us all alive."

In May 1930, seven months after the Wall Street Crash that began the Great
Depression of the 1930s, Wilson waved a Red flag and warned Tate, "I am going further and further to the left all the time and have moments of trying to
become converted to American Communism"—though he never did convert.
Referring to the 1930 manifesto of twelve Southern writers who defended the
agrarian society of the South and condemned the increasingly dehumanized
society of the North, Underwood observes: "just as Tate was becoming pre-
occupied with his aristocratic lineage, Wilson was trying to divest himself of
the stigma of his social class. Not long after *I'll Take My Stand* was published,
Wilson announced that there was 'no hope for general decency and fair play
except from a society where classes are abolished.' If Tate admired Wilson for
criticizing the status quo, he nevertheless began signing [his ironic and taunt-
ing] letters to him, 'With best wishes for a happy Revolution, and with kindest
regards to the Comrades—'I'd rather see one than be one.'"

A major North-South split in American thought, which went back to the
Civil War and still provoked hostility among friends seventy years later, sig-
naled the end of their close friendship. Tate complained that Wilson, by moving to the left, "has succumbed to all those degradations of values that are
tearing society to pieces." But Tate, while opposing Northern industrialism
with Southern agrarianism, personally perpetuated feudal conditions, and exploited both Black and white sharecroppers on his own land.

Wilson's provocative article in the *New Republic* of July 29, 1931, aimed
directly at Tate, blasted "The Tennessee Agrarians." He accused them of old-
fashioned ancestor worship, "forever feeding itself on its past," satirized their
pseudo-bohemian life in New York and Europe, and lamented their southward
retreat to sentimental and pretentious decay. He also rejected the accusation
that the North was to blame for all the social and economic problems in the
South: "after living in dark basements in Greenwich Village, floating with the
drift of the Paris cafés, they have ended by finding these sojourns both expensive and unsatisfactory, and by forming unflattering opinions of the manners
and the standards of the intelligentsia. They think tenderly of the South again;
and they come, in the end, to blame all the ills of commercialized America on

the defeat of the agrarian Confederacy by the money-grubbing merchants of New England."

The hot issues, then and now, were persistent racism and the cruel treatment of Blacks. As Wilson fiercely wrote of Tate in this article: "He feels that his tradition of living is somehow humanly right and that the modern industrial society which so flourished when his own was defeated is essentially inhuman and wrong. . . . For the Northerner, the horror of slavery still poisons the memory of that feudal society. . . . The Northerner is sure to be shocked when the Southerner speaks frankly of the Negroes as creatures—an inferior race—for whom political or social equality is utterly and forever unthinkable."

As the argument heated up in their letters, Wilson revealed that his views were provoked by personal insults as well as by ideology. He angrily complained that in February 1931, visiting his friend during his journalistic investigation of the South, Tate defended his territory, and subjected his Yankee guest to intolerable rudeness and mockery: "You people certainly take the Southern Cross. Did or did not you and John Ransom and [Donald] Davidson have the abominable manners to sit around and entertain me with prolonged head-shaking and jeering over an unfortunate Northerner who had presumed to come South and try to edit a paper, and with a sour account of other Northerners who had the effrontery to try to hunt foxes in Tennessee? And then you raise the roof when I kid you a little about General Bragg"—the Confederate officer who lost many battles and frequently retreated.

When Wilson disagreed with Tate and exposed his fatuous beliefs, Tate condescendingly dismissed his arguments instead of answering them. He told Bishop that "Edmund, sensitive and fine as he is, has always been very innocent philosophically, and now I begin to think he is an irresponsible child turned loose on things he doesn't understand." Tate then trained his artillery directly on Wilson and told him: "Not a single item of your impressionistic picture of an 'agrarian' is true, and the whole is naturally false. . . . You like to think that we are wistful boys mooning over the past. . . . We draw this moral: you are socially and spiritually bankrupt, and you won't have it that other people aren't—people who still see some hope of building on what they have." Both writers opposed capitalism that had caused the Depression, but neither had a viable alternative—Soviet or Southern.

Tate exploded again in an unconvincing diatribe to the West Virginia–born and honorary Southerner Bishop, who was caught in their whirlwind. Tate claimed that Wilson was losing his grip but, once again and with heavy irony, did not refute his attacks:

> I've had some flaming controversy with Edmund. . . . He wrote a piece about our symposium entitled "Tennessee Agrarians," the tone of which was superior wisdom before our mere ancestor worship, which is after all, of course, all that we have to offer. I scored Edmund . . . in his falling back on all the prejudices he has ever heard about the South. In general, he accuses us of day-dreaming over the past, i.e., on non-realism. I answer that we are simply calling on the traditional Southern sense of politics, which was eminently realistic, while his [communist] Planned Economy . . . is the most fantastic piece of wish-thinking I've ever seen. . . . I fear something is happening to a good man.

Though the antagonists constantly vented their anger, neither man would ever change his mind.

Tate kept putting the knife into Wilson with a torrent of 1930s letters to Bishop, who probably enjoyed their intellectual combat. Urging Bishop to enter the fray, Tate declared that attacking Wilson would be easy, that his critical assumptions were fundamentally wrong and—with backhanded praise—that Wilson's wide-ranging interests severely limited his writing: "I do think that E. has great curiosity—indispensible in a real critic. . . . But he goes from one thing to another out of curiosity, and he pauses long enough in between to be credulous. Powers of exposition, but no analytical powers (read again his essay on Valéry—juvenile, absolutely)." In fact, Wilson's analysis of Valéry's difficult poetry is quite sophisticated.

Both men were heavy drinkers and got increasingly angry as they got increasingly drunk. It was ironic that in September 1939 Tate got the teaching job that Wilson, an old Princetonian, had also applied for. The English Department at Princeton mistakenly thought that Wilson, but not Tate, was contentious and drank too much. In December the alcoholic Tate sent another shot across Wilson's bow and told Bishop, "Dr. Wilson has never been quite human, and

I am not surprised to hear that he has become a metabolic machine for the transformation of alcohol." Despite inebriation, Wilson triumphed in June 1938 when Tate and his wife, Caroline Gordon, stayed overnight with Wilson and Mary McCarthy on Cape Cod. He recited the poetry of Alexander Pushkin in Russian, which Tate could neither understand nor correct.

As both men dug in and hardened their positions, their dispute continued for the next fifteen years. At Tate's fiftieth birthday party in Princeton in 1949, they both had plenty to drink and Wilson exchanged insults with the Southern squire. Wilson regretfully said "he couldn't stay for another drink; he'd already kept his mother's chauffeur waiting too long and must get back to her house in Red Bank." Deflating Wilson's social pretentions, Tate looked out the door to see who was behind the wheel of the Cadillac and disdainfully remarked, "That's not a chauffeur, Bunny. Why that's just an ordinary field negra." During the school and college integration crises in the late 1950s, Tate felt Blacks didn't belong in white universities and imitated a Black student asking, "Is you done yo' Greek?"

Their conflict about New Criticism recurred when Wilson savaged the stodgy academic journal edited by Tate's revered teacher: "I would not write anything whatever at the request of the *Kenyon Review*. The dullness and sterility and pretentiousness of the *Kenyon*, under the editorship of Ransom, has really been a literary crime." In January 1951 Tate accused Wilson of indifference not only to his work but also to his life and wife: "I am perfectly reconciled to your almost total lack of interest in what I write; but it is a little difficult to contemplate a certain coldness, an inattentiveness to what one is, without feeling a little discouraged about it." Wilson seemed to compound his crime by making negative remarks about Caroline's books. This provoked Tate to exclaim that she would always be polite to him, but Wilson's visit to their home "would not in the end give her pleasure."

Wilson, for once, tried to lower the temperature by refuting Tate's charges, and answered Caroline's insulting demurral by inviting himself to visit them—pleasurable or not: "How on earth can you say that I've been indifferent to your work? I've often said both in print and in conversation how highly I thought of your poetry. . . . I have never said anything whatever about refuting your ideas about my criticism in my seminars or anywhere else—in fact, didn't even know you had expressed any ideas about my criticism. . . . I missed Caroline's romping dachshund and your old Confederate flag that used to hang on the wall in the back room. . . . In spite of our unusual loathing of one another's views, I'd very much like to see you."

Tate's unexpected conversion to Catholicism was another personal and extremely contentious issue. As early as 1932, after the accidental death of Wilson's second wife, Tate seemed mildly concerned with his spiritual welfare. He asked Bishop, "What do you suppose poor Edmund will do now? I wish he might be brought to some notion that would save his soul." In January 1951, personally affronted by Tate's conversion and doubting his sincerity, the ironclad atheist sent him an insulting letter. Wilson condemned the recent attacks of the Catholic Church on his novel *Memoirs of Hecate County*, published in 1946 but still banned as obscene in America. He also scorned, with three unusually hesitant "seems to me," Tate's willingness to swallow the absurdity of Christian doctrine:

> I had already heard with regret about your conversion. . . . My animus against the Catholics lately has been due to their efforts to interfere with free speech and free press. . . . I hope that becoming a Catholic will give you peace of mind: though swallowing the New Testament as a factual and moral truth seems to me an awful price to pay for it. You are wrong, and have always been wrong, in thinking that I am in any sense a Christian. Christianity seems to me the worst imposture of any of the religions I know of. Even aside from the question of faith, the morality of the Gospel seems to me absurd.

Despite Wilson's forceful disclaimers, the keen convert wanted him to enter the fold. Tate insisted that though Wilson played Satan's advocate, he was really a secret Christian and wrote in "Causerie" (chat): "None so baptized as Edmund Wilson the unwearied, / That sly parody of the devil." Wilson fiercely repudiated the imputation that he himself was a believer and mocked Tate's doomed attempt to cultivate the gentle benevolence of his newfound faith: "He makes against me a malicious, libelous and baseless charge of crypto-Christianity. It is strange to see habitually waspish people like Allen and Evelyn Waugh trying to cultivate the Christian spirit. I hope, though, that conviction will soften Allen, who has lately been excessively venomous about his literary contemporaries. He could never forgive any kind of success."

Waugh had wittily confessed, "You have no idea how much nastier I would be if I was not a Catholic. Without supernatural aid I would hardly be a human being." Tate's zealous Catholicism did not change his sexual behavior. Religion provided a sanctimonious cover for the old satyr, who went frequently to Mass, confessed and took Communion—and continued to fornicate for the next two decades.

Tate not only attacked Wilson's limitations as a critic, political and social ideas, lack of religious belief and indifference to Tate's person and poetry, but also—though Tate was more secretive and repressed—questioned his inbred puritanism. He believed that the ancestral ghost of Cotton Mather had burrowed into Wilson's conscience like a mole. He frankly told Wilson there was a sense in which, as Matthew Arnold said of the poet Thomas Gray, "*you have never spoken out. There is an area of your sensibility that you have never completely come to terms with.*" Wilson, for once, agreed with Tate. In March 1943 he conceded: "What you say about my writing is more or less true. I feel that I have not really, in general, gotten myself out in my books, and am trying to do so now." This was ironic since Wilson vividly described his sex life in *Hecate County* and his journals. By contrast, Tate did not write about his sex life, suppressed all sexual revelations by his would-be biographers and prevented the publication of his love letters.

Wilson and Tate's current reputations are very different. Tate's achievement as poet and critic has been diminished by his unregenerate racism; the second half of his biography was not completed and, except in the South, he is largely forgotten. In old age Wilson had evolved from the priggish young scholar whom E. E. Cummings called "the man in the iron necktie" into a Churchillian potentate with the fine features of a Roman senator. He published more books after he was dead than most writers publish while still alive: a novel *The Higher Jazz*, *Letters on Literature and Politics*, two editions of his correspondence with Nabokov, two collections of essays, and five volumes of his journals from the *Twenties* to the *Sixties*. He was celebrated in his centenary year, my biography was published in 1995 and a weak imitation of my book appeared ten years later. In our time Wilson's intellectual brilliance is greatly admired and his reputation is still high.

12

WILSON
—— AND ——
VLADIMIR NABOKOV

Your letter is very clever, but still you are wrong, still you
regard Onegin *from the wrong point of view.*
—PUSHKIN, LETTER OF MARCH 24, 1825

I

The dispute between Edmund Wilson and Vladimir Nabokov in 1965 recalls a time when rival views of a literary critic and a prominent novelist about a translation of a nineteenth-century poem made the news and for months occupied the pages of leading literary journals in America and England. Wilson's harsh review of Nabokov's four-volume edition of Alexander Pushkin's *Eugene Onegin*, published in the *New York Review of Books* in July 1965, destroyed his friendship with Nabokov, which had lasted through minor storms since Nabokov first arrived in America in 1940. An acrimonious correspondence took place between the two in the *New York Review of Books*, and in February 1966 Nabokov published in *Encounter* his "Reply to My Critics," which responded to all the attacks, including Wilson's, on his literal translation and extensive commentary. Wilson later reopened the wound with an account of his visit to Nabokov in *Upstate* (1971) and a critique of his novels in *A Window on Russia* (1972). Nabokov retaliated with a ferocious letter in the *New York Times Book Review* of November 1971, which concluded the most notorious literary quarrel of the century.

Despite their warm friendship, Wilson and Nabokov always had extreme intellectual differences, which fueled their protracted quarrel. But the dispute also had a deeply personal element and to be fully understood must be placed in its biographical context. In this conflict a critic with a sociohistorical approach opposed a modernist writer. But it also became a literary duel fought on various points of honor between the patrician American critic, who had great influence in the Anglo-American literary world, and the uprooted, dispossessed Russian novelist, who had established a considerable reputation with his magical English prose.

Wilson and Nabokov—like two bishops speaking ex cathedra—each had a strong didactic streak, a stubborn tenacity of opinion, a fierce pride, and a grand manner that rejected challenges and contradictions. Despite the differences in their literary and political ideas, they were intellectual equals and sympathetic soul mates. With Nabokov, Wilson abandoned his characteristic aloofness, courted his friend, and frequently invited him for stimulating visits to Connecticut, Manhattan, Cambridge, Wellfleet and Talcottville in upstate New York. Nabokov, chafing under yet grateful for Wilson's valuable patronage, responded with wary warmth and affection.

Yet the seeds of their bitter quarrel were, in retrospect, germinating from the start. Though they despised narrow-minded academics, both men were exceptionally pedantic and hair-splitting in their disputes about the fine points of Russian language and prosody. Nabokov, as touchy as a samurai, patiently endured Wilson's all-too-frank criticism of his work. But in 1965, when Nabokov's novels in English had established him as a major figure in American culture, he was no longer willing to tolerate Wilson's condescending and sometimes ill-informed remarks.

Accustomed to the potshots of their private war, Wilson was not fully aware of his own destructive impulse. An experienced journalistic warrior, he did not realize how deeply wounded Nabokov would be by the public betrayal of their long-standing comradeship. Though Wilson tried to apologize for his attack and did not respond to the harsh invective of Nabokov's parting salvo, the damage had been done and both suffered a tragic loss of friendship.

The backgrounds and personalities of the two antagonists—bulldog and butterfly—were as important in their quarrel as the issues and ideas. The evaluations by Russian specialists of Nabokov's edition of *Eugene Onegin* are useful but, like the serious reviews of *The Nabokov-Wilson Letters*, do not consider his quarrel with Wilson. The biographical essays and books on Nabokov discuss the dispute from his perspective, do not fully recognize Wilson's point of view and tend to simplify the complex motives of the combatants. Simon Karlinsky's valuable introduction to their letters gives an objective rather than analytical account of their friendship. Andrew Field, Nabokov's first biographer, offers a rather superficial view. Even Brian Boyd, in his excellent life of Nabokov, reduces Wilson's motive to simple envy.

The few critics who tried to explore the deeper motives seem to have missed the mark. To the gentle Victor Pritchett, who underestimates the seriousness of the quarrel, the row "seems more and more like a fireworks display than an attempt to draw blood." The perceptive Leon Edel calls it the product of a "protracted love-hate relationship," though there was no real hate and a great deal of sadness. Brian Boyd, who emphasizes the element of jealousy, exaggerates the comparative failure of Wilson's so-called "pornographic" fiction: "The eroticism of Wilson's *Memoirs of Hecate County* [1946] had ensured only that the book was banned from sale and forgotten. When *Lolita* [1955], by contrast, brought Nabokov fortune, fame and ringing acclaim, it sharply intensified Wilson's irritation that he could not quite compete and that Nabokov knew it."

In fact, Wilson earned the enormous sum of $60,000 from *Hecate County*. Though the book was suppressed on the grounds of obscenity, it was not forgotten. Reissued after the trial of *Lady Chatterley's Lover* by L. C. Page and W. H. Allen in 1959, it was reprinted in American paperback editions by Signet, Noonday and Ballantine. The Panther paperback edition, published in England, lists eight impressions between 1951 and 1960, and the book is still in print.

The critic and novelist were both aging and irritable egoists when their quarrel went public. But the real reasons for Wilson's attack on Nabokov's edition, which Nabokov considered "far too private to be aired in print," and for his enraged response to Wilson's account of his visit to Cornell, described in *Upstate*, have never been explained.

II

Simon Karlinsky mentions the similarities between the two men: "They came from cultivated upper-class homes within their respective cultures. Each had an interest and an involvement in the other's literature and native traditions.

Both were at home in French literature and language. Both had a skeptical, albeit divergent, view of religion and mysticism. Both were sons of jurists who were involved in politics." He could have added that Nabokov's father might have become the Russian minister of justice if the short-lived democratic government had not been destroyed by the Bolsheviks in 1917, and that Wilson's father would have been on the American Supreme Court if there had been another vacancy after Woodrow Wilson appointed Louis Brandeis in 1916.

Wilson's passionate interest in Russian politics and literature began in the early years of the Depression. He learned Russian before his disillusioning trip to the Soviet Union in 1935, which he described in the misleadingly titled *Travels in Two Democracies* (1936). He wrote his first major essay on Russian literature, "In Honor of Pushkin," that year and included it in *The Triple Thinkers* (1938). Americans knew very little about most Russian writers until after World War II. Wilson's pioneering studies reached a wide audience and "put Pushkin and Gogol on the map" in this country.

Nabokov brought to his friendship with Wilson a rare combination of qualities. Handsome, athletic and witty, sophisticated, cosmopolitan and multilingual, he had a charming personality and a brilliant mind. A wide-ranging man of letters with catholic interests in science and art, Nabokov was also a great novelist whom Wilson could respect and assist. Nabokov arrived in America, after two decades in exile, in May 1940 and soon replaced Scott Fitzgerald—who died the following December—in Wilson's emotional and intellectual life. Wilson helped Nabokov establish himself at the beginning of his American career at the same time that he was reviving Fitzgerald's posthumous reputation by editing *The Last Tycoon* (1941) and *The Crack-Up* (1945). But when the pupil no longer needed the lesson of the master and the talented beneficiary surpassed his former teacher, Nabokov—like Fitzgerald before him—aroused Wilson's jealousy and became his rival and adversary. In 1965 Wilson repeated the pattern he had formed with his Princeton disciple, turned against Nabokov and quarreled with him as he had with Fitzgerald.

At the suggestion of his cousin, the composer Nicolas Nabokov, Vladimir first wrote to Wilson on August 30, 1940. Wilson, then literary editor of the *New Republic*, responded with generous help. During the next few years Wilson used his valuable contacts to commission reviews from Nabokov for that journal, and to place his work in the *Atlantic Monthly* and the *New Yorker*. He tried to get Nabokov teaching jobs at Bennington, Yale and Princeton (while he himself was turned down for a position at Cornell) and wrote him recommendations for a Guggenheim Fellowship, including one for an edition of *Eugene Onegin*. He introduced Nabokov to editors at New Directions and Doubleday, and advised him about getting the most favorable terms for his books. Wilson also read and made useful suggestions about Nabokov's manuscripts in English, and wrote a blurb for *The Real Life of Sebastian Knight* (1941). He thought the novel was "absolutely enchanting" and compared it to Gogol, Proust and Kafka. He found a potential translator, Helen Muchnic, for Nabokov's Russian novels and loyally promoted these books, though he didn't like them. Poor himself, he offered to lend Nabokov money, which was politely refused.

Despite their formality and reserve, their friendship during the course of many visits flourished and deepened. Within eight months Nabokov was addressing Wilson as "Bunny" (a nickname used only by his oldest friends), and he was calling Nabokov "Vladimir" and the even more familiar "Volodya." On November 4, 1940, a week before his first surviving letter to Nabokov, Wilson told his old teacher and close friend Christian Gauss about Nabokov's English education and stylish book reviews, artistic reputation and political beliefs: "His English is perfect (he went to Cambridge, England)—I'm amazed at the excellence of the book reviews he's been doing for me. He is a brilliant fellow and considered by the Russians the most important talent among the émigrés. . . . His point of view is neither White Russian nor Communist. The family were landowning liberals, and intellectually the top of their class. His father was a prominent leader of the Kadets. Vladimir is in pretty bad straits." Significantly, Wilson at first grasped Nabokov's political position and then, during their subsequent argument about Communism, forgot what he had once known. Tremendously impressed by his new friend, Wilson also told his editor Robert Linscott that Nabokov was "the most brilliant man he had ever met."

When they first met Wilson was married to Mary McCarthy, who recalled their exhilarating conversations and the depth of emotions in what soon became the most important friendship in Wilson's life: "Edmund was always in a state of *joy* when Vladimir appeared; he *loved* him." Nabokov's visit to the Wilsons' in Stamford, Connecticut, on June 6, 1942, inspired Nabokov's witty poem "The Refrigerator Awakes." This visit also involved some cagey fencing and Beckett-like incongruities. Wilson asked Nabokov if he believed in God.

When Nabokov countered with "Don't you?" Wilson muttered, "What a strange question!" Wilson's marriage broke up two years later after he beat McCarthy during a drunken quarrel and she fled to New York. His resident cook, afraid she would be named co-respondent in the divorce case, threatened to leave. Wilson turned to the Nabokovs at this desperate moment and they moved into his house, before the cook moved out, for a transitional week in 1944.

The following March, shortly after the death of John Peale Bishop, another Princeton friend, Wilson, who found it difficult to express his deepest feelings, told Nabokov: "Our conversations have been among the few consolations of my literary life through these last years—when my old friends have been dying, petering out or getting more and more neurotic." Nabokov, who'd lost everything he owned, responded warmly. In the 1940s he told Wilson, "I must see you both. I miss you a lot. . . . You are one of the very few people in the world whom I keenly miss when I do not see them." He later told Andrew Field that Wilson was a very old friend, "in certain ways my closest."

Wilson's first review of Nabokov's work was a favorable notice, which appeared in the *New Yorker* on September 9, 1944, of his eccentrically perceptive study *Nicolai Gogol*. Though Wilson was "annoyed by the frequent self-indulgence of the author in poses, perversities and vanities," an annoyance that would intensify as Nabokov persisted in this habit, he praised the book and said it "takes its place with the very small body of first-rate criticism of Russian literature in English."

In November 1947 Wilson used his authority to protect Nabokov from an officious *New Yorker* editor who wanted to change the idiosyncratic style of his fiction. "I have read the Nabokov stories," Wilson imperiously told Katharine White, "and I think they are both perfect. Not a word should be changed." That same year, as Nabokov later wrote in his introduction to the *Time* paperback edition of *Bend Sinister*, Wilson read the typescript of the novel and recommended the book to Allen Tate, an editor at Holt, who published it in 1947. The proud Nabokov, who did not find it easy to express his gratitude, freely acknowledged throughout his life his enormous debt to Wilson. In March 1943, for example, he gratefully told Wilson, "I have noticed that whenever you are involved in any of my affairs they are always successful."

Their passionate common interest in Russian literature led Wilson in November 1943 to suggest that they collaborate on a "Siamese" book in which he would write the critical essays and Nabokov do the translations. Though they signed a contract with Doubleday (which Nabokov called "Dayday") for this joint project on 1944 and received an advance of $750 each, the book was never completed. "The only time I ever collaborated with any writer," Nabokov said in his *Paris Review* interview, "was when I translated with Edmund Wilson Pushkin's [short verse play] *Mozart and Salieri* for the *New Republic* twenty-five years ago [in April 1941], a rather paradoxical recollection in view of his making such a fool of himself last year, when he had the audacity to question my understanding of *Eugene Onegin*."

In September 1948 Wilson revived the idea of a collaboration and helped to inaugurate Nabokov's edition by suggesting that they work together on a prose translation, with scholarly notes, of *Eugene Onegin*. Yet when Nabokov took up this idea on his own, and devoted more than a decade to this project, Wilson admonished him for spending so much time on *Onegin* instead of writing his own novels. Fitzgerald had given Wilson a similar warning in August 1919, just after completing *This Side of Paradise*, when he told him: "For God's sake, Bunny, write a novel and don't waste your time editing collections [of war stories]. It's getting to be a habit."

III

Though Wilson and Nabokov were intimate friends who admired and respected each other, their friendship was not based on similar views on life and art. Throughout the years they argued, in person and by mail, gently and harshly, about punning, pronunciation, pornography, approaches to literature, taste in authors, the meaning and value of Nabokov's works, and Russian politics. They also fought about two issues that would recur in their quarrel about Pushkin: the fine points of English and Russian versification and Pushkin's knowledge of English. Commenting in his capacity as editor of the *New Republic* on Nabokov's first review, Wilson advised him, in his very first letter, to give up his lamentable propensity to pun. Twelve years later the incorrigible Nabokov was still referring to Pushkin's poem as "You gin? One gin." Much later in their friendship, Wilson ticked off Nabokov about the correct way to pronounce "nihilist" in English and about the correct meaning of the French *faux ami: fastidieux*.

Their different—indeed, antithetical—approaches to literature were a more serious problem. In his diary of 1956, as well as in his essay on Nabokov in *A*

Window on Russia, Wilson compared Nabokov's involuted novels to an out-moded decorative object of the Czarist era. He condemned the fabulous artificer's idea of a literary work as "something in the nature of a Fabergé Easter egg or other elaborate knickknack." The historically minded Wilson, who emphasized the author's biography and milieu rather than his style and technique, condescendingly asked Nabokov how he could "pretend that it is possible to write about human beings and leave out of account all question of society and environment." He concluded that Nabokov mindlessly "took over in your youth the *fin de siècle* Art for Art's sake slogan and have never thought it out."

Nabokov, carefully replying to his "fellow magician," argued on the contrary that "a critic's duty should be to draw [the reader's] attention to the specific detail, to the unique image, without . . . which there can be no art, no genius." In his commentary on *Eugene Onegin* he hit directly at Wilson's influential approach by regretting that Pushkin "is treated by Russian pedants as a sociological and historical phenomenon, typical of Alexander I's regime (alas, this tendency to generalize and vulgarize the unique fancy of an individual genius has also its advocates in the United States)." In 1959, six years before their dispute exploded in public, Nabokov asked his editor not to seek an endorsement of his novels from Wilson, whose "symbolico-social criticism and phony erudition in regard to *Doctor Zhivago*" inspired his "utter disgust."

Their letters became bitter and even insulting when the two extremely contentious, competitive and dogmatic friends disagreed about the merits of both classic and contemporary authors. Wilson would enthusiastically recommend his favorite authors and Nabokov—who had an exalted idea of his own work and loved to demolish the reputations of great writers—would attack them and condemn Wilson's crude taste. When Wilson called André Malraux "the greatest contemporary writer," the bristling Nabokov (who probably thought he himself was the greatest) asked if Wilson was kidding, and called *Days of Wrath* and *Man's Fate* a "solid mass of clichés." When Wilson praised Faulkner's genius, Nabokov could not believe that he took Faulkner seriously and dismissed *Light in August* as "trite and tedious." Wilson disliked Stevenson and Kafka, whom Nabokov admired. "You and I differ completely," he told Wilson, "not only about Malraux [Pasternak and Henry James], but also about Dostoyevsky, Greek drama, Lenin, Freud and a lot of other things—about which, I'm sure, we'll never be reconciled." Wilson finally persuaded Nabokov to include Jane Austen and Dickens in his course on the novel at Cornell. And they did manage to agree about a few immortals: Pushkin, Flaubert, Proust and Joyce.

Both men had a taste for "indecent" literature, from *The Story of O* to Jean Genet; and Wilson once suggested an obscene, Genet-like interpretation of the title of one of his books: *The Bit Between My Teeth*. Wilson's *Hecate County* and Nabokov's *Lolita* were considered pornographic and ran into trouble with contemporary censorship, but both authors were severely critical of each other's work in that genre. Wilson complained to the poet Louise Bogan that Nabokov, ignoring the serious intent of his book, thought he had tried to imitate the pornography of John Cleland's eighteenth-century novel *Fanny Hill*. Nabokov, using a masochistic image, tactlessly told Wilson that his book had failed to arouse erotic interest: "I derive no kick from the hero's love-making. I should have as soon tried to open a sardine can with my penis. The result is remarkably chaste, despite its frankness." Eight years later Wilson gave an imperceptive and similarly cutting response to *Lolita* (which both Mary McCarthy and his fourth wife Elena both admired): "I like it less than anything else of yours I have read. . . . Nasty subjects may make fine books; but I don't feel you have got away with this."

Their political disagreements were intensely personal and bitterly contested. "In historical and political matters," Nabokov told Wilson, stressing Wilson's ideological rigidity, "You are partisan of a certain interpretation which you regard as absolute. This means that we will have many a pleasant tussle and that neither will ever yield a thumb (inch) of *terrain* (ground)." Wilson had first recognized (in his letter to Christian Gauss) and then forgotten (when he dug in his heels against Nabokov) that the *intellectual* tradition in Russia, with few exceptions like Gogol and Dostoyevsky, was always liberal; and that an important democratic tradition—which Nabokov's father had belonged to and died for when he was assassinated in Berlin in 1922—stood between the czarists and the communists. Wilson, strongly influenced by the Marxist doctrines that swept America in the 1930s, tended to see Nabokov as a reactionary White Russian monarchist. "Your conception of Russian history is all wrong," he told Wilson, with his usual bluntness, "being based on the stale Bolshevist propaganda which you imbibed in your youth. . . . [You have] a complete ignorance of the . . . liberal movement that started in the time of Alexander I," who reigned from 1801 to 1825.

Despite these severe strictures, Wilson naively sent Nabokov a copy of *To the Finland Station* (1940), his massive study of the intellectual and political movements that led to the Russian Revolution. Though the book (in Nabokov's view) was fatally based on communist sources, and portrayed Lenin as a warmhearted humanitarian and freedom-loving democrat, Wilson inscribed it "to Vladimir Nabokov in the hope that this may make him think better of Lenin." In 1971 Wilson finally recanted his views and admitted (indirectly) that Nabokov had been right about the ruthless Lenin. Alluding to Nabokov as well as to other critics, Wilson awkwardly wrote in his introduction to a reprint of the book: "I have been charged with having given a much too amiable picture of Lenin, and I believe that this criticism has been made not without some justification." He also confessed, "I had no premonition that the Soviet Union was to become one of the most hideous tyrannies that the world had ever known."

Provoking, stimulating, offending and even outraging each other was an essential element in the Wilson-Nabokov friendship, which survived for twenty-five years despite their profound disagreements. "We have always been frank with each other," Nabokov told him, "and I know that you will find my criticism exhilarating." After the extraordinary success of *Lolita* enabled Nabokov to give up teaching at Cornell and move to a suite in the Montreux Palace Hotel, Edmund and Elena Wilson visited him in Switzerland. In January 1964 they had friendly luncheons and dinners and met for the last time. But Nabokov felt betrayed and wounded when he discovered that Wilson had written, but did not mention, the attack on his edition of *Eugene Onegin*.

IV

The *Eugene Onegin* controversy began with a preliminary skirmish between Nabokov and Walter Arndt, who published a verse translation of Pushkin's poem in 1963. Like Nabokov, Arndt was an ardent antifascist and cosmopolitan exile who became an academic in America. But these similarities did not save him from a savage review by Nabokov in the *New York Review of Books* of April 30, 1964. Announcing his own long-gestated and soon-to-be-published translation, Nabokov mercilessly flayed the verbal gobbets of the "pitiless and

irresponsible paraphrast," who had just won the Bollingen Prize for translation. He attacked Arndt's anachronisms, absurd scansion, burlesque rhymes,
crippled clichés, vulgarisms, howlers, lamentable Russian and wobbly English.

After the assault on Arndt's workmanlike translation, Nabokov was under
considerable pressure to produce a superior work of his own. But his word-for-
word prose translation in 1964 was generally condemned as a misconceived
failure. Most critics felt the elaborate commentary in his great Gothic cathedral
of an edition (complete with the rose windows and gargoyles) was seriously
compromised by Nabokov's eccentricities and vendettas, and by his venomous
criticism of innocent predecessors.

The root of the problem was Nabokov's absurd yet dogmatic desire to produce a literal "rendering, as closely as the associative and syntactical capacities
of another language allow, of the exact contextual meaning of the original.
Only this," he insisted, "is true translation." Nabokov, the greatest Russian
prose stylist of the century, was willing to sacrifice everything—"elegance,
euphony, clarity, good taste, modern usage, and even grammar"—on the altar
of literalism. He felt he would reap his greatest reward if students used his
deliberately dull version of Pushkin's sparkling stanzas as a lame trot.

Virtually all the Slavic experts agreed that the translation was hopeless.
Even the partisan Brian Boyd conceded defeat and later explained: "Unquestionably Nabokov's lines are not only unrhymed but often flat and gracelessly
awkward, unlike Pushkin's, and it was this that many reviewers found a cruel
betrayal of Pushkin and sufficient reason to prefer Arndt's nonsense jingles."
Nabokov's friend Gleb Struve believed that Wilson "was right in criticizing
Nabokov's translation . . . for the use of rare, unfamiliar, outlandish and . . .
unPushkinian words."

Robert Conquest agreed that it was "too much a transposition into Nabok-
ovese, rather than a translation into English." Edward Brown, writing in the
Slavic Review about the revised edition, was even more severe. He asserted
that "this translation of *Eugene Onegin*, by one of the craftsmen of our time is
execrable. . . . [He] systematically abandons poetry and does so on the basis of
a shallow and spurious 'theory' of translation." The Harvard economist Alexander Gerschenkron, in what Wilson considered the most intelligent review,
perceived that "what Nabokov sacrifices so lightheartedly and so disdainfully

is not his own elegance and clarity, and euphony, but Pushkin's." Gerschenkron concluded with a convincing catalogue of Nabokov's defects: "It is indeed deplorable that so much of Nabokov's great effort is so sadly distorted by the desire to be original at all cost, by confused theorizing, by promises that never could be redeemed, by spiteful pedantry, unbridled emotions, and, last but not least, by unrestrained egotism. All this is bound to annoy some readers; it will revolt others."

All the verbal artistry that should have been applied to the translation Nabokov lavished on his learned commentary on the poem. In doing so, he surpassed his academic colleagues—who had been reluctant to recognize either his creative or his scholarly achievements—by applying to the text of Pushkin the minute taxonomic details he had so ably used in his scientific study of butterflies. He observed, for example, that in chapter 3 of *Eugene Onegin*, the "vigorous flow of events constitutes a most harmoniously constructed entity with a streamlined body and symmetrical wings."

Nabokov's extremely digressive commentary not only mimicked the Byronic digressions in Pushkin's poem but, as Clarence Brown observed, imitated and re-created the satiric tone and scholarly structure of his brilliant novel *Pale Fire* (1962): "This work consists of an introduction by [Dr.] Kinbote, a narrative and ruminative poem entitled 'Pale Fire' by John Shade, a much longer, very detailed, even more ruminative, certainly more narrative, and I think more poetic commentary by Kinbote, and, finally, a hilarious index to the whole book."

Nabokov's commentary made two significant references to Wilson, which influenced Wilson's review. In the first, friendly reference (2.391), Nabokov recalled a Russian actress reading Pushkin on "a wonderful record (played for me in Talcottville by Edmund Wilson)." In the second, slightly critical reference (2.474), he stated that Pushkin's famous "description of the coming of winter . . . is well translated (with a few minor inexactitudes)" by Edmund Wilson. Wilson's brief translation, in his essay on Pushkin, had remained unchanged since its publication in 1936. But it seemed to deteriorate, in Nabokov's view, between his original edition of 1964, which provoked Wilson's hostile review, and his revised edition of 1975. In the later edition Wilson's description of winter was "translated" (rather than "well translated") with "a number of inaccuracies" (rather than "a few minor inexactitudes"). The later, retaliatory note lumped Wilson with the rest of the dunces in the commentary.

V

Nabokov, battered by the professional Slavicists, hoped that Wilson would respond favorably in the influential *New York Review of Books* to the edition that had cost so much time, thought and labor. But in August 1964 Nabokov warned his editor that the Bollingen Foundation—which had supported and copublished his edition, but also awarded the translation prize to Arndt—"keeps looking forward to the Edmund Wilson article; but as I have mentioned before his Russian is primitive and his knowledge of Russian literature gappy and grotesque." He also quite accurately told Andrew Field that "there were the two mirages of Wilson. That he knew Russian history better than I because of his Marxism, and that he knew at least as much about Russian literature as I." But Wilson—who felt he could hold his own with any authority when discussing a subject he had carefully studied—had confidently disputed Marxist philosophy with Sidney Hook. He now committed, according to Clarence Brown, "the almost unbelievable *hubris* of reading Nabokov several petulant little lessons about Russian grammar and vocabulary, himself blundering all the while."

Despite his limited knowledge of Russian, Wilson scored several direct hits in his lengthy attack on Nabokov's edition of Pushkin, the writer who had first drawn them together and then become the cause célèbre of their quarrel. Wilson's immediate response, which resembled storm warnings off the Cape, mentioned several criticisms that would find expression in his forthcoming review. As he told Barbara Epstein, his editor at the *New York Review of Books*: "Just looking through it, I can see that Volodya's translation, sometimes in the same way, is almost as much open to objection as Arndt's. It is full of flat writing, outlandish words and awkward phrases. And some of the things he says about the Russian language are inaccurate." Though Wilson realized he did not like the book, he could not resist the opportunity to beat Nabokov at his own game and chose to write a negative review—which might threaten and even extinguish their friendship.

Wilson's measured opening paragraph established the harsh tone of the review, which appeared on July 15, 1965, and seemed more appropriate to dealing with inept translators and doltish scholiasts than for judging the work of an intimate friend. Wilson justified his censorious tone by citing the precedent of Nabokov's assault in his commentary both on Arndt and other unfortunate meddlers with Pushkin. Wilson revealed his ambivalent feelings about

Nabokov, expressed disapproval of his bad manners, and suggested his own more objective view by minimizing his own hostility and rhetorically balancing "does not propose to mask his disappointment" with "does not hesitate to underline his weaknesses."

> Vladimir Nabokov's translation of Pushkin's *Eugene Onegin* is something of a disappointment; and the reviewer, though a personal friend of Mr. Nabokov—for whom he feels a warm affection sometimes chilled by exasperation—and an admirer of much of his work, does not propose to mask his disappointment. Since Mr. Nabokov is in the habit of introducing any job of this kind which he undertakes by an announcement that he is unique and incomparable and that everybody else who has attempted it is an oaf and an ignoramus, incompetent as a linguist and scholar, usually with the implication that he is also a low-class person and a ridiculous personality, Nabokov ought not to complain if the reviewer, though trying not imitate Nabokov's bad literary manners, does not hesitate to underline his weaknesses.

In his blurb for *The Real Life of Sebastian Knight*, Wilson had compared his friend to three writers that Nabokov greatly admired: Gogol, Proust and Kafka. But in his review of *Eugene Onegin*, Wilson deliberately wounded Nabokov by comparing him to three writers his friend particularly disliked: Marx, Dostoyevsky and Sartre. (In 1939 Sartre had dismissed the French translation of Nabokov's *Despair*, and Nabokov had retaliated in 1949 with "Sartre's First Try," a hostile review of the American edition of *Nausea*.)

Like most other critics, Wilson found the "bald and awkward language" of Nabokov's translation, "which has nothing in common with Pushkin's or with the usual writing of Nabokov . . . more disastrous that Arndt's heroic effort." He criticized Nabokov's addiction to unfamiliar and inappropriate words, and gave several examples of his uneven and at times banal translation:

> You will agree, my reader
> That very nicely did our pal
> act toward melancholy Tatiana.

He then spent several pages defending the words and phrases that Nabokov disapproved of in Wilson's own ("well" or inaccurately) translated stanzas of Pushkin's verse.

Wilson next zeroed in on the "lack of common sense" in Nabokov's tedious and interminable appendices about Pushkin's African ancestor and about Pushkin's prosody. The two antagonists had been heatedly arguing about Russian versification since the early 1940s, when Nabokov sent Wilson an eight-page lesson, complete with charts and diagrams. He tried to tell Wilson "you are as wrong as can be," but his lecture had been ignored. In 1950 Wilson admonished Nabokov, "You are all off, as usual," but was now weary of arguing about this stalemated subject. Nabokov's editions forced him to resume their disputations and, once again, to condemn as "ridiculous" the system of prosody invented by his old adversary. Both men loved to instruct others, but Nabokov had much more to teach Wilson, since his English was far superior to Wilson's Russian. But according to Simon Karlinsky, Wilson was right—and Nabokov wrong— about two crucial points: Pushkin *did* know English, and English versification *is* different from Russian.

Wilson also felt the (somewhat parodic) commentary was "overdone" and showed "remarkably little sensitivity to the texture and rhythm of Pushkin's writing, to the skill in manipulating language." But he conceded, if one skipped the *longueurs*, that it makes "very pleasant reading, and represents an immense amount of labor." Toward the end of the review, Wilson struck at Nabokov's *déraciné* style by remarking: "What he writes is not always English. On the other hand, he sometimes betrays . . . that he is not quite at home with Russian." He tried, however, to conclude on a more positive note by portraying Nabokov in the role he himself had assumed—that of cultural interpreter and intermediary: "In spite of his queer prejudices, which few people share—such as his utter contempt for Dostoyevsky—his sense of beauty and his literary proficiency, his energy which never seems to tire, have made him a wire of communication which vibrates between us and that Russian past." The contentious Mary McCarthy, amused and delighted by Wilson's polemic, urged him to continue the controversy.

Nabokov—though intensely aware of his own status and dignity—had put up with Wilson's ill-tempered criticism in their private correspondence.

Though the hostile off-the-cuff (or off-the-Nabokov) remarks in their letters could be tolerated, he considered Wilson's public attack a personal insult. Wilson's offensive tone, Nabokov angrily explained to Barbara Epstein, "compels me to be quite ruthless in regard to his linguistic incompetence." But he decided, at first, to limit his letter in the *New York Review of Books*, on August 26, 1965, to refuting only the "Russian"—or weakest—part of Wilson's review, adding: "Though well aware of the real reason behind this attack, I consider this reason far too sad and private to be aired in print."

The petty philological squabbles in their letters to the editor were not nearly as interesting as the major resumption of hostilities, which took place in the spring campaign of 1966. Unwilling to leave the battlefield to the apparently victorious Wilson, Nabokov changed the venue to England (where few readers would have closely followed their controversy in America) and replied at great length in the February 1966 issue of *Encounter*. He began his "Reply to My Critics" by stating that Wilson's ill-advised attack was a "polemicist's dream come true" and that he would be a "poor sportsman to disdain what it offers." He also began, as Wilson did, by mentioning their friendship and by conceding that Wilson had generously promoted his work: "I have always been grateful to him for the tact he showed in not reviewing any of my novels while constantly saying flattering things about me in the so-called literary circles where I seldom revolve." He continued in this personal vein by mocking Wilson's absurd attempt to pronounce Pushkin's poetry and seriously questioning his competence on this subject: "Upon being challenged to read *Evgeniy Onegin* aloud, he started to perform with great gusto, garbling every second word, and turning Pushkin's iambic line into a kind of spastic anapest with a lot of jaw-twisting haws and rather endearing little barks that utterly jumbled the rhythm and soon had us both in stitches." Nabokov asserted from personal experience that Wilson "is incapable of comprehending the mechanism of verse—either Russian or English."

Nabokov's tone became venomous as the attack shifted from Wilson himself to his review of *Eugene Onegin*. He resented Wilson's insinuation that Nabokov had read neither Theocritus nor Virgil; jeered at Wilson's ignorant Russianisms; insisted that Wilson "knows nothing" about Pushkin's knowledge of English; condemned Wilson's "ludicrous display of pseudo-scholarship"; and defended his own savage digs at established reputations—including Wilson's. In 1949 he had told Wilson that "I liked your book [*The Triple Thinkers*] very much." But in his *Encounter* "Reply," he emphasized their different approaches to literature and mocked "the old-fashioned, naïve, and musty method of human-interest criticism championed by Mr. Wilson . . . [and exemplified by] Wilson's extraordinary misconceptions in *The Triple Thinkers*."

Nabokov concluded by referring to Wilson's letter in the *New York Review of Books* of August 26, 1965—which suggested that Wilson had miscalculated both the severity of his attack and the bitter wound it inflicted on Nabokov—and loftily withdrew from the conflict: "Mr. Wilson says that on rereading his article he felt it sounded 'more damaging' than he had meant it to be. His article, entirely consisting, as I have shown, of quibbles and blunders, can be damaging only to his own reputation—and that is the last look I shall ever take at this dismal scene."

Nabokov's and Wilson's antithetical approach to *Eugene Onegin* concentrated on the most dramatic event in Pushkin's "novel in verse": the fatal duel between Onegin and Lenski. Both authors, themselves engaged in an intellectual duel, believed their personal honor was involved. Both not only used Pushkin's duel as a symbol of their own conduct but also interpreted it in a way that (perhaps unconsciously) revealed their own motivation. In his 1936 essay on Pushkin, Wilson had observed: "Evgeny had killed in the most cynical fashion a man whose friend he had believed himself to be and whom he had thought he did not want to kill. . . . Evgeny had been jealous of him, because Lensky has been able to feel for Olga an all-absorbing emotion, whereas Evgeny, loved so passionately by Tatyana, has been unable to feel anything at all."

In his review published thirty years after his essay on Pushkin, Wilson criticized Nabokov's failure to interpret the fundamental point of the central situation: "He finds himself unable to account for Evgeni's behavior." Wilson then repeated his original interpretation, which took on a new meaning in the context of the quarrel between the intellectual critic (Onegin-Wilson) and the passionate artist (Lenski-Nabokov). Onegin "thinks Lensky a fool yet he envies him. He cannot stand it that Lensky . . . should be fired by ecstatic emotion. So, taking a mean advantage—raising slowly, we are told, his pistol, in malignant cold blood—he aims to put out that fire." Just as Wilson's review inadvertently revealed his own "malignant cold blood," so Nabokov's commentary on *Eugene*

Onegin suggests his motives for changing his mind, airing the "sad and private" reasons for Wilson's attack and bitterly answering his old friend: "In modern Russia little remains of the idea of honor—pure personal honor. . . . Lenski's course of action [in challenging his dearest friend, who had recklessly flirted with Lenski's fiancée], far from being a temperamental extravaganza, is the only logical course an honorable man could have taken." In "Reply to My Critics" Nabokov notes that "Pushkin stresses the fact that Onegin 'sincerely loves the youth' but that *amour propre* is sometimes stronger than friendship."

VI

Wilson did not reply to Nabokov's "Reply, "and their lively and affectionate correspondence inevitably ceased. But five years later, in March 1971, Nabokov responded to news from their mutual friend Harry Levin that the seventy-six-year-old Wilson was seriously ill with heart disease. In his last letter to Wilson, Nabokov made a magnanimous gesture of reconciliation: "A few days ago I had the occasion to reread the whole batch . . . of our correspondence. It was such a pleasure to feel again the warmth of your many kindnesses, the various thrills of our friendship, that constant excitement of art and intellectual discovery. . . . Please believe that I have long ceased to bear you a grudge for your incomprehensible incomprehension of Pushkin and Nabokov's *Onegin*." Wilson, always more belligerent, was glad to get Nabokov's letter. But in *his* last letter he warned his old comrade-in-arms that he would soon have two pieces on Nabokov in press. He was revising his review of *Eugene Onegin* for *A Window on Russia*—correcting his own errors in Russian and "citing a few more of your ineptitudes"—and had included an account of his 1957 visit to the Nabokovs at Cornell in the forthcoming *Upstate*. "I hope it will not again impair our personal relations," he told Nabokov—but he seemed to fear that it would. Ten days later, Wilson bitterly informed Helen Muchnic: "Nabokov has suddenly written me a letter telling me that he values my friendship and that all has been forgiven. He has been told that I am ill and it always makes him cheerful to think that his friends are in bad shape."

The two proud peacocks had always been hypersensitive about each other's behavior. In the early 1940s, when Wilson and Mary McCarthy were in the front seat of the car and the Nabokovs in the rear, Vladimir "leaned forward and nimbly removed Wilson's awful brown hat." Ignoring Nabokov, Wilson

turned to Vera and said: "Your husband has a rather strange sense of humor."
(Wilson's response to such pranks was remarkably like his father's. When
called to the window by his wife, who claimed to have seen an accident and
then cried "April Fool!" Edmund Senior sourly said: "Madame, I don't think
that's funny!") On another occasion, when Mary McCarthy had gone to great
trouble to prepare cherries jubilee for the Nabokovs, Vladimir had mocked
the absurdly hot and cold American confection. Though testy himself about
Nabokov's behavior, Wilson noted in the 1971 addition to his review of *Eugene
Onegin*: "Like all persons who enjoy malicious teasing and embarrassing practical jokes, [Nabokov] is invariably aggrieved and indignant when anyone tries
anything of the kind on himself."

Wilson's visit to Cornell in late May 1957 got off to a bad start. He had a
painful attack of gout and Nabokov met the wrong train. In his account of this
visit in *Upstate* (1971) Wilson noted that his friend was exhausted from over-
work, that his nerves were on edge and that he suddenly shifted from a benign
to an aggressive temper. Nabokov told Wilson that Onegin was going to marry
Lolita, whom he had met at the University of Alaska. He "was at first amusing and charming, then relapsed into his semi-humorous, semi-disagreeable
mood, when he is always contradicting and always trying to score, though his
statements may be quite absurd." The devoted Vera, as usual, sided with her
husband and became hostile if anyone argued with him. Wilson's gout forced
him to eat dinner on the couch, with his leg on a footstool; and he thought,
"It irked Vera a little to have to serve me thus. She so concentrates on Volodya
that she grudges special attention to anyone else, and [a bit of a governess and
prude] she does not like my bringing him pornographic books."

Wilson not only mildly criticized Nabokov's moods, hospitality and wife
(about whom Nabokov felt very protective), but also offered a Freudian theory (which Nabokov particularly disliked) about Nabokov's years in exile in
order to account for the repulsive aspect of his fiction: "I always enjoy seeing
them—what we have are really intellectual romps, sometimes accompanied by
a mauling—but I am always afterwards left with a somewhat uncomfortable
impression. The element in his work that I find repellent is his addiction to
Schadenfreude [malicious pleasure]. Everybody is always being humiliated. He
himself must have suffered a good deal of humiliation." Despite this criticism,
Wilson concluded his description with a tribute to Nabokov's personal courage

and dedication to his art: "He is in many ways an admirable person, a strong character, a terrific worker, unwavering in his devotion to his family, with a rigor in his devotion to his art which has something in common with Joyce's. . . . The miseries, horrors and handicaps that he has had to confront in his exile would have degraded or broken many, but these have been overcome by his fortitude and his talent."

The aristocratic Nabokov had always controlled his interviewers and bi-ographers by demanding that they submit their questions in writing and in advance, and by revising whatever they had written about him. The sugges-tion—in Wilson's ambivalent though essentially sympathetic memoir—that he was rude and inhospitable was, he believed, an invasion of his privacy, an insult to his wife and an affront to his honor. Vera may also have been offended by *Upstate* and urged Nabokov to retaliate. He felt that after forgiving Wilson's vicious review and renewing their friendship—as Wilson himself should have done—he had once again been subjected to an unprovoked assault. Nabokov had not, in fact, taken his last look at the dismal scene. But as he explained to the editor of the *New York Times Book Review*, which published his corrosive letter on November 7, 1971, he was not merely "airing a grievance but firmly stopping a flow of vulgar and fatuous invention on Wilson's part."

Nabokov's last letter to the press is more fierce and furious than anything he ever wrote about Wilson. Believing that he had been victimized by Wilson's "conjecture, ignorance and invention," he once again rejected Wilson's views on Russian versification, defended his wife against Wilson's criticism and con-demned his theory of humiliation:

> His muddleheaded and ill-informed description of Russian prosody only proves that he remains organically incapable of reading, let alone understanding, my work on the subject. Equally inconsistent with facts—and typical of his Philistine imagination—is his impression that at parties in my Ithaca house my wife "concentrated" on me and grudged "special attention to anyone else."
>
> A particularly repulsive blend of vulgarity and naïveté is reflected in his notion that I must have suffered "a good deal of humiliation" be-cause as the son of a liberal noble I was not "accepted (!) by the strictly illiberal nobility."

Wilson's published diary was so "vindictive and fatuous," Nabokov exclaimed, that—had he known Wilson was nourishing such hostile feelings—he would have immediately asked him to leave his house. Returning to the concept of honor that defined Onegin's character, Nabokov bitterly concluded: "I am aware that my former friend is in poor health but in the struggle between the dictates of compassion and those of personal honor the latter wins."

Wilson's great authority as a critic enabled him to make or break reputations of contemporary writers, and he was usually very generous about his friends' work. Nabokov had consistently praised Wilson's books; and in letters written to Nabokov between 1945 and 1953 Wilson repeatedly mentioned that he planned to write a long essay about Nabokov for the *Atlantic* or the *New Yorker*. Although Wilson liked *The Real Life of Sebastian Knight*, he was "disappointed" (his favorite word about Nabokov's works) by *Bend Sinister* and the later novels. Since he could not help Nabokov by giving his frank opinion, he thought it best not to review his books. Wilson disliked the elaborate artifice and lack of social context in Nabokov's novels. He was unsympathetic to the satiric portrayal of a series of fictional heroes who were, like Wilson himself, highly intellectual and emotionally repressed.

Wilson had the last word in their quarrel—after his death in June 1972. He did not make restitution, as he had done with Fitzgerald, but finally delivered in the form of a critical time bomb the judgment of his work that Nabokov had awaited for thirty years. In the posthumously published *A Window on Russia*, Wilson for the last time attacked Nabokov's belief that Pushkin knew almost no English, and remarked on his surprisingly limited knowledge of Russia. He "despises the Communist regime and, it seems to me, does not even understand how it works or how it came to be." Turning to Nabokov's works, Wilson ignored his early masterpiece *The Gift*. He found the other Russian novels—*Mary*; *King, Queen, Knave*; *Invitation to a Beheading* and *The Defense*, which ache with pain for the loss of Russia—static and disappointing, and dismissed them all in less than two pages. When examining the English novels (in only one page), he ignored the dazzling *Pale Fire*, revived the *Schadenfreude*-humiliation theory he had first expressed in *Upstate*, dismissed *Bend Sinister*, *Pnin* and *Lolita*, and found *Ada* stupendously boring.

In 1976, four years after Bunny's last word, in a letter to the English novelist and critic John Wain, Volodya alluded to, but did not explain—the real reasons for Wilson's attack. The Pushkin controversy, Nabokov wrote, "revealed not only ignorance of Russian on EW's part, but also a bizarre animosity that he appears to have been nursing since the late nineteen-fifties." Since he dates Wilson's animosity from the time of his own astonishing success with *Lolita*, Wilson's envy of Nabokov and desire to pull down the high-flying novelist cannot be dismissed. But Wilson's motives were more complex than that. Well aware of what he called Nabokov's "insatiable and narcissistic vanity," he certainly underestimated the "damaging" effect of his review and naively thought their friendship could somehow survive it. As late as 1971 he tried to minimize his own responsibility and claimed, with disingenuous innocence, that his "attempts to tease Nabokov were not recognized as such but received in a virulent spirit, and his retaliation was protracted."

The remark of another touchy beneficiary, Edward Dahlberg, illustrates Wilson's generous but patronizing attitude to Nabokov: "He never ceased to show me kindnesses . . . and [was] quite ready to help a writer provided he felt he was superior to him." When Wilson had all the advantages (an established reputation, extensive contacts, an editorial position and considerable influence in the literary world), he could afford to be generous to the proud Nabokov, who had come from an immensely rich family and had been forced at first to live on charity in America. But when Nabokov refused to become his disciple and then surpassed him—as Fitzgerald had done—in art, wealth and fame, Wilson became embittered and vindictive.

Wilson had the "intellectual arrogance and unconscious assumption of superiority" that he attributed to Lincoln in *Patriotic Gore*, and his "impulse to wound," as he said of Ambrose Bierce, "was involved with a vulnerable pride." The intensely competitive Wilson, who always (as Hannah Arendt told Mary McCarthy) wanted to prove how intelligent he was, boldly challenged Nabokov on his own scholarly turf. Wilson's old friend Lillian Hellman, though not discussing his relations with Nabokov, penetrated to the core of their quarrel when she observed that Wilson was always gallant with women, but "if you were a man and not prepared to pay him proper obeisance, he would have to knock you down intellectually by demonstrating that he knew more about your subject than you did, had read key books that you hadn't in languages you didn't know, and otherwise establish himself as the brightest guy on the block."

The real beneficiaries of the *Eugene Onegin* quarrel were the literary editors who got all the controversial letters and profitable publicity for nothing (even Robert Lowell jumped into the fray on Wilson's behalf), and the readers who delighted in the cut and slash, the revelations and insults of two great literary figures. But when the dust had settled, the lives of Wilson and Nabokov had each been diminished by the loss of a treasured and irreplaceable friend. Wilson once told Nabokov that he had had "great fun during the *Onegin* exchange." But Nabokov disagreed and failed to relish the controversy as Wilson did. Nabokov found it intellectually exciting but quite ghastly, and was horrified when his intimate companion suddenly and incomprehensibly attacked him. In July 1972, a month after Wilson's death, Vera tried to calm the troubled waters of the past by writing to Wilson's half-Russian wife: "I would like to tell you . . . how fond Vladimir has always been of Edmund despite the unfortunate turn in their late relations. We always think of Edmund in terms of past friendship and affection, not of the so unnecessary hostilities of recent years." In May 1974, when Wilson's widow was gathering their letters for publication, Nabokov, saddened by their quarrel, wrote: "I need not tell you what agony it was rereading the exchanges belonging to the early radiant era of our correspondence."

13

NABOKOV

——— AND ———

BALTHUS

I

Despite their idiosyncratic characters, the close contemporaries Vladimir Nabokov (1899–1977) and Balthazar (Balthus) Klossowski (1908–2001) had a surprisingly similar background, life, character, art and career. Jed Perl, in *Paris Without End*, is completely mistaken when he claims that "Balthus' adolescents have little in common with the Lolita of Nabokov's novel." In fact, both author and painter were exceptionally handsome, with elegant manners and regal demeanor, and had sophisticated wit, comic irony, perverse ideas and lubricious work.

Nabokov was born in St. Petersburg. His father, who belonged to the Russian nobility, was a Liberal lawyer, statesman and writer, and member of Alexander Kerensky's doomed cabinet in March 1917. In the days before the Revolution the wealthy family took many holidays in Europe, and had fifty full-time servants in their St. Petersburg mansion and their country estate fifty miles from the capital.

Balthus also had a cosmopolitan Slavic background. His maternal grandfather Abraham Spiro, born in Russia, was a Jewish cantor and two of his thirteen children became opera singers. (Nabokov's wife was Jewish and his son Dmitri became an opera singer in Milan.) Balthus' Russian-Jewish mother was born in Breslau, East Prussia, now Wroclaw, Poland. A professional artist, she used the name of Baladine, which means dancer and whose first three letters echo

Balthus. His Polish-Catholic father, also born in Breslau where he met and married his wife, was an art historian.

Balthus was born in Paris and, like Nabokov, moved frequently throughout his life to Switzerland, Germany, France, Italy and back to Switzerland. Both were able to work anywhere. During his boyhood and teenaged years Balthus' talent was nourished and promoted by the distinguished Austrian poet Rainer Maria Rilke. After Balthus' parents separated, Rilke became his surrogate father and his mother's lover. Balthus' biographer Nicholas Fox Weber writes, "Balthus, a French citizen at birth, from a Polish family, found Japan in many ways to be his spiritual home, Italy his source of inspiration, and Switzerland his refuge."

Nabokov and Balthus had an idyllic but fatally disrupted childhood. Taught by a British nanny, they were multilingual with English as their first language. Nabokov knew Russian, French and German; Balthus surpassed him with a knowledge of Latin, Polish, French, German, Italian, Japanese and some Arabic. Both men were forced into exile during the chaos of World War I. In 1914 Balthus' father, a German citizen, had to move his family from Paris to Berlin and lost all his possessions. After the Russian Revolution of 1917 he also lost all his money, which had been invested in Russian railways, and was reduced to humiliating poverty.

Nabokov's uncle left him a few million dollars and a 2,000-acre estate. He lost it all when his family was forced to leave Russia and they escaped by ship from the Crimea in 1919. After the cataclysmic Revolution had completely obliterated his stable and idealized world, Nabokov began stepping westward to Cambridge University (1919–22), Berlin (1922–37), Paris (1937–40) and America in 1940.

Though Nabokov and Balthus moved in different circles and never met, they lived at the same time and for several years in Berlin and in Paris. Accustomed to great wealth, both were desperately poor in postwar Berlin, disliked Germany and the Germans, and did not participate in the flowering of Weimar culture in the 1920s. Nabokov lived in furnished rooms, wrote novels in Russian for a limited audience of Russian émigrés, and survived by giving lessons in English and tennis. In March 1922 his father, who'd lost his political influence in exile, was assassinated in Berlin by czarist anarchists. Three months later, during wild inflation and a continuing wave of terror, the

German finance minister Walter Rathenau was assassinated in an attempt to provoke a civil war.

In 1937 Nabokov, his wife Vera and three-year-old son Dmitri (born in Berlin) moved to Paris. In May 1940, as the German army advanced toward the city, they managed to board the last ship sailing from St. Nazaire to the safety of America. This narrow escape by sea reprised his flight from the Crimea and voyage to Europe in 1919. Even when teaching at Cornell University, Nabokov continued to move around constantly. He rented a different house every year and hunted butterflies in the Rocky Mountains every summer.

Balthus served in the French artillery in Fez and Kenitra, on the west coast of Morocco, during 1930–31. When World War II broke out in September 1939 he was mobilized. He served near Saarbrucken in Alsace, and had to clear the battlefield of mutilated and dead bodies. After several weeks he suffered a leg injury from an explosion down a mine, had a nervous breakdown and received a medical discharge. He recuperated in Switzerland and returned to Paris in March 1940. In June, a month after Nabokov escaped from France, Balthus fled from Paris when the Germans occupied the city, which echoed his flight from Paris to Berlin with his German-born parents in 1914. Though Nabokov and Balthus experienced the horrors of the Russian Revolution and two world wars, including agonizing exile, and saw their ancestral countries ravaged and nearly destroyed, they spent a safe war in America and in Switzerland, and eliminated politics from their art.

Balthus and Nabokov created dramatic narratives that transformed their ideas and emotions into paint on canvas and words on paper. During the 1930s Depression and the conservative Eisenhower 1950s, they imposed their enchanted yet melancholy vision on the world, and made people see things they would rather not recognize or prefer to hide. They craved privacy and disliked public disclosures, but gave many interviews that carefully constructed their aristocratic, mysterious and glamorous public image. Both were supposedly hostile to biography but cooperated with biographers—Nabokov with Brian Boyd, Balthus with Nicholas Fox Weber—whom they thought they could control. Balthus' hospitable help came with a generous serving of lies that Weber had to investigate and disprove. Their fascinating lives, in fact, aroused great interest and sent people back to their art.

Their precise and exact work portrayed violation and disaster—with powerful males, captive but crafty females—and was always tantalizing. The tone of their art was both ambiguous and disturbing, mischievous and seductive. They liked to conceal, disguise and dissemble, and throw curious critics off the scent. Nabokov loved puns, puzzles, cryptic and often obscene allusions, and anagrams such as Vivian Darkbloom for his own name. He even enthusiastically praised V. Sirin, the pseudonym he used for the Russian novels, in his autobiography *Speak, Memory*.

Both men were exceptionally intelligent, charming and talented. Nabokov, more of a loner, was ensconced with his family. Balthus, an amiable genius and prima donna, had an insatiable appetite for admiration. He loved to be entertained and his favorite word for congenial friends was "amusing." After Rilke's death in 1926, Balthus became close to many leading writers and artists in France: André Gide, Antonin Artaud and Albert Camus; André Derain, Joan Miró and Alberto Giacometti. Picasso bought his painting *The Children* (1937) in 1941, and Balthus was revered by his fellow-realist Lucian Freud.

Both Balthus and Nabokov were secretive and, when they could afford it, maintained tight control of the world around them. Each made a sudden transition from relative obscurity to an exalted existence. André Malraux, the minister of culture, appointed Balthus director of the French Academy in the splendid Villa Medici in Rome, where he reigned from 1961 to 1977. Nabokov moved to a luxurious suite in the Montreux Palace Hotel in Switzerland in exactly the same years: 1961 to 1977. Though he had no moat and drawbridge, he was content to reside in the palatial hotel, comfortably attended by a cadre of obliging servants. Balthus would have tried to buy the place. Their residences in Italy and Switzerland recreated the grand life they had lost in war and revolution. Nabokov, a real aristocrat, was treated like royalty by a humble visiting scholar who recalled, "I was received by Vladimir Nabokov and his wife Vera in the Montreux Palace Hotel." Balthus, a pretentious aristocrat, puffed himself up by adopting a bogus title, the Comte de Rola.

The self-educated Balthus believed that university titles were a sham, but that his sham title was real. Denying his Jewish heritage and making anti-Semitic remarks to cover his tracks, he created a fantasy lineage that was sometimes Scottish-Byronic, sometimes Russian-Czarist. Weber notes that Balthus' pater nal Polish ancestors (like those of Joseph Conrad) belonged to a "huge, unwieldy landed class that was a lesser rank of nobility called the *szlachta*. . . . Though seventy-three families bear the Rola coat of arms, they never held a title." On this shaky foundation Balthus awarded himself the title of Comte de Rola. In any case, if such a title had actually existed, it would have belonged to his older brother.

Two other sources may have inspired Balthus' title. His first wife, Antoinette de Watteville (with whom he remained on good terms), lived in *Rolle* on the northwest shore of Lake Geneva in Switzerland, for the last decades of her life. More significantly, Balthus found the title and subject of Henri Gervex's erotic and notorious painting, *Rolla* (1878, Musée d'Orsay, Paris) extremely attractive. This picture was inspired by Alfred de Musset's poem of that name (1833), which rejects Christian repression and celebrates the delights of the flesh, and depicts the woman in her "garb of pure and spotless youth" who "found again her long lost juvenility."

Like François Boucher's *Mademoiselle O'Murphy* (1751), *Rolla* portrays a gorgeous, pearly-skinned, post-coital nude spread out on a sumptuous canopied silken bed. She has one leg raised and bent, the other dropping off the side of the bed, and the sheet barely covering her pudenda. Her hair is tangled, her eyes closed. Her jewelry lies on the bedside table, and she's carelessly thrown her red bodice and lingerie on the floor next to the bed. A self-portrait of the artist, tall and slender with angular features and dark eyes, dressed in dark trousers and white shirt open at the neck, stands at an open balcony door, with Paris houses rising in the background. He looks down at his sleeping lover, as if waiting for her to awake and resume their pleasures. This painting strongly appealed to Balthus. It had a suggestive title he would have been pleased to adopt, great technical skill in portraying female flesh, the sensual nude's sexy raised-leg pose which Balthus often used, the resemblance of the male figure to himself and the scandal when the picture was rejected by the Salon of 1878.

Balthus' artistic reputation did not completely satisfy him. The soi-disant Comte de Rola—or Rolla—bought a series of castles to confirm his title and emphasize his nobility. Claiming that his art was more important than a workman's food, he egoistically declared, "I have a greater need for a château than a laborer for a loaf of bread." In 1953 he bought the Château de Chassy, near Nièvre in the remote Morvan region of central France, 150 miles southeast of

Paris. The huge three-story manor house had thick walls and round pointed towers on all four sides.

In 1970, while living in the sumptuous Villa Medici, Balthus acquired and restored the thirteenth-century stone Castello di Montecalvello, near Viterbo, fifty miles north of Rome. He finally left Italy in 1977 and bought a fifty-room ruin, the Grand Chalet in Rossinière, Switzerland, thirty miles east of Montreux. When his desire for self-promotion surpassed his wish for privacy, he had his three châteaux photographed in *House and Garden* and the French *Vogue*. Balthus always insisted that his servants and suppliants address him as Comte. Though the title was meant to enhance his stature and the no-account count clung to this role till the end of his life, his false claim made a ludicrous impression and was mocked by his old friends.

Nabokov and Balthus had unusually long and productive careers, and moved from riches to poverty, from obscurity and back to wealth. Like the English writers Kipling, Lawrence and Auden, who spent years in America, Nabokov finally returned to Europe. Though Scott Fitzgerald bitterly remarked that Switzerland was "a country where very few things begin, but many things end," Nabokov and Balthus always associated it with luxury and security. Both men, who lived quite near each other in 1977, died in Switzerland: Nabokov at 79; Balthus, looking like a withered Voltaire, at 93.

II

Nabokov and Balthus were intellectually and emotionally connected by their lifelong interest in Lewis Carroll and Edgar Allan Poe, and by their hatred of Sigmund Freud. Carroll epitomized the surprisingly large group of sexually repressed, dysfunctional and miserable English writers in the Victorian age, including Carlyle, Ruskin, Swinburne, Pater, Hopkins, Wilde and Housman. Carroll was a pseudonym, like Balthus and V. Sirin. A Cheshire cat appears in *Alice in Wonderland* and in many pictures by Balthus. At Cambridge, Nabokov translated *Alice* into Russian, and he describes Lolita as "a half-naked nymphet stilled in the act of combing her Alice-in-Wonderland hair."

Carroll, whose temperament was morbid and taste perverse, liked to photograph half-naked pubescent girls. His provocative image of the beautiful Alice Liddell, the model for the fictional Alice, foreshadowed Balthus' paintings and was the visual representation of Lolita. The photograph shows a very young girl in a pose and dress completely opposed to Victorian standards of respectable behavior. Alice wears a ragged, knee-length, Gypsy-like skirt and very low-cut top showing her left nipple. She has her hand on her hip, bare feet, a pouting and seductive appearance. For unknown reasons, probably connected to Carroll's provocative images of Alice, her family severed relations with him. Nabokov was delighted to learn that the name of Alice's governess was Miss Prickett. Balthus must have noticed that Carroll anticipated the facial distortions in Picasso's portraits when Humpty Dumpty says, "if you had the two eyes on the same side of the nose . . . that would be *some* help" in recognizing you.

Poe, a favorite writer of both Nabokov and Balthus, helped them recapture the past. In *The Great Gatsby*, Nick Carraway warns Gatsby, who's courting his youthful love, "You can't repeat the past," and he replies, "Can't repeat the past? Why of course you can!" Poe portrayed in his last poem "Annabel Lee," whose name with its labials suggests *Lolita*, a longing for his lost childhood sweetheart. "In a kingdom by the sea" he grieves for the death of a beautiful and innocent girl: "And this maiden she lived with no other thought / Than to love and be loved by me." Poe had loved his cousin Virginia when she was a child. She had been his thirteen-year-old child bride and died young of tuberculosis. Poe had both poetic and carnal relations with Virginia, and realized his adult fantasies by combining pedophilia with quasi-incest.

In *Lolita* Nabokov brilliantly transforms the slim, Southern Edgar Poe into another awkward outsider, the middle-aged European Humbert Humbert, and the childish dying Virginia Poe into the naive yet knowing Lolita. In the novel Humbert attempts to recapture his childhood love Annabel Leigh through his adolescent stepdaughter Lolita, and recalls: "there might have been no Lolita at all had I not loved, one summer, a certain initial girl-child. In a *princedom by the sea*." Humbert's pleasure is intensified through sadomasochistic sex with Lolita. He rapturously explains that "when my hand located what it sought, a dreamy and eerie expression, half-pleasure, half-pain, came over those childish features." After Humbert loses Lolita, he murders the guilty Quilty in a decayed Gothic mansion that resembles Poe's crumbling House of Usher.

Recalling his idyllic childhood, Balthus declared, "God knows how happy I would be if I could remain a child forever." In his 1949 essay, Camus emphasized Balthus' Poe-like nostalgia and obsession with "the emotional world of the adolescent, particularly the intensity of adolescent love." In his *Large*

Composition with Raven (1986) Balthus pays a macabre tribute to Poe's most famous poem. He portrays the raven, a sinister omen that Poe called a symbol of "Mournful and Never-ending Remembrance," pointing its sharp beak at a naked girl's genitals as if he were about to penetrate her.

Both men loathed Sigmund Freud's psychoanalytic theories, which Balthus called "the curse of modern thought" and Nabokov condemned as the work of a Viennese quack. They believed Freud perversely shifted the emphasis from art to the artist, and offered pseudoscientific speculations about the creator's inner life. Nabokov mocks Freud throughout *Lolita*, especially in the lecture to Humbert by the headmistress of Beardsley School, Mrs. Pratt (English slang for buttocks), who regrets that Lolita is not developing sexually and believes the innocent child should be given sexual instruction.

Nabokov detested the fictional use of symbols and allegories that also distracted attention from his work. He hated "the vulgarity of human interest" and categorically dismissed all social, political and philosophical subjects as extraneous to art. Balthus firmly agreed, and in his 1984 exhibition catalog insisted, "I very much disapprove of the habit of feeding the public with details and anecdotes on a painter's private life together with the implication that the latter somehow explains his paintings."

Though the shocking display of bare vulvas are the main focus of interest in his pictures of naked girls, Balthus tried to purify them by denying the obvious sexual content: "Some have claimed that my undressed young girls are erotic. I never painted them with that intent, which would have made them anecdotal, mere objects of gossips. I aimed at precisely the opposite, to surround them with a halo of silence and depth, as if creating a vertigo around them. That's why I think of them as angels."

Balthus' erotic work belongs to a significant but scandalous modern literary and artistic tradition. Frank Wedekind's play *Spring Awakening* (1891) deals realistically with the surge of sexual feelings and erotic fantasies in puberty. Felicien Rops' *The Temptation of St. Anthony* (1894) portrays a crucified naked woman with bare breasts and cleft vulva. Edvard Munch's *Puberty* (1895), not as bold as Balthus, shows a round-faced, wide-eyed pubescent girl who exposes her budding breasts but covers her genitals with crossed arms. Jules Pascin's *Caress* (1925) reveals a woman lying on her back, her open vagina at the viewer's eye level as she pleasures herself with her finger. Similarly, in Christian Schad's

Two Girls (1928) one woman in her twenties, facing the viewer with open legs, fingers her exposed hairless vulva while another naked woman, reclining behind her, simultaneously satisfies herself.

In James Joyce's *Ulysses* (1922) Gerty MacDowell raises her legs and exposes herself to the wildly excited voyeur Leopold Bloom. Joyce's orgasmic description of Gerty, "bent so far back" like Balthus' naked girls, alludes to French can-can dancers and to Jean-Honoré Fragonard's *The Swing* (1767): "she let him and she saw that he saw . . . she was trembling in every limb from being bent so far back that he had a full view high up above her knee where no-one ever not even on the swing or wading and she wasn't ashamed and he wasn't either to look in that immodest way like that because he couldn't resist the sight of the wondrous revealment half offered like those skirtdancers behaving so immodest before gentlemen looking and he kept on looking, looking"—until he finally ejaculates. Like Joyce, Balthus allows us to see what is usually hidden and forbidden in life and art.

In 1934, following this erotic tradition, Balthus first exhibited his daydreaming, seductive and naked pubescent girls. Later on, he also painted his thin, small-breasted Japanese wife without adult pubic hair. By rejecting Jonathan Swift's command to hide "those Parts that Nature taught us to conceal" and revealing female genitals in a libidinous way, Balthus allows the voyeuristic viewer to violate their Eve-like innocence. His friend Antonin Artaud, inventor of the Theater of Cruelty, emphasized Balthus' disturbing content, his use of "the technique of [Jacques-Louis] David's era at the service of a violent, modern inspiration, of a sick era, in which the artist only uses reality in order to crucify it more effectively."

Balthus painted his six most erotic works in his greatest era, the 1930s. Combining the superb draftsmanship of Ingres and the sensuality of Modigliani, he created comatose pubescents with awakening sexual awareness and sinister overtones. In *André Derain* and *Cathy Dressing* the men look away from the girl; in *The Guitar Lesson* the lesbian is sexually engaged with her. The genitals of the girls, who present themselves like animals in heat, are the center of attention and draw the spectator into the pictures.

Thérèse Blanchard, the eleven-year-old model for *Girl with a Cat*, was the daughter of a neighborhood waiter in Paris. She wears a green skirt and red sweater over a red shirt. Her oversized head, above a shrunken torso, is framed by thick brown hair curling onto her forehead. She has a blunt nose, thick lips and widely spaced eyes, and a sullen pouting expression. She crosses her arms and locks her fingers behind her head to lift her budding breasts. Reclining on a chaise longue with her left leg characteristically raised (as in *Rolla* by Henri Gervex), she rivets our attention on her panties, and what they suggest and scarcely hide. The bright red tongue of the brown tabby at her feet matches the girl's red shirt and sweater, and reflects the features of her face and colors of her knee socks. Like "pussy" in English, *chatte* (female cat) in French slang means vagina.

Thérèse Dreaming portrays the same young model with another erotic gray cat lapping milk from a saucer on the floor. Thérèse reclines on the same chair with arms crossed behind her head, and raises her left leg to reveal her undies and lace-trimmed slip between her red skirt and red pom-pom slippers. There's a hint of adolescent hair beneath her raised left arm. She wears a white buttoned shirt open at the collar and leans uncomfortably back on a large green cushion. Seen in profile with closed eyes, she now looks prettier, and her pose suggests that she's dreaming about sex. To her right, in front of brown and red-striped wallpaper, a green-topped wooden table holds a carelessly folded white cloth, red and gray canister, tall blue frill-topped vase and delicate orange single-stem vessel thinned out in the middle like a woman's waist.

Alice depicts a girl, certainly not in Wonderland, combing her tangled hair and cornered between empty walls and stark floor. She has an oval face; curved upper lip; glaucous, closed Modigliani-eyes and sleepy expression. She pulls up the bottom of her transparent chemise, lowers the top and exposes one full breast. Her other breast, covered by her right arm, is much smaller and asymmetrical. Raising her thick, muscular, trunk-like left leg with rough red knees onto a fragile cane-seated chair, she boldly exposes her pubic hair (a rare exception in Balthus) and her dark vulva that hangs down like a fissured scrotum. Antonin Artaud described the element of threat in this picture: "By the light of a wall, a polished floor, a chair, or an epidermis he invites us to enter into the mystery of a human body. That body has a sex, and that sex makes itself clear to us, with all the asperities that go with it. The nude has something harsh, something tough, something unyielding, and—something cruel. It is an invitation to lovemaking, but one that does not dissimulate the dangers involved."

The subject of *André Derain*, the Fauve artist and close friend of Balthus, was fifty-six when his portrait was painted. He is clean-shaven, very tall and broad, with a massive chest and shoulders. He has black hair, huge forehead, greenish jowly face, glaring pouched asymmetrical eyes, long straight nose, downturned mouth and double chin. This monumental man, facing the viewer and nearly filling the frame, wears a heavy brown-and-red-striped belted bathrobe, which recalls the wallpaper in *Thérèse Dreaming*. In a Napoleonic pose his large spread-fingered left hand is placed between his robe and the white shirt beneath it, and penetrates the slit of his shirt to suggest the sexual act. His paintings are turned against the side wall.

Behind the much older man and nearly pushed out of the picture, an exhausted pale-skinned girl, half his size, sits submissively on a wooden chair. She has blushing cheeks, sad expression and downcast eyes that shut out her grim situation. She exposes one full breast and seems to be preparing herself for the next sexual assault by the monstrous Derain. By contrast, Balthus' contemporary painting of a fellow artist, *Joan Miró and His Daughter Dolores*, portrays a young girl in a striped dress who replicates Joan's flat face, high forehead, small mouth and strong chin. She rests her right hand on his hand and her left hand on his knee, while he embraces her waist. The picture describes tender love, rather than sexual exploitation, of father and daughter.

In *Cathy Dressing* the elongated Cathy, her unruly reddish hair combed and arranged by a grim-looking maid, stands with one extended slipper-clad foot in the circle of a colored carpet and grasps the erect mirror handle. She tilts her masklike head, has a troubled expression and wears an open flesh-colored silk gown. She boldly exposes her large projecting breasts and erect nipples, her elongated Lucas Cranach–like torso with slightly protruding belly and, by contrast to her well-developed chest, her bare clefted vulva. In *Lolita* Nabokov describes the pleasure of watching such a girl: "there is always delight in the semitranslucent mystery, the flowing [veil] through which the flesh and the eye you alone are elected to know."

Cathy is wanton, her maid severe. The maid's hooded eyes, long nose, thin face, narrow mouth, strong chin and harsh expression are modeled on the woman in Honoré Daumier's *The Third Class Carriage*. (Balthus' father published a monograph on Daumier in 1923.) Weber notes, "The maid's tight grey bun is in marked contrast to the seductress's flowing blond tresses. Her gray and black uniform and white apron invoke rules and restraint." The maid and Cathy, absorbed in her toilette, look away from and ignore her suitor.

The brooding man with a dark face, a self-portrait of Balthus, is dressed in a white shirt, black jacket and bow tie. Seated next to the naked lady, he anxiously wraps his hands around the posts on the back of his chair. Mixing memory and desire, he looks away from her and thinks of the pleasures to come. But his indented trouser leg and her bent right leg fit together across the space between them. He clenches his fists, as if angry about her slow progress that both prepares for and delays their erotic encounter. This picture was influenced by Edouard Manet's *Nana* (1876), in which a client in her dressing room watches impatiently as she prepares her toilette. Like the Balthus-figure, the gentleman is ready to pounce and will undress her soon after she dresses herself.

With the yellow guitar and upright piano abandoned, the musical tuition in the sensational *The Guitar Lesson* turns into a perverse sexual lesson—a grotesque version of the sexually seductive music in Leo Tolstoy's "The Kreutzer Sonata." An older lesbian, whose grim expression and shadowy face are an androgynous self-portrait, pulls the young girl's hair that falls to the floor. The girl's head—between piano and guitar—is low; her bare, bald and bifurcated vulva is high. The teacher's fingers on the girl's upper thigh are about to penetrate her vagina, and she spreads her legs as if she were playing her victim's body like a cello. The girl, her dark skirt pulled up to her navel, is "bent so far back" like Gerty MacDowell. Uncomfortably sprawled across the woman's lap, she has a dazed, open-mouthed, orgasmic expression. Her wool-lined slippers, high white knee socks, bows in her hair and shirt accentuate her youthful innocence. Her underwear is not visible, and may have been removed to prepare for her erotic training. Her bruised red knees suggests she's been kneeling in a previous sexual rite. Her limp open hand touches the floor and suggests complete surrender.

Despite her swoon, the girl massages the nipple of one cantilevered naked breast that projects from the top of the teacher's gray silk dress. The nipple of her clothed breast is also erect. In this blasphemous *pietà*, simultaneously stimulating and punishing, the lesbian seems to be providing pleasure and inflicting pain. Her mood is both seductive and sadistic as she forces the girl to submit to a masturbatory orgasm. Weber notes that the strictly alternating zebra-striped piano keys, which echo the vertical stripes of the wallpaper, are not realistic;

that the guitar's tight strings resemble the girl's pulled tight hair, her cleft is echoed in the cleft on the top of the guitar's arm, and the instrument is curved and indented, like a human form, with a dark hole in the center. Both Balthus and Nabokov invite the viewer or reader to vicariously participate in forbidden pleasures.

During the scandalous exhibition at Pierre Loeb's gallery in April 1934 the explicit sexual provocation was greeted with both outrage and delight. *The Guitar Lesson* remained in the back room and was shown only to privileged clients. The picture was exhibited for the first and only time at the Pierre Matisse Gallery in New York in 1957 when an ecstatic mob lined up to see it. Once owned by the director Mike Nichols, it now belongs to the Greek shipping magnate Stavros Niarchos, who keeps it well hidden in the bedroom of his luxurious New York apartment.

Brian Boyd reports that Nabokov knew and admired the paintings of Balthus who, he self-reflectively said, "at this late stage in the history of art could still find new poses and moods and implications for the human body." In *Strong Opinions* Nabokov confirmed what Balthus denied, "A contemporary artist I do admire very much, though not only because he paints Lolita-like creatures, is Balthus."

When he was fifteen Balthus described, like Humbert, his ecstatic and inspiring physical embrace of an eleven-year-old model: "After holding him in my arms and sensing his shapely limbs with my body and arms, my pencil is more knowledgeable, for touch is as important as sight." He ridiculed false rumors that in adult life he had sexual relations with his pubescent girls, though in 1949 he did sleep with his teenaged female model Laurence Bataille.

Many normal men are attracted to pretty young girls, but Balthus and Nabokov sublimated their longings into high art. Sabine Rewald describes the ambiguous feelings provoked by Balthus' work, which turned the young girls "into archetypal nymphets observed by a voyeur. The strange dichotomy between the painter's desire for and empathy with his adolescent models finds a pictorial analogy in their titillating postures . . . the contradictory spell of their sexual power and vulnerability."

Robert Graves' poem "The Naked and the Nude" describes the similarities between Nabokov's novel and Balthus' pictures. In both works,

Lovers without reproach will gaze
On bodies naked and ablaze. . . .
The nude are bold, the nude are sly
To hold each treasonable eye.

Balthus' erotic paintings, whose sharp and clear images suggest sexual ambiguity, inspired Nabokov's similar descriptions of Lolita. The "dreamy sweet
radiance of all her features," for example, vividly recalls *Thérèse Dreaming*. The
predator-prey relations of the girls in Balthus' art also recur in *Lolita*. Balthus'
The Moth (1960) combines Nabokov's two personal and literary interests: the
hunt for lepidoptera and for nymphets, both with short lifespans. The white
flame of the tall cylindrical oil lamp shines on the long high-breasted torso of
a female nude and attracts an elusive semitransparent moth. With her hand
grasping the tall bedpost and right arm extended, she's either trying to capture the fluttering moth or to protect it from flying into the fatal flame. The
upside-down glass on the bedside table could confine the moth if she manages
to catch it.

Balthus' pictures were inevitably connected to Nabokov's sensational novel
when *Lolita* was published by the Olympia Press in Paris in 1955 and by Putnam's in New York in 1958. Alluding to Balthus' favorite painter, one critic
called him "a curious mix of Piero della Francesca and Humbert Humbert."
Lucian Freud wrote that Balthus' exhibition in London "showcased Humberts
and Lolitas." The artist, however, denied that their themes and mood were
similar, and condemned the "Humbert Humbert school of critics."

But in a late interview of 1996, Balthus admitted that he created *The Guitar
Lesson* in 1934 to shock spectators and establish his artistic reputation: "This
one I painted because I was very hard up and I wanted to be known at once.
And at that time you could be known by a scandal. The best way to get known
was with scandal. In Paris." In Balthus' *New York Times* obituary of February 19,
2001, John Russell quoted the artist insisting, with an important qualification:
"I really don't understand why people see the paintings of girls as Lolitas. . . . I've
never made anything pornographic. Except perhaps *The Guitar Lesson*."

Nicholas Weber deftly describes the achievement of both men. Balthus
frequently repeated "that all comparisons to Nabokov are entirely off base,

yet like the worldly and erudite author of *Lolita*, he, too, has had the bravery and magnificent effrontery to acknowledge that grown men can be sexually attracted to young girls, and to make great art of that taboo. In a disarmingly tasteful style of painting, he has tackled without equivocation an apparently tasteless subject. Like Nabokov, he has brought intense culture and intelligence to the revelation of raw emotion."

III

The names of the characters in *Lolita* are erudite, suggestive and amusing. Nabokov resisted giving the homicidal Humbert Humbert—who adopts the first name of Edgar—the hometown of Baden Baden. His name, often jumbled in the novel, recalls the meditative "hmm," the ironic "humble" and the accurate "humbug." It echoes the great German scientist Alexander von Humboldt, to whom Edgar Poe dedicated his last major work, *Eureka*, "With Very Perfect Respect." It also recalls Umberto, the last king of Italy; the minor Georgian poet Humbert Wolfe; and most cunningly the witty and macabre Edwardian satirist H. H. Munro, known as Saki. The photos of notable homosexuals in the studio of Humbert's friend Gaston Godin at (Aubrey) Beardsley College include "Harold D. Doublename." "Harold" was the name of Charlotte Haze's late husband; "Doublename" stands for both "H. H." and Munro-Saki. Like Balthus, Godin paints "sliced guitars and blue nipples."

Lolita—short for Dolores, which means "pains" in Spanish—has the euphonious labials and vowels sounded in the first sentence of the novel: "Lolita, light of my life, fire of my loins. My sin, my soul. . . . Lo. Lee. Ta." Lola Montez was the sexy and notorious Irish dancer and mistress of mad King Ludwig of Bavaria. Lola Lola, played by Marlene Dietrich, was the destructive heroine of *The Blue Angel* film in 1930. Algernon Swinburne's poem "Dolores, Our Lady of Pain" was blasphemous and sadomasochistic. Lolita's full name also recalls Bathus' major painting *Joan Miró and His Daughter Dolores*. Though Nabokov didn't know the background, Balthus actually inflicted pain on Dolores by putting her in a sack when she did not sit still. Miró, who put art before children, did not object to Balthus' cruel treatment of his daughter.

Lotte, the familiar name of Humbert's pretentious, short-lived wife Charlotte Haze, sounds like the name of her sexual rival, Lolita. It also ironically recalls Charlottenburg, the posh district with elegant shops in Berlin, where

Nabokov lived from 1922 to 1937. Charlotte, who longs to absorb European culture through the sophisticated Humbert, has the name of the hero's lover in Goethe's *The Sorrows of Young Werther* and his *Elective Affinities*. Nicholas Weber repeatedly uses "haze" to describe Balthus' art. The variants of the word can mean cloudy and blurred, obscure and confused, teased and tormented. In *Lolita* "haze" describes Humbert's ambiguous motives, feelings and relations with both Lolita and Charlotte.

The names of Clare Quilty come from the mad nineteenth-century poet John Clare, and from Quilp in Charles Dickens' *The Old Curiosity Shop* and Quint in Henry James' "The Turn of the Screw," both of whom prey on children. Lolita's husband *Rich*ard F. (for Fried*rich*) Schiller is, to use the German poet's terms, "naïve" and unaware of her shocking past while she maintains a "sentimental" but not passionate attachment to him. Richard's deafness corresponds to Friedrich Schiller's fatal tuberculosis.

On their wandering journey Humbert is propelled by sex as much as by car. He has to keep Lolita sequestered, and constantly pleased with new clothes, junk food, childish movies and comic books so she doesn't get bored and reject her companion, an un-Easy Rider, On the Road trip. Meanwhile, except for the considerable delights of sex and the distraction of perpetual movement, he's also rather bored and culturally debased. So the volatile Humbert must play many different roles: cultured European, college professor, diarist, French scholar and translator; husband, stepfather, kidnapper, chauffeur, seducer and seduced; benefactor, avenger, murderer, prisoner and confessor. In the course of the novel he changes from benign to sinister to pathetic, from predator to lover to prey.

Humbert at first merely stares at pubescent girls with the perfect impunity that is only granted in dreams. He quotes the French Renaissance poet Rémy Belleau when dreaming of Lolita's secret place: "the hill velveted with delicate moss . . . traced in the middle with a little scarlet thread." After sleeping with her, he ecstatically declares that her skin "presented to me its pale breast-buds; in the rosy lamplight, a little pubic floss glistened on its plump hillock." Aroused by fantasies and poetry, he confesses, "there is no other bliss on earth comparable to that of fondling a nymphet."

Humbert realizes his wildest fantasies and satisfies his mad obsession. He recaptures the idealized girl of his childhood, indulges in forbidden sexual pleasures and takes ecstatic delight as Lolita's lover. His amorous techniques, if not his potency, must have been infinitely superior to the desperate groping of Charlie in the summer camp near Climax, and he attempts to give Lolita intellectual as well as sexual lessons (museum, boredom). But he must pay the fatal price for his outrageous acts.

Humbert's dangerous behavior, like feasting with panthers, is part of the excitement. The Mann Act of 1910 made it illegal to transport women across state lines for immoral purposes. Though the Act could not prevent the obsession of Humbert, who crossed a great many state lines, it could certainly punish him. At the climactic conclusion of Part One, Lolita smiles sweetly at him and declares with an ironic, half-serious threat: "You revolting creature. I was a daisy-fresh girl, and look what you've done to me. I ought to call the police and tell them you raped me. Oh you, dirty, dirty old man."

During our current epidemic of child molestation it's difficult for readers to see that Lolita makes the first sexual advances to Humbert while Charlotte is still alive. She loses her virginity and becomes sexually experienced after sleeping with Charlie. As Humbert declares, "I am going to tell you something very strange: it was she who seduced me." The apparently innocent orphan manipulates and eventually dominates the cosmopolitan sophisticate. She now has Humbert in her power, could expose him and send him to jail at any time, then live with either the Fowlers in Ramsdale or with the family of her friend Mona Dahl in Beardsley. But she prefers an itinerant life with Humbert, and after her escape continues to travel with Quilty.

In a poignant passage just before their final farewell, Humbert expresses his profound love for the pregnant housewife, though she's no longer a nymphet: "I loved her more than anything I had ever seen or imagined on earth, or hoped for anywhere else." He then begs her to run away with him, "Come just as you are. And we shall live happily ever after." His pathetic plea echoes Christopher Marlowe's lyrical "Come live with me and be my love," but does not allude to the following line that suggests her sexual submission: "And we will all the pleasures prove." Referring to Quilty, who never really loved her, Lolita refuses to forgive Humbert and exclaims, "*He* broke my heart. *You* merely broke my life." By giving Quilty's address to Humbert, Lolita revenges herself and dooms both of them.

Like Humbert, Quilty adopts many roles: playwright, literary celebrity, inquisitive hotel guest, vigilant detective, fake uncle, cunning kidnapper, vile seducer, owner of a ghoulish mansion and murder victim. Lolita tricks Humbert in childish ways; Quilty deceives him with more sophisticated techniques. In the Enchanted Hunters hotel, he immediately perceives that Humbert and Lolita are not really father and daughter, and teases and detains Humbert, who is anxiously waiting to have sex with Lolita. Determined to possess Lolita, Quilty takes great pleasure in pursuing, tormenting and threatening to expose Humbert before stealing her. Humbert captures Lolita from camp, Quilty captures her from the hospital.

Like a Jacobean revenge tragedy, most of the characters die in *Lolita*. Humbert's first wife Valeria dies in childbirth. His mother is suddenly struck dead: "(picnic, lightning)." His childhood sweetheart Annabel Leigh dies euphoniously of typhus in Corfu. Charlotte is accidentally killed: (rain, car). Lolita descends from an innocent child to sex with Charlie, Humbert and Quilty, to marriage and death in childbirth. Humbert calls Quilty an "inhuman trickster who had sodomized my darling," and kills the man who defiled her in a cruel and perverse way. Humbert dies of a coronary thrombosis while awaiting his trial for murder and the likely sentence of death. Like the Marquis de Sade, Humbert confesses in prison. Balthus' older brother Pierre was an authority on the work of the divine marquis, and it's quite possible that Nabokov read Pierre's book *Sade My Neighbor* (1947).

In a crucial passage Humbert naively argues that "the majority of sex offenders that hanker for some throbbing, sweet-moaning, physical . . . relation with a girl-child, are innocuous, inadequate, passive, timid strangers who merely ask the community to allow them to pursue their practically harmless, so-called aberrant behavior, their little hot wet private acts of sexual deviation without the police and society cracking down upon them." Despite his "merely ask" and "practically harmless," Humbert expects us to accept his argument. But the pathetic justification for his admittedly deviant behavior gives him away and reveals Nabokov's devastating irony.

Weber, clinching the connection between Balthus and Nabokov, observes, "The use of his 1937 *Girl with a Cat* on the widely distributed Penguin paperback of *Lolita* was anathema to him. Balthus maintained that there is not a hint of lasciviousness in this portrait he made of a girl Lolita's age—in which the viewer is at eye level with the child's crotch. . . . Of the way that the child flashes her bare thighs at an alluring angle and flaunts her underwear-covered labia, he blithely commented, 'That's how little girls sit.'" But Balthus must have wanted the excellent publicity and granted permission for the Penguin cover in 1995. The deletion of the sexy cat merely intensified the focus on his nymphet.

The erotic images of the paintings and novel continue to haunt us. The scandalous publication of *Lolita* provided a new way to look back and reinterpret the art of Balthus. His paintings were the visual equivalent of the novel; *Lolita* was the verbal complement of the paintings. Balthus portrayed climactic scenes; Nabokov, influenced by Balthus, told the full story of sexual seduction, and created an ironic tragedy out of the erotic relations of man and child.

14

ERNEST HEMINGWAY

—— AND ——

JOHN HUSTON

Andrew Sarris called John Huston "a Hemingway character lost in a Dostoyev-sky novel." Norman Mailer—who portrayed Huston as Charles Eitel in *The Deer Park* (1955)—observed that he is "the only celebrated film artist to bear com-parison with Hemingway. His life celebrates a style more important to him than film." In an interview Huston said of Hemingway, "I was very influenced by his writing and by his thinking. . . . His values, his reassessment of the things that make life go." These suggestive statements merely hint at the strik-ing parallels between the two men. Both sought to live a life filled with the action, adventure and romance they created in their work. Keen sportsmen who courted danger and took risks, they enjoyed early success, cultivated a Byronic persona and knew the satisfactions of celebrity and the perils of fame. Hemingway's character, virile ethos and code of honor strongly influenced Huston, whose best films can be thematically defined by Hemingway's titles: *Men Without Women* and *Winner Take Nothing*.

I

Both Hemingway and Huston had grandfathers who fought with the Union army in the Civil War, and both men were born in the Midwest at the turn of the century: Hemingway in 1899, Huston in 1906. Their mothers had domi-nant personalities and professional careers. Both men refused to attend college, set out to learn from direct experience in the world, lived in Paris in their twenties and began their writing careers as journalists. Both were enthusiastic about Latin culture: Hemingway about Spain and tropical Cuba, Huston about tropical Mexico, where he made four movies and spent the last years of his life.

Both were powerful boxers in their youth and in later life. Hemingway's opponents included Ezra Pound, William Carlos Williams and the Canadian novelist Morley Callaghan, with Scott Fitzgerald as incompetent timekeeper. The young Huston won twenty-three out of twenty-five amateur bouts, breaking his nose in one of them, and became a ranking California lightweight before abandoning the sport. Both were heavy drinkers, but did not let alcohol interfere with their work.

Huston shared with Hemingway a fascination with cruelty, wounds and death. Hemingway witnessed this as a Red Cross volunteer on the Italian front in World War I. Huston had ridden with Mexican cavalry in his early twenties. Both participated in fierce fighting in World War II in Europe, Hemingway as a war correspondent, Huston as a documentary filmmaker. They enjoyed testing their own courage in difficult situations, and liked to subject their friends to danger to see how they'd react. Their overpowering personalities dominated everyone around them. Hemingway constantly challenged competitors. Huston took great risks with the lives and health of his actors and crew. On separate occasions both men intimidated Tennessee Williams with their aggressive *machismo*.

Hemingway and Huston felt compelled to demonstrate their toughness and strength. Huston followed Hemingway, made his own way through the Master's tumultuous wake and practiced the same dangerous masculine pursuits: bicycle racing, horseback riding (and betting on horses), marlin fishing, bullfighting, hunting elephants and big cats. In December 1954 a friend wrote that the forty-eight-year-old Huston had actually "fought a bull in Madrid, made quite a few good passes and has the photos to prove it."

The Maharajah of Cooch Behar, a bullfight *aficionado* and friend of Hemingway, organized a tiger hunt in Assam, in the foothills of the Himalayas, for Huston. On August 25, 1955, Huston sent an enthusiastic cable to Clark Gable, a keen hunter, urging him to join their expedition: "Am seizing opportunity and joining Maharajah of Cooch Behar hunt on 18th. This last of great hunts sixty elephants all the trimmings. Only be four guns. One gun still open. Would you like me to make res for you." Gable, confined by a movie contract, was forced to refuse.

After Huston had climbed the ladder to the shooting platform on his elephant, the huge beast (he wrote) "suddenly began to trumpet . . . and out came [the tiger], fast as a flaring bird. . . . As I pulled the trigger, my elephant swayed wildly, throwing me to one side. I fired again, knowing I'd miss, as the yellow-and-black devil darted away into the brush. . . . He'd covered 200 yards in under 10 seconds." Though Huston missed his first shot, he got his second and bagged a tiger that was eight-and-a-half-feet long. In Peter Viertel's novel *White Hunter, Black Heart* (1954), the character based on Huston says that Hemingway's "Francis Macomber experiences the greatest sensation of his life after he has killed his first buffalo. He has overcome fear. We're after those same sensations."

Both men, for all their obsession with courage, danger and the elemental struggles of mankind, had romantic natures and domestic inclinations. Hemingway had four wives, Huston had five (and all five divorced him). Hemingway shot a lion; his fourth wife ate lion; Huston's fifth wife boldly *rode* a lion—and has the photos to prove it. Each married increasingly younger women and, while married, fell in love with a series of women even younger than their wives. Huston, however, was unashamedly promiscuous, while Hemingway was a guilt-ridden serial monogamist. Both had three children and were difficult, demanding and frequently absent fathers. Both owned large houses and retreats from the world, which displayed their trophy wives and hunting trophies, and both were connoisseurs of art and had fine collections of modern paintings. Hemingway had a grand house in Key West, and then the Finca Vigía near Havana, and owned works by Klee, Gris, Braque, Miró, Masson and several valuable bullfight posters. Huston owned St. Clarens, his Georgian mansion in Ireland, where he displayed works by Klee, Gris, Monet, Modigliani, Chaim Soutine and several night-life posters by Lautrec.

The novelist and screenwriter Peter Viertel, their mutual friend, introduced the eccentric and ebullient Huston to Hemingway in May 1948, when Huston was in Havana to make *We Were Strangers* (1949), a movie about Cuban revolutionaries. At the time Viertel was more worried about Huston's reaction than Hemingway's. "I was never quite sure how [Huston] would react in any given situation," Viertel recalled. "I knew he could be violent if provoked." But Huston loved trials, hardships and disasters, and was soon given the chance to test his strength and courage. At first Hemingway challenged him to a boxing match and threatened to "cool" the gangling lightweight. Anticipating Huston's tactics, he said, "With those long arms you might just stand off and keep jabbing me in the nose, mightn't you? Maybe cut me up?" Huston chivalrously replied, "I wouldn't dream of doing that, Papa." But the match did not come off. Mary Hemingway told Huston that Papa was ill and begged him not to fight.

Inevitably the two, so similar in character, engaged in a competitive test. Hemingway invited Huston and Viertel on his boat, the *Pilar*, where they discussed Havana and war, writing and potential movie deals. Huston shot an iguana, and Hemingway insisted he retrieve it. Huston and Viertel searched for it in the crevices of the rocks and saw some spots of blood, but gave up after forty minutes and swam back to the boat. Though dissatisfied with their inept performance, Hemingway did not send them back. Instead, he himself searched for two more hours, among the rocks and under the blazing sun, put a bullet through its head and brought back the hideous trophy.

It may have seemed pointless, even foolish, to search through burning rocks for a dying iguana instead of enjoying the tropical breeze, cool shade and icy drinks on his boat. But the arduous quest was an important example of Hemingway's personal courage, showy endurance, sense of duty and moral lesson to his younger disciples. In this Day of the Iguana episode, Hemingway also meant to humiliate Huston by showing that he was (though seven years older) a tougher man who lived by his own virile code. In *Green Hills of Africa* (1935), Hemingway—wounded in the Great War—justified his passion for hunting when he identified with his wounded prey. He remarked, "I did nothing that had not been done to me. I had been shot and I had been crippled and gotten away."

Huston liked the challenge of shooting his films in distant and difficult locales, and his reading of Hemingway had drawn him to Africa. The burning of the missionary outpost in *The African Queen* (1951) was filmed in Butiaba, near Lake Albert and Murchison Falls in Uganda, where Hemingway had two plane crashes (and was reported dead) in January 1954. Hemingway's pilot, Roy Marsh, was the same former RAF officer who'd flown Huston around central Africa. And the *Murchison*, the boat that rescued Hemingway after a plane crash, was the same one that Huston had rented while making *The African Queen*.

Huston always tried to keep in touch. In 1954, amidst his hectic film schedule, he reminded himself: "11:00. Call Papa—Palace Hotel, Madrid." Later that year, on November 21, he congratulated Hemingway on winning the Nobel

Prize and mentioned the overwhelming problems on his current picture: "*Moby Dick* is a tough one to make. I have been at the actual shooting four months now and don't see daylight even yet. Misfortunes multiply as we go along; the only thing that hasn't happened yet is for somebody to get killed"— though there were a few close calls. In 1956, when *Moby Dick* was released, an English journalist, sensing the parallels between Hemingway's work and Huston's films, parodied the style of *The Old Man and the Sea* when describing Melville's novel: "He was an old Huston who filmed alone, and he had gone many days now without making a film. . . . 'I fear the Dick of Moby,' the boy said, 'It is difficult to make and will cost many dollars.' 'I do not fear,' said the old Huston, 'I know many tricks and I have faith.'"

On the last day of 1956, Huston suggested meeting for a drink before he started to read the Pulitzer Prize-winning *Old Man and the Sea* (actually, one of Hemingway's worst books): "It seemed to me, before starting one of your finest books, I should talk or anyway have a drink with you. I even imagined that you would consider my not coming to see you a rudeness. . . . In any case, there was no thought in my mind of asking for your help on the screenplay. I mean, I only wanted to come in and get warm." He didn't want to seem as rude as David O. Selznick, who had infuriated Hemingway by failing to stand up when his wife Mary came into the room. But Hemingway did not know that Selznick, in his underwear, had good reason to stay where he was.

Huston was one of the best screenwriters in the business, and Hemingway had never written a screenplay (and was proud of it). But Huston—who deferred to no one but his actor-father, Walter Huston—felt obliged to assume an extremely deferential tone with the hypersensitive novelist and assure him that he was *not* seeking help with a script. Aware of Hemingway's touchiness and competitiveness, and admiring his writing, Huston had a unique relationship with him.

Though they met only a few times and corresponded rarely, Huston (with some exaggeration) claimed that Hemingway "was a very close personal friend of mine." He then nailed down Hemingway's impact: his values, ideals and courage. "I've enormous admiration for Hemingway," he said, "and to my generation he was a great influence. . . . Hemingway laid down a certain set of standards for my time, standards of behavior. He made some effort to describe tastes and the good things of life and put them down on record, evaluating their importance. . . . It was important for a man to be brave and have valor. . . . They influenced my generation to the point of being . . . almost a new religion."

When Hemingway committed suicide, Huston "approved completely." He felt that if Hemingway could not live a heroic life, it was better not to live at all. Best, Huston felt, to die while sane than exist while crazy: "He knew he was on the way out; his mind was gone. Papa had been having persecution complexes, phobias, and life was dreadful for him. He had a moment or two of sanity and killed himself on one of those moments."

II

Both Hemingway and Huston admired Kipling, a major influence on their work, who taught them a colloquial and laconic, sceptical and stoical, belligerently masculine style. Huston, director of *The Man Who Would Be King*, was repeatedly drawn to a group of intensely masculine writers—Melville, Crane, Kipling and Hemingway—whose adventurous heroes stood at a slight angle to the universe. His early fiction portrayed this type of character, who often reappeared in his films.

Huston's two early boxing stories—"Fool" (March 1929) and "Figures of Fighting Men" (May 1931)—published in H. L. Mencken's prestigious *American Mercury*, were strongly influenced by Hemingway's prose style, bitter stoicism and theme of defeat in victory. In the second story Huston wrote that "a second-rater dipped his gloves in rosin and rubbed them in the old-timer's eyes during a clinch. His sight was ruined, but his fighting days were not over. Now he showed them he could take it. He became a punching bag in the small clubs. His pretty-boy face was knocked lop-sided. In a few months he was one of the old men of the ring."

The blasphemy at the end of the first story—the idea that Christ and Judas were in cahoots and the Crucifixion was fixed—recalls the blasphemy in Hemingway's playlet, "Today is Friday" (1926), in which three Roman soldiers callously discuss the Crucifixion in a modern idiom. He later made an excellent picture about washed-up boxers, *Fat City* (1972). James Agee, Huston's most perceptive critic, alluded to Hemingway's famous phrase "grace under pressure" and seemed to be talking about the novelist when describing Huston's films: "his movies have centered on men under pressure, have usually involved violence and have occasionally verged on a kind of romanticism about danger."

Most of Huston's films were adaptations of serious novels. As a reader, writer and director with a powerful connection to literature, Huston liked to quote Hemingway's views on writing. "There was no greater feeling in the world," Hemingway said, "than anchoring your words firmly on paper . . . when the words took wing." Comparing Hemingway to his leading contemporary, Huston told the screenwriter of *Under the Volcano* that Hemingway's work was essential to his own filmmaking: "Scott Fitzgerald is not as visceral as Hemingway, who gets you into the scenes, not just into the words." He later added that Hemingway had an uncanny ability to bring scenes and characters to life: "Certain American writers have . . . a peculiar ability to re-create, to make you feel that you are actually present in something. If Hemingway had anything, he had that." This was the great goal of twentieth-century moviemaking: to give the audience an even more intimate and immediate connection with the characters and action on the screen than readers could have with a novel.

Huston specialized in movies about male comradeship during violent conflict: *The Treasure of the Sierra Madre* (1948), *The Red Badge of Courage* (1951), *Moby Dick* (1956), *The Man Who Would Be King* (1975) and *Victory* (1981). Hemingway was also a great admirer of Crane's work, and of the coarse-grained texture and white sky of the Mathew Brady photographs that inspired both the novel and Huston's film. In his Introduction to *Men at War* Hemingway observed: "Crane wrote [*The Red Badge of Courage*] before he had ever seen any war. But he had read the contemporary accounts, he had heard the old soldiers, they were not so old then, talk, and above all he had seen Matthew Brady's wonderful photographs. Creating his story out of this material he wrote that great boy's dream of war that was to be truer to how war is than any war the boy who wrote it would ever live to see. It is one of the finest books of our literature."

The Killers (1946), directed by Robert Siodmak, could have been an ordinary *film noir* but, elevated by the screenplay written by Huston with his friend and longtime collaborator Anthony Veiller, became an important picture. It was the only film based on his work that Hemingway actually liked. In Hemingway's story (which reads like a screenplay) the killers, awaiting the arrival of their victim, taunt and intimidate the workers in a diner with a series of insults that require immediate assent. One of the killers—imitating gangster movies like *Little Caesar* (1930) and *Public Enemy* (1931)—tells George, "Ever go to the movies? . . . You ought to go to the movies more. The movies are fine for a bright boy like you."

In the film version Huston recreated Hemingway's hardened hero, torn between ironic fatalism and despairing courage, who seeks authentic values and adheres to a strict code of honor. *The Killers* opens as the gangsters enter a diner that recalls a classic Edward Hopper painting. They are not smartly dressed, as in the story, but make a lot of menacing wisecracks. The workers, who are frightened and don't understand what's going on, are ironically called "bright boy." The haunted victim, played by Burt Lancaster, is about to be murdered for stealing the gang's money after a successful robbery (rather than for failing to throw a fight and betraying the gamblers, as in the story). Just before his death Lancaster, with stoic resignation, says, "There's nothing I can do about it. . . . Once I did something wrong. . . . I'm through with all that runnin' around." After he's killed, the insurance investigator, played by Edmund O'Brien, discovers through a series of flashbacks the reason for his death.

Huston planned to make another movie based on three Hemingway stories, which would be directed by himself and two Europeans: his mentor William Wyler and his friend Billy Wilder—a strange choice for a work by Hemingway. On July 5, 1954, Huston wrote to his longtime agent, Paul Kohner, "I would be delighted to do either 'Fifty Grand' or 'The Undefeated.' Now it's up to them to make their choices." These stories of courageous losers had a strong appeal. In "Fifty Grand" (1927) an aging boxer bets $50,000 against himself in a hopeless match. He almost wins when he's fouled by a painful low blow, but survives to lose the fight and win his bet. In "The Undefeated" (1925, also in *Men Without Women*) an old wounded bullfighter attempts a comeback in a Madrid night fight. Though tossed twice and gored, he kills the bull on the sixth try and is rushed to the hospital. "'I was going good,' Manuel said weakly. 'I was going great. . . . I didn't have any luck. That was all.'" Though the subject, style and theme of these stories were a perfect match for Huston, the movie—because of complications with the other directors—was never made.

In 1954 Huston also tried to coax Hemingway, who staunchly resisted all temptations from Hollywood (and condemned Faulkner for swallowing the bait and selling out), to take part in another film based on the greatest bull-fighter of the time: "I think the idea of you and Peter [Viertel] and me doing the one with [Luis Miguel] Domínguín is great and an absolute must." Huston, a keen *aficionado*, had also been considering Barnaby Conrad's bestselling *Matador* (1952), based on his career as an American bullfighter. But Huston told Kohner that he preferred the Hemingway project: "I don't think [*Matador*] would have the immediate and widespread appeal as *Death in the Afternoon by Ernest Hemingway*. And I believe Papa could be coaxed into doing the script himself or perhaps himself with Peter. If the three [Hemingway] stories idea falls by the wayside, I would like to aim for that. I couldn't guarantee it would come off, but, if it did, it would certainly be big medicine." The producer Harold Mirisch was keen on this idea and cabled Huston: "Everyone here terrifically enthusiastic over Hemingway idea. You have our blessings. Investigate possibilities of subject." But Hemingway could not be coaxed and the project was dropped.

Huston was asked to direct *The Old Man and the Sea*, with a screenplay by Peter Viertel, "but couldn't see the old Cuban fisherman played by a [professional] actor, and the studio couldn't risk doing it without one." In 1958 the movie, leadenly directed by John Sturges, starred the rotund, red-faced and absurdly miscast Irish-American, Spencer Tracy, who owned the rights and was coproducer.

Despite these ill-fated setbacks, Huston was still determined to make a Hemingway film. The producer David Selznick, a kind-hearted companion and long-standing friend, wanted to remake *A Farewell to Arms* (the 1932 movie had starred Gary Cooper and Helen Hayes) starring Rock Hudson and his own adored wife, Jennifer Jones. The budget was $4.2 million and Huston's unusually high fee was $250,000. On October 25, 1956, Selznick cabled Huston: "Could you concentrate wholly on *Farewell* [*to Arms*] until completion photography, after which believe you would feel safe leaving post-production, including editing, entirely in my hands?"

Far from feeling safe with Selznick, who wanted complete control and appropriated the power that traditionally belonged to the director, Huston sensed the danger and felt extremely uneasy. Selznick, hand over heart, falsely claimed "there have been few books ever transcribed to the screen with the studied and loving care that [Ben] Hecht and I gave this one through many weary months." But Huston realized at the outset that their debased version had turned one of Hemingway's greatest novels into a banal and cliché-ridden romance. In his autobiography, *An Open Book*, Huston recalled, "From the moment I saw the script, David and I were in conflict. Through David's influence on Hecht, the Hemingway story had simply become a vehicle for the female lead—Jennifer Jones." Well aware of the challenge, the strong-willed Huston pretended to agree with Selznick while plunging ahead and making the movie his own way.

Selznick's biographer remarked that Huston criticized all the material which was not in the novel and which Selznick and Hecht had put into their ninth draft. Following his habitual method, he insisted that "they should stay as close as possible to Hemingway's original scenes." In typical Hollywood fashion, which Huston strenuously opposed, Selznick had paid a fortune for a brilliant novel and then ruined it with his own inept additions.

Selznick's biographer also explained the irreconcilable differences between the two powerful egos: "Huston liked to keep himself open to any new ideas he might have until just before shooting a scene, which meant that camera set-ups could be—and usually were—changed, lines of dialogue altered, blocking and other staging details revamped, thus giving his scenes an edgy, almost improvised spontaneity. Selznick, on the other hand, wanted as much control as possible." After spending an entire day with three secretaries, Selznick sent Huston a tedious and offensive sixteen-page memo that criticized Huston's careful planning and accused him of procrastination. The secretaries warned Selznick that the memo would have a disastrous effect, but he preferred a showdown and sent the ultimatum.

> I should be less than candid with you [Selznick wrote] if I didn't tell you that I am most desperately unhappy about the way things are going. It is an experience completely unique in my very long career. It is an experience that I feel is going to lead us, not to a better picture . . . but to a worse one.
>
> Fervently as I want you to direct the picture, I would rather face the awful consequence of your not directing it than to go through what I am presently going through.

Though Selznick emphatically maintained, "I have learned that *nothing matters but the final picture*," the only thing that really mattered to him was Jennifer Jones.

Before he'd finished the memo, Huston—generous, extravagant and always short of cash, but unwilling to bend the knee—immediately packed his bags, left the film and surrendered his lucrative fee. Unable to protect the integrity of the novel, he was immensely relieved to abandon the project that he knew Hemingway would hate and that would destroy their precious friendship. Huston was replaced by the plodding Charles Vidor. Released in 1957, the picture did not make a profit and Hemingway never got the additional $100,000 that Selznick had promised to give him. When describing his response to this debacle, Huston quoted Hemingway's story about a *picador*'s comments after his *matador*'s disastrous performance: "There was a division of opinion. Some wanted to shit on his father, some wanted to shit on his mother."

Though Huston had failed to direct a film by Hemingway, he did play him on the screen. In the early 1970s Huston took on the role of James Hanneford, a movie director modeled on Hemingway in Orson Welles' *The Other Side of the Wind*. Welles had observed Hemingway and his followers at bullfights in Spain. But Welles, who had more unfinished projects than Leonardo da Vinci, never completed this picture.

Hemingway was writing his Venetian novel, *Across the River and Into the Trees* (1950), his first book since the tremendously successful *For Whom the Bell Tolls* (1940), when he first met Huston and they had discussed the possibility of making a film of the book. In 1975–76 Huston and his longtime mistress, secretary and collaborator, Gladys Hill, worked on a script of the movie that he planned to direct. He knew the difficulties—no real action and a lot of repetitive scenes and boring dialogue—and explained that Hemingway "was trying something that didn't come off—it's an experiment, a kind of indulgence." He also told the *New York Times* that "the book, which was largely a disaster, is a dialogue between a colonel who is dying and a very young Italian girl. Papa was very dejected by the reception of the book and I've got correspondence from him [now lost] which was written when he was so down about it. I know the background, a lot of personal things. He really exposes himself in the book and it is hard to draw the line between Hemingway and the old colonel." Armed with inside knowledge, Huston cut to the essence of the novel. The film would show "the compassionate and sensitive side" of Hemingway and define "what it means to be a soldier."

It's interesting to see how, with all their considerable skill, Huston and Hill failed to master a hopeless project and dramatize dead words and lifeless scenes. (I've tried to write the script myself; it can't be done.) In this case,

Huston (awed by Hemingway) followed the novel too faithfully instead of inventing new scenes (as he did in *The Killers*) to flesh out and vitalize the story. The 117-page typescript in the Herrick Library begins with Colonel Richard Cantwell driving in a jeep with Sergeant Jackson and remembering his past. There are flashbacks to battles in World War II; an allusion to duck shooting in the Venetian marshes; and a reference to the always obliging porter and bartender in the luxurious Hotel Gritti on the Grand Canal. There's a good deal of arch conversation, and scenes in the streets of Venice and in Harry's bar. Cantwell talks to his friend Alvarito; meets the beautiful young aristocrat Renata (his rebirth) and asks her, "Would you ever like to run for Queen of Heaven?" (28).

After another flashback to the war, Cantwell says, "I don't care about our losses—because the moon is our mother and our father" (43). (Imitation bad Hemingway is even worse than real bad Hemingway.) Renata keeps asking him to recount his tedious war exploits. Thus encouraged, Cantwell disparages the generals who destroyed his career. He then tells her, "We are devotees of the pictorial arts" (57). They take a gondola ride (like a couple of tourists) and she urges him to "hold me tight and try to love me true" (64). When they dock at St. Mark's Square, Cantwell, despite his weak heart, gallantly punches two American sailors whom he thinks have made insulting remarks about his true love. He and Renata admire her portrait, which he has commissioned; and he ungallantly tells her younger sister Vittoria (Huston's invention), "You are so god-damned beautiful it's heart-breaking. Also, you are jail bait" (75).

Well aware of his physical decline, Cantwell tells himself, "You are half a hundred years old, you beat up old bastard you" (79). Hemingway reveals in this autobiographical novel that he regarded himself as old and finished at fifty, his age when he wrote the book. Cantwell makes plans for the future in America. He talks to the headwaiter at the Gritti, whom he elevates to *Gran Maestro*, and discusses their fanciful *Ordine Militare*. He bitterly and obsessively recalls the hopeless attack whose failure demoted him from general to colonel. The duck hunt, the best scene in the book, is shifted to the end of the film, and the boatman, who suggests Charon, the oarsman of the Underworld, foreshadows the colonel's death. The script returns to the opening scene, and Cantwell dies in the jeep, leaving written orders to give the portrait to Renata and his guns to Alvarito. As the jeep drives off, the movie ends. The second version, dated

April 2, 1976, is revised but essentially the same. Huston could not solve the intractable, impossible problem: that nothing much, and nothing interesting, ever happens in the novel or the film.

Huston confessed in an interview that, with all his strenuous efforts, "I never got a proper script. I worked on it myself, but I never got it. . . . I did use flashbacks, but the script never came off." It was terribly sad for the careers of both Hemingway and Huston, despite the perfect match of novelist and director, that none of Huston's ambitious and promising projects to put Hemingway on film was ever realized. For all his admiration and passionate commitment to Hemingway, Huston never directed a film based on his friend's work.

Hemingway and Huston lived egoistic, adventurous and dangerous lives. They nurtured in themselves and their friends a cult of masculinity and often reckless courage, which inspired some of their finest artistic achievements. They were lionized in the 1940s, but Lillian Ross, of the *New Yorker*, wrote satiric portraits of Hemingway in 1950 and of Huston in 1952. Both men, toward the end of their lives, had some failures, and both had an entourage of courtiers and camp followers, flatterers and parasites. But after being written off, they made a strong finish: Hemingway with the posthumous *A Moveable Feast* and Huston with a final cinematic masterpiece, *The Dead*.

15

HEMINGWAY

——— AND ———

GARY COOPER

I

Hemingway and Cooper, born at the turn of the century, were sons of professional men: a doctor and a judge. They achieved early fame in their twenties. *The Sun Also Rises* and Cooper's first important film, *The Winning of Barbara Worth*, both appeared in 1926. Tall, athletic and extraordinarily handsome, they loved the American West. Cooper was born and raised in Helena, Montana; Hemingway, beginning in 1928, spent part of the year in Wyoming and Idaho. They shared a passion for rifles, hunting and sports, and decorated their houses with stuffed trophies and mounted specimens.

They also had a powerful bond from their experience of hunting big game in East Africa. Cooper, who spent five months in Kenya and Tanganyika in 1931, had eighty kills, including two lions, and brought home a pet chimpanzee. Two years later Hemingway went on a two-month safari, shot three lions, a buffalo and twenty-seven other beasts, and wrote about his adventures in *Green Hills of Africa* (1935).

Cooper starred in the first two films based on Hemingway's work: *A Farewell to Arms* in 1932 and *For Whom the Bell Tolls* in 1943. Hemingway formed platonic friendships, fueled by lust, with Marlene Dietrich and Ingrid Bergman, both of whom became Cooper's lovers. After World War II, Cooper planned to form a film company with Hemingway and star in their own production of *Across the River and into the Trees*. Cooper sought Hemingway's advice during two crucial episodes of his life: his affair with the actress Patricia Neal and his conversion to the Roman Catholic Church. After more than twenty years of friendship (unusual for Hemingway, who tended to break with his former pals), they had a poignant reunion, as old comrades will do, when plagued by illness at the end of their lives.

Though Hemingway admired Cooper's restrained yet heroic performance in *A Farewell to Arms*, he hated the screen version of the novel. He condemned the fake morality, phony marriage ceremony, Rinaldi's withholding of the lovers' letters and Frederic Henry's preposterous desertion from the army, and was disgusted by the attempts of the studio press agents to publicize his own boxing ability and exploits in war. In a letter to a journalist, Hemingway said "the movie hero deserts because his girlfriend wouldn't write him any letters. When he goes to look for her, the entire army tags along so he won't get lonely."

Hemingway first met Cooper in September 1940 in Sun Valley, situated amidst the spectacular scenery of the Sawtooth Mountains of south-central Idaho. It had been opened as a ski resort in 1936 by Averell Harriman and the Union Pacific Railroad. The company, eager for publicity and well aware of Hemingway's reputation as a sportsman, paid all his expenses there, beginning in 1939, in return for using his name in their advertisements, and many film stars—including Clark Gable and Ingrid Bergman—soon followed in his wake. Idaho had excellent shooting and fishing, and offered a stimulating change from the hot and humid weather of Cuba and Los Angeles. Cooper spent part of the fall and winter in Sun Valley just before and after the war as well as many autumns, for hunting and good talk, in the 1950s.

Sun Valley reminded Cooper of his boyhood ranch, north of Helena. He also loved the big open country, south of the resort, that was filled with jackrabbits, bobcats and golden eagles. The landscape of the Rockies put Hemingway and Cooper in touch with the quintessential characteristics they had known in their youth: virgin land, heroic origins, traditional Indians, pioneer solitude and individualistic triumph. Both loved, as Hemingway wrote in "The Snows of Kilimanjaro," "the ranch and the silvered gray of the sage brush, the quick, clear water in the irrigation ditches, and the heavy green of the alfalfa. The trail went up into the hills and the cattle in the summer were as shy as deer."

In October 1940, two weeks after they met, Hemingway told his editor that Cooper's character matched his screen persona. Hemingway was better at gracefully swinging a shotgun to kill ducks and pheasant but conceded the keen-eyed Cooper's superiority with a rifle. Always intensely competitive,

Hemingway could beat Cooper—who had a hip injury from a teenage car accident—in tennis. He also threatened to get his friend, who weighed forty pounds less than he did, into the boxing ring (Gary, valuing the fine bone structure of his face, wisely declined): "Cooper is a fine man; as honest and straight and friendly and unspoiled as he looks. . . . Cooper is a very, very fine rifle shot and a good wing shot. I can shoot a little better than he can with a shotgun but not nearly as good with a rifle due I guess to drinking too much for too many years."

Both men had suffered numerous injuries: Hemingway, from engaging in dangerous activities while drunk; Cooper, from doing riding stunts and carrying out romantic exploits in movies. Patrick Hemingway recalled that his father asked Cooper about how they staged fist fights in movies and made them look real. Cooper explained that the realistic sound of a punch came from the blow of a mallet on a grapefruit. Both men had risked their lives pursuing wild animals in Africa. They loved to recall their adventures (one paid for by Hemingway's rich uncle-in-law, Gus Pfeiffer; the other by Cooper's millionaire mistress, the Countess di Frasso), and Hemingway claimed his lesser kudu was greater than Cooper's greater kudu. Inscribing a copy of *Green Hills of Africa* (now owned by Cooper's daughter), Hemingway wrote: "To Gary Cooper, hoping it will remind him of Tanganyika. With very best wishes. Ernest Hemingway."

Both men were targets of ambitious women, who often pursued and sometimes seduced them. Hemingway's glamorous third wife, Martha Gellhorn, who unkindly called him "The Pig," urged him to smooth his rough edges and follow Cooper's elegant example. "Since Marty has been around with the Coopers," he told Charles Scribner, and "seeing that Gary, she wants me to have clothes and be handsome and that sort of thing." The Sun Valley photographer "Pappy" Arnold reported that Hemingway (like an eastern dude) imitated Cooper's role as Wild Bill Hickok in De Mille's Western of 1936: "He went all out, had several things made, including a white capeskin hunting shirt—'going Hollywood' to quote him—'don't you think I'm as handsome as Plainsman Hickok Cooper in this fancy shirt?'"

Toward the end of his life Cooper recalled one of Hemingway's indelicate aphorisms: "Always stand in the back of the man who fires a gun and in front of the man who shits. Then you won't get shot at or shit on." He also described a shooting expedition in the fall of 1941, commanded by Hemingway, who could not resist the opportunity to take unsporting advantage of his famous guests:

> The party included Hemingway, Martha Gellhorn, Bob Taylor, Barbara Stanwyck, Rocky [Gary's wife] and me. Pheasant was our objective, and Hemingway so impressed Bob and me with his knowledge of pheasant hunting that we didn't have a word to say. He deployed us like a general directing maneuvers. Bob and Barbara down the slope about a quarter of a mile to a patch of likely-looking cover. Rocky and me to a blackberry patch straight across the field.
>
> "And Martha and I will take the upper corner," Hemingway said. "I know this field, and it's real good. Don't shoot if you flush a bird or two. In fact, don't shoot until you hear me holler. Is that clear?"
>
> We started out. Bob and Barbara got to their patch of brush just as Rocky and I reached ours. As I looked at Bob to see how he was coming, the air around him exploded with birds. If he hadn't been holding his gun, he could have caught a dozen in his bare hands. Rocky made a move, and there was another explosion of pheasant all around us. They nearly blew my hat off. I held my gun poised, waiting for Hemingway.
>
> He knew his pheasant, all right. Far beyond Bob's or my range, the two flocks joined and swung right over his head.
>
> "Fire!" he yelled, and let go with both barrels. It took a minute for the air to clear of feathers.
>
> I looked down at Bob and he looked back at me. The Nebraska boy and the Montana boy, raised in pheasant country, had been took.

Hemingway told a friend, early on, "if you made up a character like Coop, nobody would believe it. He's just too good to be true." But as his initial enthusiasm wore off, he became more critical of his gentle friend. "Cooper is wonderful and fine company to hunt with," he told his editor in 1941, using a down-home Arkansas expression. "Also as tight about money as a hog's ass in fly-time." Hemingway hated the right-wing Sam Wood, who directed the apolitical and extremely Wooden film version of *For Whom the Bell Tolls*, and told Cooper that Wood "was an ignoramus, devoid of both intellect and charm."

When Cooper tried to defend his colleague by saying, "Well, Sam's a lot like me," Hemingway tartly replied: "No, Coop, you *do* have charm."

Hemingway's youngest son, on the scene at Sun Valley (where, as an adolescent, he ran up an enormous bar bill) observed that Cooper had a soothing effect on his belligerent companion: "Though they had little in common intellectually, a kindness and gentleness seemed to exist between them." Both had healthy but discriminating appetites; and their feast of smoked goose and Chablis, devoured when they were locked in by a blizzard, inspired Cooper to observe: "Ain't this Mormon country wonderful! they know how to live." "I'm practically one myself," Ernest said. "Had four wives, didn't I?" They swapped barbed jokes, revealed amorous intrigues and struggled against the depredations of time.

Hemingway lived and wrote about, while Cooper portrayed in film, the life of a romantic hero. And it was good for the careers of both image-conscious men not only to be together but to be seen together by millions of their fans. A four-page spread in *Life* magazine of November 24, 1941, had twelve photographs, by Hemingway's Spanish War comrade Robert Capa, of the two handsome men and almost-as-handsome wives hunting, eating, drinking, dancing and loafing in Sun Valley. This kind of valuable publicity continued into the 1950s. After Hemingway had won the Nobel Prize and Cooper his second Oscar, *Newsweek* of March 12, 1956, ran a photo of a valet-like Hemingway helping the bare-chested Cooper into a Cuban shirt. Three years later, on February 16, 1959, *Life* showed Hemingway, at a Sun Valley cocktail party, playfully tossing an olive into Cooper's open mouth.

II

Hemingway had admired Cooper's performance in *A Farewell to Arms*, read about him in the newspapers and heard about him from Marlene Dietrich before they met. And he modeled certain aspects of Robert Jordan—a lean, laconic native of Montana—on Gary Cooper. In *For Whom the Bell Tolls*, Hemingway describes Jordan as a "young man, who was tall and thin, with sun-streaked fair hair, and a wind- and sun-burned face." When the novel was published, a month after he met Cooper, Hemingway told the *Kansas City Times* that "Cooper rather fitted the character of Robert Jordan." He inscribed one of the advance copies: "To the Coopers, to make something to supplement the

Idaho Statesman as reading matter. With good luck always. Ernest Hemingway. On the day we got books. October 5, 1940."

Hemingway naturally urged Cooper to play Jordan, opposite the Swedish-Spaniard Ingrid Bergman, in the screen version of the novel. He sold the rights for $150,000 to Paramount, Cooper's studio, so that he would have the starring role, and both author and actor would have some influence in choosing the director. In January 1941, en route to report the war in China, Hemingway stayed at Cooper's house while conferring with Paramount executives about the film. On January 30, just before embarking from San Francisco, he met Bergman and enthusiastically recommended her for the part. After telling her that her hair would have to be cut short, he asked to see her ears (Cooper would ask to see much more than this) and found them as delightful as the rest of her. Gregory Hemingway said that when Bergman confided, "I always carry an extra pair of stockings in my bag," Hemingway, "whose only possible interest in her lingerie was how to get it off her," would say, "Yes, Ingrid, that's a very practical thing to do." He inscribed a copy of the novel "For Ingrid Bergman, who is the Maria of this story." After casting the leading roles, he flew off to the "bad earth" of China.

Both Hemingway and Cooper wanted the sportsman Howard Hawks (who had helped Cooper win an Oscar for *Sergeant York* and would later do a fine version of *To Have and Have Not*) to direct *For Whom the Bell Tolls*. So in October 1941, Hemingway's third consecutive season in Sun Valley, the three men met to discuss the project, formulate a clear interpretation of the film and try to convince the studio to hire Hawks. Resisting the pressure of author and actor, Paramount first chose Cecil B. De Mille and then gave it to the stolid Sam Wood. Completely out of sympathy with Hemingway's political views, he produced a slow-paced version of 170 minutes, which one critic called "a studio-bound and mock Spanish rendering of Hemingway." Even worse, the role of Maria was given to the Norwegian ballerina, Vera Zorina. After two weeks of shooting, Cooper threatened to leave the film and Zorina was suddenly replaced.

Bergman, who came from her dazzling success with Bogart in *Casablanca* to the Sonora Pass in the High Sierras of California, said "we worked twelve weeks in the mountains and later twelve weeks in the studios, Paramount spending three million dollars on their biggest film. . . . It was so primitive and romantic up there among the stars and the high peaks before the winter snows cut off the whole region." Bergman often told her accommodating first husband that "she couldn't work well unless she was in love with either the leading man or the director." She soon fell in love with Cooper, who usually had brief affairs with his leading ladies—from Clara Bow and Lupe Velez to Tallulah Bankhead and Grace Kelly.

Bergman later praised Cooper's physical beauty as well as his effectively understated acting: "The personality of this man was so enormous, so overpowering—and that expression in his eyes and his face, it was so delicate and so underplayed. You just didn't notice it until you saw it on the screen. I thought he was marvellous; the most underplaying and the most natural actor I ever worked with." Cooper returned the compliment by stating: "She is one of the easiest actresses to do a scene with. . . . She lifts the scene. That's because she is so completely natural."

Bergman's adoration of her leading man was all too apparent to her confidante, who warned her: "You must stop looking at him like that. You sit there just looking! I know you are supposed to be in love with him in the picture, but not too much in love with him." Though Bergman's passion for Cooper shone through on the screen, the unbelievably healthy and radiant actress scarcely looked as if she had recently been raped by a gang of fascists and was living a primitive existence in the remote fastness of the Spanish mountains.

Bergman spent all her free time with Cooper, eating evening meals and preparing her role with him. Since the film was shot far from the prying eyes of Hollywood, she escaped the scandalous rumors in the gossip columns. Cooper's liaison with Bergman, as with Dietrich, intensified Hemingway's competitive instinct. As he longed for the two beautiful women Cooper had so easily taken to bed, he became more critical of his friend.

Since America was fighting German and Italian Fascism while the film was being made, Hemingway naturally thought the political themes of the novel were more urgent than ever. But, after Franco's victory in the Civil War, Paramount wanted to soften the political implications of the film in order to avoid a boycott by the Spanish government. The film critic James Agee quoted Adolph Zukor, the head of the studio, who rather fatuously exclaimed: "It is a great picture, without political significance. We are not for or against anybody." The screenplay by Dudley Nichols not only ignored the political ideas and stressed

Jordan's conflict with Pablo and love for Maria, but also omitted Hemingway's poignant personal memories of his grandfather and father.

Despite the "political castration," Franco's American agents tried to prevent the production of the film. The screen version of *For Whom the Bell Tolls*—like *A Farewell to Arms*—infuriated Hemingway. Paraphrasing an unpublished letter, one biographer wrote that when Hemingway first read the script, "Nichols' love scenes struck him as astonishingly inept, while his picturesque conception of the appearance of the Spaniards could only have been derived from fourth-rate productions of Bizet's *Carmen*. . . . In place of the red bandannas prescribed by Nichols, the actors must all wear grays and blacks, and the whole emphasis must be on the native dignity of the Loyalists."

Though the performances of Cooper and Bergman, both of whom were nominated for Academy Awards, made *For Whom the Bell Tolls* "a little less awful" than the earlier film, Hemingway mocked the all-too-discreet love scene in which Cooper, bowing to the prevailing· censorship, didn't even "take off his coat. That's one hell of a way for a guy to make love, with his coat on—in a sleeping bag. And Ingrid, in her tailored dress and all those pretty curls—she was strictly Elizabeth Arden out of Abercrombie and Fitch."

The Hemingway-Cooper friendship thrived, despite the novelist's condemnation of the film, when the two friends met again after the war. Both men had always admired Kipling—Cooper kept a copy of "If" in his dressing room, and Kipling was a major influence on Hemingway's work—and retained in adult life Kipling's taste for boyish adventure as well as a streak of his cruelty. Cooper's fellow actor Joel McCrea said that when deep-sea fishing his friend "liked to tie pieces of meat to each end of a piece of string. He would then throw them overboard and chuckle quietly to himself as he watched the squabbling of a couple of outraged sea gulls who have gobbled them up and are, therefore, 'tied' together." Durie Shevlin, who spent her 1947 honeymoon aboard Hemingway's boat, the *Pilar*, recalled that when he "saw two turtles mating on a Caribbean beach, he immediately rowed ashore in a dinghy, disturbed their congress, captured one for cat food and carried it aboard. He turned the turtle on its back; and it became pink, then purple, smelled horribly and died slowly."

Bergman's first husband, Petter Lindstrom, on a hunting expedition with Hemingway, Cooper and Clark Gable in the spring of 1946, was shocked by the unsportsmanlike and indiscriminate slaughter: "We drove along the power lines in a jeep," Lindstrom recalled, "and they shot eagles off the power lines using telescopic sights and rifles resting on tripods. Another day we went rabbit hunting. They engaged these farmers to ride in trucks chasing the rabbits towards them. I didn't shoot a single shot, either day. They killed maybe fifty rabbits. Nobody wanted them."

McCrea, who knew Cooper well, also emphasized the actor's unwillingness to confide in anyone about his personal dilemmas: "He never kicks. He never mentions, even to me, any sort of problem or difficulty he may have encountered. He never discusses anything personal with anybody." Despite his characteristic reserve, Cooper brought Pat Neal to Cuba in 1950 to introduce her to Hemingway and ask his advice about whether he should leave his wife and marry the young actress with whom he had fallen deeply in love. Neal (who had a three-year affair with Cooper, after which she returned to his wife) observed: "I just know Gary was telling him that he wanted to marry me. He was asking for Papa's blessing, and I was sure he was getting it. . . . Gary and I were escorted to the little guest house and found it had one double bed, which had been turned down for us to share. Years later I read that Ernest Hemingway disapproved of our affair. He did not then." Hemingway was ambivalent about Cooper's situation. He had left the older Hadley Richardson for Pauline Pfeiffer in 1926 and (as he wrote in *A Moveable Feast*) felt intensely guilty about it. He understood Cooper's feelings, but found it somewhat difficult to encourage Cooper to do what he himself had done. He also, in 1949, had fallen in love with a young Italian girl, Adriana Ivancich, but she had kept the affair platonic.

Neal also revealed a defect in Cooper's character—his craving for wealth— which Hemingway emphasized when anatomizing the personality of his friend. "He adored people with money," Neal wrote. "That was what had happened with the Countess de Frasso. When he met Rocky, he knew her step-father was rich, rich, rich and he wanted to marry her and, in fact, they were very happy. When you met him, he pretended not to care about money, but he loved it. He loved to live well, and he did live well: fabulous suits, ties, shirts and shoes which he had made for himself. He was the best dresser I have ever known."

Hemingway, who disliked Gatsby-like attire and dominating women, resented Rocky, who would sometimes jerk the chain and cut short an all-male hunting trip so that Gary could return in time for a social event in Sun Valley. Hemingway tried to support Cooper when they later discussed his intention to convert to Catholicism, partly to please his wife and daughter and to heal the wounds caused by his affair with Pat Neal. But he disapproved of Rocky's influence on Cooper's religion and sardonically remarked that by entering the Church Coop could have "all that money *and* God." Hemingway told another friend that Cooper now loved money more than most people loved God. He felt especially bitter about Cooper's conversion to Catholicism to please his wealthy wife because he had done precisely the same thing when he married Pauline Pfeiffer in 1927.

III

High Noon, Cooper's greatest film, opened in New York in July 1952; *The Old Man and the Sea*, Hemingway's most popular novel, was serialized in *Life* that September. Kenneth Lynn noted the similarities between the heroism of the characters Cooper played and Hemingway created: "Just as Will Kane has to do, Santiago sets out alone to do battle, against an adversary that turns out to be the most formidable of his career. And once again like Kane, he both wins and loses, for the flesh of his record-breaking marlin is totally devoured by sharks."

Eager to play the embittered hero of Hemingway's projected postwar novel, *Across the River and Into the Trees*, Cooper, as early as May 1945, urged Hemingway to join him in producing the picture, controlling the artistic quality and reaping most of the profits: "I am sure that if any important yarn of yours is done on the screen the next time it would be a great advantage all around if you were here on the spot to be part of the company which creates it. . . . I would like nothing better than to produce a picture with you which both of us would make and share in the results. . . . I've had various reports on your activities from time to time and all sound very interesting and weird. I'm sure you're coming out with a hot one about the thing in Europe." Hemingway, who had just returned to Cuba from reporting the war in Europe, was planning to marry his fourth wife and had not even started the novel, did not respond to this proposal.

Shortly after their meeting in 1956 at the Ritz in Paris, where Cooper was filming *Love in the Afternoon*, Cooper again tried to draw Hemingway into the movie business. This time the hot property was *The Leopard Woman* and the draw was not only money but also Cooper's companionship on another safari to Africa:

Would you be interested in doing it with me on a participating set-up, tossing in your ideas and some writing and perhaps, if you feel up to it, going to Africa when it is made and getting some good plinking [pistol shooting] and bird shooting at the same time?

The condition of the picture business today makes it possible to come off with some real money if you have got a movie a real cut above the average. . . . Ever since *For Whom the Bell Tolls* I have felt that you have never gotten your share of what you have contributed to stories of yours that have been made into pictures. . . .

If you think you want to yak a bit about the African picture, I am always ready to jump aboard and come down to see you [in Cuba].

Hemingway felt morally superior by remaining aloof from Hollywood and had condemned Faulkner for taking money to work on the screenplay of *To Have and Have Not*. He had been seriously injured and reported dead after two plane crashes during his second trip to Africa in January 1954 and was about to leave on a futile journey to Peru in search of huge jumping marlin for the film version of *The Old Man and the Sea*. As soon as he received the letter he wisely wrote Cooper that he would have nothing more to do with the disgusting producers who made movies: "Coops the picture business is not for me and no matter how much dough we could make, how would we spend it if we were dead from dealing with the characters we would have to deal with. After *The Old Man and the Sea* is finished I will not ever have anything to do with pictures again so Help Me God. God is Capitalized."

Despite Hemingway's forceful rejection of both *The Leopard Woman* and Hollywood, Cooper revived his old plan to make a film based on *Across the River and into the Trees* (published in 1950) in Sun Valley in the fall of 1958. He discussed the idea with Hemingway during their annual hunt and the project made some progress. By March 1960 Cooper was actively trying to acquire the screen rights of the novel and Hemingway was calling him in London to find out about the deal. In October, Hemingway's emissary, after meeting Cooper in London, announced that the contracts would soon be drawn up in Hollywood.

But in the fall of 1960, when both men became desperately ill, the project had to be cancelled. In April and again in June 1960, as the disease began to spread through and ravage his body, Cooper had major operations for cancer of the prostate and of the colon. On May 2, while recuperating from the first surgery, he tried in a letter to Hemingway to make light of his condition: "I was hooked up to a P[iss] bottle with a tube coming out of 'you know what' and I looked like some sort of 'still' making a low-grade grape juice." In the summer and fall of 1960, while Cooper was recovering, Hemingway began to suffer from obsessions, delusions, paranoid fears of poverty and persecution, inability to work, severe depression and suicidal impulses. In late November 1960 he entered the Mayo Clinic and endured a disastrous series of shock treatments which obliterated his memory and intensified his depression. In late December, while Hemingway was in the Mayo, Rocky Cooper was told that Gary had fatal cancer. Two months later, as his pain became intolerable, she told him the truth.

On January 9, 1961, the Friars Club gave Cooper a testimonial dinner at the Beverly Hilton Hotel, where he was honored by Audrey Hepburn, Greer Garson, Sam Goldwyn and Carl Sandburg. Hemingway printed out a strained message in childish capital letters. "DEAR COOPS. MARY AND EYE COULDNT BE PROUDER OR HAPPIER AND ITS WONDERFUL TO HAVE THE FIRST GUY HONORED. DESERVE IT COMPLETELY AS MAN AND SO MUCH FINER ACTOR THAN ANYBODY KNOWS INCLUDING YOU. LOVE FROM US BOTH AND SEE YOU AND ROCK SOON AT THE VALLEY. PAPA." In late January, after Hemingway was released from the clinic, the two doomed friends met in Sun Valley to hike, hunt and talk for the last time.

On April 17 Hemingway, watching television at his home in Ketchum (next to Sun Valley), saw James Stewart accept an honorary Oscar for Cooper, who was too ill to attend the ceremony. When Stewart suddenly broke down and cried: "We're all very proud of you Coop . . . all of us . . . terribly proud," revealing that Cooper was close to death, Hemingway was devastated.

Pappy Arnold recalled: "There was a noticeable wincing in Papa, a squirming—in his chair at the moment—an odd little utterance, like an 'mmmph!' But it was not particularly alarming, even when he got up, paced about, joining the normal comments about Coop. . . . Mary [Hemingway] suggested a call be put through to Coop—congratulate him, cheer him up. . . . Papa resisted strongly." But Mary called anyway, talked to both Rocky and Cooper, then handed the phone to Hemingway: "It was torture to poor Papa. . . . 'What will I say to Coop, what can I say?'" Obsessed by the illness of the always strong Cooper— who was close to death and grimly predicted "I bet I make it to the barn before you"—Hemingway, using gambling and boxing metaphors, exclaimed that his friend "had been dealt the Big C but would go fifteen rounds with it."

A week later, on April 25, Hemingway reentered the Mayo for the second and even more disastrous series of shock treatments. Now it was Cooper's turn to offer condolences. On the 29th, the Coopers sent a sympathetic telegram: "DEAR PAPA. WHAT'S THERE TO SAY EXCEPT THAT YOU HAVE OUR LOVE. GARY AND ROCKY." Sustained by religion as he was devoured by cancer, Cooper provided a terrifying warning to Hemingway. He kept his word and died on May 13. Hemingway was too ill to attend Cooper's funeral and, less than two months later, shot himself. It was left to Rocky to say: "I know there was no person that Gary held in greater regard."

Cooper, whose parents were English and who had spent three years at an English public school, created a new film persona by combining an English gentleman with a Montana cowboy. Hemingway created tough heroes, torn between ironic fatalism and despairing courage, who sought authenticity and adhered to a strict code of honor. Both actor and artist forged a modern masculine style and, influenced by their personal friendship, became two of the preeminent image-makers of the twentieth century.

16

SEAMUS HEANEY
—— AND ——
ROBERT LOWELL

I

In *Stepping Stones* (2008), Dennis O'Driscoll's excellent book of interviews, Seamus Heaney recalled that he first met Robert Lowell in 1972 at Sonia Orwell's party to celebrate Lowell's wedding to Caroline Blackwood. Heaney was young enough to be Lowell's son and from a rural Irish background, remote from Lowell's patrician pedigree. He had not been invited to that grand occasion, but was staying with Karl Miller, editor of the *Listener*, who was on the guest list and brought him along. He was shy of meeting Lowell "because of that nimbus of authority that ringed his writings and his actions," but "actually got into a corner with him for about half an hour and did the laundry list, as [Joseph] Brodsky used to say—checking out what was to be said about which poets. . . . It was a genuine enough meeting, and he was immensely charming and even more immensely intelligent." Later, on several manic and memorable occasions, the two developed a close friendship that influenced and inspired Heaney's poetry. At the party Heaney was not only introduced to distinguished poets, but also gained insight into the politics of poetry: the prestige and power that controlled lucrative teaching jobs and lecture tours, fellowships and honors, of which he would later reap the full harvest. After Lowell's untimely death in September 1977 Heaney wrote two essays, a memorial address and two poems about him.

Lowell had social and political as well as poetical influence. Heaney remarked that "Lowell was the last American to be a dual citizen of the university and the world beyond it, at home in Harvard, but also at home among the metropolitan set, a figure to be photographed at cocktail parties and on marches to the Pentagon." He used Keats' description of Wordsworth to describe Lowell's distinctive genius, and also explained why Lowell's reputation, though not his poetry, fell after his death when fashions changed and standards declined: "Lowell is taking the punishment that's always handed out to the big guy eventually; so no, I'm not surprised. Lowell was a white Anglo-Saxon Protestant male, a Eurocentric, *egotistical sublime*, writing as if he intended to be heard in a high wind. He was on the winning side from the start: Boston Brahmin, friend of Eliot, part of the literary establishment on both sides of the Atlantic." When Heaney's reputation later soared, he too took his share of low blows.

Caroline Blackwood, a witty and talented writer, was also a considerable figure. Her wealthy and aristocratic family came (like Heaney's) from Northern Ireland, but her father, killed in Burma in World War II, was the 4th Marquess of Dufferin and Ava. An heir to the Guinness brewery fortune, she was also a great beauty. Her first husband, Lucian Freud, had painted her portrait that was as stunning and sensuous as Botticelli's Venus.

In August 1975 Heaney invited Lowell to a poetry festival in Kilkenny, Ireland. As Lowell feared from past experience, the event became a week of drunken and quarrelsome reelings and writhings. Heaney expected Lowell to arrive for his midweek performance, but he came on the previous Sunday and stayed with him through the next weekend. Heaney's nine-year-old son Michael, with unusually formal diction, told Lowell that he preferred soccer to sonnets: "I know you are a famous poet, but it's my ambition to meet a famous footballer." During that prolonged visit Lowell, a wayward and distant father to his own daughter and son, envied Heaney's close family life and sadly remarked, "You see a lot of your children"—as if that were a rare event.

Heaney said that Lowell "had a wonderful way of coming close, personally and critically," and he valued both aspects of that intimacy. In a letter of September 11, 1975, a month after the Kilkenny chaos, Lowell advised Heaney to follow Lowell's practice of salvaging the best parts of his discarded work: "Your Nature pours out images with a full hand. . . . You should be able to mine many poems out of your many strong lines." But in 1975 even Lowell's gratifying praise provoked jealousy and contention. As Heaney noted, "Lowell boosting me after *North* as 'the best Irish poet since W. B. Yeats' . . . rankled all round and . . . helped to sharpen the quills of the honest Ulstermen. At the time, I didn't take aboard just how badly Lowell had rocked the boat."

Heaney, who began to read Lowell when he was an undergraduate at Queen's University in Belfast, freely acknowledged his early interest in Lowell's poetic freedom and personal example: "'The Quaker Graveyard at Nantucket' I had known since I was an undergraduate, so for me that poem and its author were the real canonical goods. All through the sixties I was reading him, constantly—*Life Studies, Imitations, For the Union Dead*—books that were just part of the air we breathed." (Hopkins, Heaney's mentor, had compared the Blessed Virgin to the "Air We Breathe.") He was also generous and specific about Lowell's imprint on his work: "You can see the influence in the second half of *North*, in the blank verse, 'why not say what happened' bits of the 'Singing School' sequence, and in particular in the 'Fosterage' section. That one is an unrhymed sonnet, modelled on those unrhymed sonnet-portraits of writers in *Notebook* and *History*—'Robert Frost,' for example," about Frost's tragic family life. "Why not say what happened" comes from Lowell's "Epilogue," the last poem in his last book *Day by Day*, and is followed by commanding and inspiring lines: "Pray for the grace of accuracy / Vermeer gave to the sun's illumination / stealing like the tide across a map." Lowell described Vermeer's picture, *The Art of Painting* (1668), where the light flows into the room from behind the heavy drawn curtain and from the white window on the left. (The title of Heaney's first "Singing School" poem, "The Ministry of Fear," adopted the title of Graham Greene's novel, 1943).

Lowell not only encouraged Heaney to write unrhymed sonnets, but also to translate cantos from Dante's *Inferno*. (Ezra Pound had started the dubious but sometimes successful practice of translating from languages the poet did not know.) Heaney recalled, "The bit of Lowell translation that had the most impact on me was his version of the Brunetto Latini canto in *Near the Ocean*. If I hadn't encountered that, there would have been no 'Ugolino' in *Field Work*." In "Brunetto" Lowell self-reflectively wrote:

This much I know: If I can bear the stings
of my own heavy conscience, I will face
whatever good or evil Fortune brings.

In "Ugolino" Heaney emphasized the disgusting details:

The sinner eased his mouth up off his meal
To answer me, and wiped it with the hair
Left growing on his victim's ravaged skull.

Finally, Heaney allowed that Lowell was the exemplary creator of crushing and massive, not cautious and minute, poetry: "Lowell went head-on at the times—there was no more literary poet around but at the same time he was like a great cement mixer: he just shovelled the world in and it delivered. Now that's what I yearn for—the cement mixer rather than the chopstick."

Heaney published all his enthusiastic writing about Lowell after his unexpected death. In his review of *Day by Day* (*Irish Times*, 1978), he noted the change in taste after Lowell had dominated the poetry scene for two decades: "There was perhaps a conflict between . . . his predilection for the high rhetorical modes of poetry and the age's preference for the democratic and the demotic." He then praised Lowell's personal commitment to his art and courage when overcome by episodes of madness: "Lowell was exemplary in his dedication and achievement . . . in the integrity and passion with which he pursued his artistic ambitions. . . . Lowell's bravery was different from the bravery of [the suicides] John Berryman or Sylvia Plath. They swam . . . towards death, but Lowell resisted that, held fast to conscience and pushed deliberately towards self-mastery."

"Lowell's Command," a more ambitious essay, was one of Heaney's T. S. Eliot Memorial Lectures at the University of Kent in October 1986. He observed that the searing and innovative *Life Studies* had led the way to a new kind of self-probing poetry that became part of the modern tradition: "noted at first for the extremity of its candour, so apparently private and self-absorbed, [it] now stands as firm and approachable as a public monument. . . . Lowell deliberately occupied—sometimes by public apostrophe and rebuke, sometimes by introspective or confessional example—the role of the poet as conscience." Heaney concluded by stressing Lowell's combative stance as a political poet: "Lowell was always the one to call out the opposition, to send the duelling note; so there was an imperious strain even in his desire to embrace the role of witness."

II

Since I was exactly two weeks older than Heaney and he granted me Confucian respect for an elder, he agreed to answer my queries. In a letter to me of August 11,

2013, written only two weeks before his death, he began by using the title of the first poem in his first book: "To be 'digging' as vigorously as ever in your senior (to me, at any rate) position is enviable, so I am honestly well disposed to agreeing to your invitation to talk on the phone about Lowell." He then convincingly discussed the sensitive question of why he was chosen to deliver the Memorial Address on Lowell at St. Luke's Anglican Church in London on October 5, 1977:

> I was not sure why I was picked. I assumed there were just too many contenders on the ground for any one of them to be chosen above the others, so somebody from "outside," as it were, might ease the situation. Ease it for those I'm thinking of as being on the "inside"—people like Ian Hamilton, Al Alvarez, Grey Gowrie, [Jonathan] Raban himself. I did know, however, about the two widows being at the New York service. . . . But I had no special insight or information at the time, just the high octane literary gossip that surrounded the whole coterie.

Blackwood and Elizabeth Hardwick chose Heaney because he was the best poet and the best speaker. He also quoted Blackwood's witty remark about all the literary celebrities who turned up in the church: "'My dear, you could tour it,' Caroline said, the one jag I remember."

With an oratorical grandeur worthy of his subject, Heaney placed Lowell in the modern poetic tradition. He spoke of Lowell's lineal descent from Frost, Pound, Eliot, Ransom and Tate; and of the oracular and penitential voice whose purpose was redemptive. He wove personal memories with poetic praise, described their recent meeting and his response to Lowell's death, and reflected on his themes of memory, history, love and renewal. He ended with Lowell's theme of guilt and with a surprising revelation about the origin, in the editors of Shakespeare's First Folio in 1623, of his famous line:

> This man whom we so gratefully praise thirsted for accusation. That line in the concluding sonnet of *The Dolphin* which says, "My eyes have seen what my hand did" branded itself upon me when I read it. . . .
> The man who spoke of "the brute push of composition," was ruefully aware that that push could bruise others, others who were perhaps even the very nurturers of his poetic gift and confidence. When I praised the

line to him, he gracefully diverted the credit for it from himself and said, "Well, it's something like what Heminges and Condell said about Shakespeare ["His mind and hand went together"], isn't it?"

As Eliot asked about guilt and redemption in "Gerontion," "After such knowledge, what forgiveness?"

In the mid-1970s, when Lowell and Blackwood got bored in Castletown, her huge and isolated Irish house, they'd visit Heaney in Dublin for a taste of normal life, copious drink and stimulating talk. Heaney recalled, "Their life was pretty turbulent, wherever they were, and they probably regarded Marie and me as freakishly domesticated. . . . Six days before he died, Lowell and his wife Caroline had spent a happy, bantering evening with us in Dublin. I felt that something in our friendship had been fulfilled and looked forward to many more of those creative, sportive encounters, [to] his wise and wicked talk, his obsessive love and diagnosis of writing and writers, the whole ursine force of his presence." But tragedy suddenly struck and the poets had no future together. Heaney sensed "with the aid of gossip then going the rounds, that the relationship with Caroline was about to end. . . . He seemed just that bit flaccid, but only in the body, and I certainly had no sense that he was near the end. . . . 'Will I be seeing you soon again?' I asked and he replied, with that high neigh that sometimes came into his voice, and one of his lightning-flicker looks over the glasses, 'I don't think so'"—the exit line of an actor leaving the stage.

In "Lowell's Command" Heaney wrote that in "Ulysses and Circe" the hero is "a kind of correlative for the poet caught between his marriages and his manias." Lowell is the wily and wandering Ulysses, torn between Blackwood, the alluring and seductive Circe, and Hardwick, the faithful wife Penelope. On the lofty occasion of his Memorial Address, Heaney confined himself to Lowell's calling and conduct as a poet. He didn't mention Lowell's notorious madness or marriages, two vital sources of his poetry, though his manic episodes were the most fierce and fascinating aspects of their brief but intense friendship.

Paul Mariani quoted Heaney's vivid recollection of Lowell's weird behavior. After Lowell had evaded his nurse's scrutiny and they swigged some perfumed alcoholic substitute, they sped off to an uncertain destination, where the passive victim was manhandled by a couple of spooky frauds:

I went with him in January 1976 to two acupuncturists in Harley Street. He was at that time confined in a small private hospital where I had called to see him earlier in the afternoon and had been given a restorative nip from his Imperial After Shave bottle, which he had assured me contained Benedictine. Then, almost it would seem to atone, he carried me away in a taxi, with his ever present male nurse. And the next thing we had penetrated to the inner sanctum of two friendly and slightly quackish acupuncturists, stealthy, stooped and vaguely insinuating elders from the city of Leeds. They called him Professor. They spoke calmingly to him and he became calm. He answered their questions about what they called his tension with an unexpected childlike candor. He allowed them to palp along the line of his neck and over the temples and down the back of his skull. He took off his shirt. He bowed a little and accepted the needles, one by one, in a delicate gleaming line, from the point of his shoulder to the back of his ear.

Heaney thought Lowell resembled Gulliver captured and confined in Lilliput: "Disabled, pinned down, yet essentially magnificent. An emblem of his afflicted life, his great native strength and his sorrowful, invigilated helplessness, Robert not himself, then Robert himself again." In this brilliant passage, Heaney used sacred diction—Benedictine, atone, sanctum, temples, pinned down, bowed and accepted the needles—to describe his friend's symbolic Calvary.

Most spectacular of all Lowell's manic behavior was his breakout from Greenways, a private clinic in London, in the summer of 1970. He was supposed to present Heaney with the Duff Cooper Prize. Despite his illness and contrary to all expectations, Lowell managed to find his way to the proper place and fulfill his obligation to a friend and fellow poet. Heaney recalled the bizarre aspects of the chaotic scene:

He had agreed to do the presentation, but when the time came he was in one of his "high" periods and confined to a nursing home. Then—on the afternoon of the day in question—he disappeared, much to the distress of his wife and friends, who eventually found him in the room in London University where the award ceremony was to take place. It was a sad, mad event. Lowell going about with a jacket over his pyjama tops; Diana Cooper [Duff Cooper's widow] with a Chihuahua on her arm, telling him at some point that the prize was to be presented by some mad American; Lowell, wild-eyed and nodding, "I know, I know!"

Seamus Deane, Heaney's close friend since prep school and university and the less famous Seamus, observed that Heaney greatly admired Lowell's boldness and daring in both life and art, qualities which he timorously and conspicuously lacked:

Heaney revered Lowell's patrician authority, his Daedalus-Icarus combination of the classical and the Romantic, repeatedly driving itself to the point of breakdown. I guess Heaney showed too much respect for people who took risks, because he disliked in himself a characteristic that he felt was a failure. He was, indeed, as cautious as a cat, and instinctively played safe, was nice to everyone, entertained . . . multitudes of people at his [Dublin] home, among whom the percentage of hangers-on must have been considerable. But, as usual, Heaney was also fomenting a little rebellion in his more recondite provinces of feeling. Heaney, the man who writes poems, can sometimes rail at Heaney the Poet, the public persona. The authority of reputation is not identical with the authority of the writer's voice; it may undermine it. What Heaney observed and admired in Lowell was his way of dealing with this conflict. (New Yorker, March 20, 2000)

Heaney's first poem about Lowell, "Pit Stop at Castletown," used the feudal word "demesne" to describe Blackwood's grand house. He mentions Lowell's "high neigh," and portrayed in rough rhymes a moment of comradely intimacy and revelation:

Robert Lowell's incomparable high
What? Pitched voice? Destiny? Mania and style?
Under midnight beeches billowing darkly
We made our pit stop about half a mile

From the demesne gates, pissing like men
Together and apart against the wall. . . .
He intimated he'd probably not be
Returning to Caroline. (*Agni*, April 2003)

Heaney compared Lowell's poems to Marlowe's mighty line and, quoting "like
ghosts from an enchanter fleeing" from "Ode to the West Wind," to Shelley's
political idealism. With his stormy marriage ended, Lowell planned to return
to his second wife, Elizabeth Hardwick, in New York. Heaney said that after
his Memorial Address, Hardwick's close friend Mary McCarthy "Took my rhet-
oric and wrung its neck: 'The biggest cover-up since Watergate.'" But on that
solemn occasion it would have been inappropriate to mention Lowell's notoriously callous behavior to Hardwick—to whom he repentantly returned in a
Manhattan taxicab, dead-on-arrival from a heart attack. Heaney's poem also
gives mythic significance to another meaningful micturition. In *Ulysses* James
Joyce wittily connects Tom Moore's poem "The Meeting of the Waters" to a uri-
nal. In the "Ithaca" chapter the two heroes also unite, together and apart: "first
Stephen, then Bloom, in penumbra urinated, their sides contiguous." Then
Bloom returns to his wife as Lowell planned to do.

Heaney's "Elegy" for Lowell in *Field Work* (1979), written in fourteen short
uneven quatrains, was dominated by nautical imagery. It echoed Lowell's
adoption of Melville's exalted themes and Hopkins' pulsating rhythms in "The
Quaker Graveyard in Nantucket": the dorsal nib, swaying tiller, fear of water, thudding Irish Sea and symbolic dolphin that turn Lowell into a plashing
helmsman, amphibious adventurer and sturdy ship:

Two a.m., seaboard weather.
Not the proud sail of your great verse . . .
No. You were our night ferry
thudding in a big sea,
the whole craft ringing
with an armourer's music
the course set willfully across
the ungovernable and dangerous.

Heaney alluded to the famous guilt-ridden lines in Lowell's *Dolphin*, "Your eyes saw what your hand did," to Lowell's translations of Osip Mandelstam's Russian poems, and to his "heart-harrowing" book about his estranged wife and daughter *For Lizzie and Harriet*. He then quoted Lowell's pervasive fear in "Fall 1961" that nuclear weapons would destroy the world: "*A father's no shield / for his child.*" Though a lapsed Catholic, like Lowell, Heaney ended with his hopeful salutation "I'll pray for you."

Heaney witnessed Lowell's best and worst moments. Branded and blessed, he carried the traditional laurels that Lowell once wore. He too became a great performer, always in demand, and a professor at Harvard, admired by his students, and he surpassed Lowell by winning the Nobel Prize.

17

HEANEY

—— AND ——

JOSEPH BRODSKY

Seamus Heaney first met Joseph Brodsky at the Poetry International Festival in London in June 1972. Heaney recalled, "My first impression of him . . . was of a slight, somewhat nervous fellow about my own age, shooting the half-tentative, half-suspicious glances that any young poet shoots at a big-deal poetry reading." Heaney, who had published three highly praised books of poetry, was fascinated by the unprepossessing Brodsky—short, red-haired, balding and with Russian clothes and a strong Russian accent: "There was something mysterious and enlivening about this fair-faced, trimly built man in a red shirt, born [in 1940] a year later than I but already marked for and propelled into history."

Brodsky had been denounced and imprisoned as a social parasite for declaring himself a poet, and could say with Walt Whitman, "I am the man, I suffered, I was there." Heaney wrote that Brodsky's "arrest and trial by the Soviet authorities in the 1960's and his subsequent banishment to a work camp near Archangel had specifically to do with his embrace of poetic vocation—a socially parasitical vocation according to the prosecution. This had turned his case into something of an international cause célèbre and insured him immediate fame when he arrived in the West." He saw Brodsky as a legendary *poeta non grata*, as a courageous warrior and martyr who'd sacrificed his freedom for his art: "Joseph was a kind of poetry samurai, totally alert, totally trained in his art, a bit of a dazzler and a bit of a danger. We'd heard of his defiance of the Soviets, and regarded these things as the boy-deeds of a poetry hero."

While writing my biography of Robert Frost I asked Brodsky if he'd met the older poet on his visit to Russia in August–September 1962, when Frost had the famously contentious tête-à-tête with Nikita Khrushchev. In a letter of February 11, 1995, Brodsky wrote, with irony and wit, "Alas, I have to inform you that I did not meet Frost on his visit to Russia. At the time of his sojourn in my home town [Leningrad] I was behind bars." Brodsky's hero Osip Mandelstam, who died in 1938 from cold and hunger in the Gulag, remarked that "poetry is respected only in Russia—where people are killed for it."

Like a prince who'd inherited a prestigious dynasty, Brodsky had received the laying on of hands from Anna Akhmatova and Mandelstam's widow Nadezhda in Russia, and from Auden in America, and became the filial successor to two great poetic traditions. Heaney noted that "we were all conscious of Brodsky as the man of the moment, ever since he'd landed in Austria as the guest of Auden." Casually describing the violence in Northern Ireland as if it were a party, he speculated "that my Belfast address may have been of [political] interest to him, since the bombing and shooting were by then in full swing."

In his influential Foreword to Brodsky's *Selected Poems* (1973), Auden vaguely but enthusiastically called him a traditionalist, interested "in personal encounters with nature, human artifacts, persons loved or revered, and in reflections upon the human condition, death, and the meaning of existence. . . . I have no hesitation in declaring that, in Russian, Joseph Brodsky must be a poet of the first order."

Though Brodsky was egotistical and pugnacious, Heaney admired his faults and always gave him generous respect and precedence. The two poets had important traits in common. The Irish Catholic and Russian Jew, born a year apart and far from the centers of Anglophone poetry, were both caught up in violent politics. They bonded through their keen interest in Dante and Donne, and both published (with Derek Walcott) their tripartite *Homage to Robert Frost* (1996). Heaney praised Brodsky in interviews and wrote a tribute when he won the Nobel Prize. He patiently tolerated Brodsky's dogmatic and sometimes ignorant assertions as well as his lame English verse, defended his attack on Yevgeny Yevtushenko and expressed sympathy when Brodsky's mother died. He wrote Brodsky's obituary, spoke at his memorial service, visited his old flat in Petersburg and composed two poems about him. Though Heaney translated Sophocles, Virgil, Dante, Beowulf, Irish poets, the Scottish Robert Henryson, Polish and Czech writers, he never translated Brodsky—who would have insisted on correcting his work. The self-absorbed and self-promoting Brodsky did not write about Heaney. Without an edition of Brodsky's letters and a thorough biography, we see their friendship only from Heaney's worshipful point of view.

Brodsky, the perennial outsider in Russia, was enthusiastically adopted in America. He was translated by distinguished poets like Richard Wilbur and Anthony Hecht, and gave sixty poetry readings during the first eighteen months in his new country. He published his work in the *New York Review of Books*, was chosen as poet laureate of the United States, and won distinguished professorships, a Guggenheim fellowship, membership in the American Academy, the National Book Critics Circle Award for Criticism, honorary doctorates from Oxford and Yale, a MacArthur award and the Nobel Prize—which W. H. Auden, whom Brodsky rightly considered infinitely superior to himself, never received. In short, after his change of empires, he reaped every reward and honor the American artistic and intellectual world could give a poet.

Except for physical beauty and a successful suicide (though he did once cut his wrists), Brodsky had every nonliterary quality that enhanced his reputation. He dropped out of school at fifteen, which allowed his originality to flourish, and gained unusual experience as a geologist in Siberia. His poems were condemned, suppressed and confined to the underground in Russia. He showed courage and a stoical lack of complaint as a Jewish victim of Soviet persecution, became a legend when the transcript of his trial was published in the West, spent time in psychiatric hospitals and prisons, and was sent into harsh exile in the Arctic Circle. He derived tragic authority from several heart attacks, heart operations and the threat of an early death. He lived modestly, generously helped Russian exiles, was an overwhelming personality, charismatic in speech and in the strongly accented, bardic chanting of his poems. He quickly learned English and published extensively in his new language. Though his involuntary exile was a fortunate escape and his life in America infinitely better than in Russia, he'd lost his country, his language, his parents, his lovers and his children.

Like most people, Heaney was deeply impressed by Brodsky's electrifying character and conversation, by his fiery performance and teaching. He was a brilliant speaker who made everyone race to keep up with his verbal pyrotechnics. Heaney said Brodsky was "like a star, an exhilaration, a transformer. The pace quickened when he entered a company, the bar was raised, the daring increased, the feats became more spectacular. . . . It was as if some underground cable had started to carry the full voltage and the whole grid was sizzling. . . . His intellectual readiness was almost feral. Conversation attained immediate vertical takeoff and no deceleration was possible. . . . Words were a kind of high octane for him, and he loved to be propelled by them wherever they took him."

But there was also a penalty clause to Brodsky's unrepentant *diktats*. He claimed to know more about English poetry than the best poets writing in English. He'd been oppressed and felt the urge to dominate. "Joseph liked to lay down the law; certainly," Heaney allowed. "Even among friends, he would act the boss poet; but if you had his respect, he would take what you had to give. He couldn't help speaking ex cathedra [or ex synagoga], trampolining off his own brilliance." Brodsky also had the stubborn and exasperating blind spot about Heaney's favorite poet: "He told me once that Yeats' rhymes left something to be desired and at that stage I felt he was too far gone in certitude to be educable."

Heaney took the title of Albert Lord's influential book *The Singer of Tales* (1960), about the Balkan bards who chant their poetry, for his tribute after Brodsky won the Nobel Prize. He compared his performance to the music of a Russian balalaika: "He brought a new vitality and seriousness to the business of poetry readings. . . . It was as if a hard-grained, thick-stringed and deeply tuned instrument were given release. There was lament and tension, turbulence and coherence. I have never been in the presence of a reader who was so manifestly all poet at the moment of reading."

Brodsky was an inspiring teacher at the University of Michigan and Mount Holyoke College, and Heaney gave a positive spin to his dogmatic declarations: "Nobody enjoyed laying down the law more than he, with the result that his fame as a teacher began to spread and certain aspects of his practice came to be imitated. In particular, his insistence that students learn and recite several poems by heart had considerable influence in creative writing schools all over the United States, and his advocacy of traditional form, his concentration on matters of meter and rhyme, and his high rating of nonmodernist poets like Robert Frost and Thomas Hardy also had the general effect of reawakening an older poetic memory." Unfortunately, Brodsky's salutary advice did not take hold, and the endlessly proliferating creative writing courses encouraged self-indulgent free verse, without technical skill, that was little more than "sensitive" prose in broken lines. Heaney could have added that Brodsky, who adored Czeslaw Milosz, aroused Anglophone interest in East European writers, who were enthusiastically promoted by Ted Hughes and Philip Roth.

In June 1987, a few months before Brodsky won the Nobel Prize, he got into a fierce public controversy with Yevgeny Yevtushenko, the older Soviet poet and cultural ambassador. Loyally defending Brodsky, Heaney—who would never have attacked a fellow poet—declared: "He was scornful, but didn't go on about it. His actions spoke louder than his words. He resigned from the American Academy of Arts and Letters when Yevtushenko was elected a member. When he talked about them, it was like Virgil talking to Dante about the damned in their circles: he instructed you to observe and pass on quickly." In fact, in the *New York Times* of June 20, Brodsky did go on about it and made a loud, rather brutal assault: "I cannot in good conscience sustain membership in an organization which has thus so fully compromised its integrity. . . . Yevtushenko is a high member of his country's establishment, and he lies terribly about the United States to his Russian readers. . . . He throws stones only in directions that are officially sanctioned and approved. To have him as an honorary member of the American academy, as though he represents all Russian poets, seems to me unseemly and scandalous." Though Yevtushenko was well known in Western literary circles for his poems exploring Soviet anti-Semitism and Stalinist terror, Brodsky claimed that "he adopted both positions only when it was safe to do so."

As usual, Brodsky provided no evidence for his attack and for challenging the Academy's right to elect its own members. Since Brodsky reigned in America, Yevtushenko did not "represent *all* Russian poets," and his poems condemning anti-Semitism and Stalinist terror were certainly not "officially sanctioned and approved." Though Brodsky, according to Heaney, assumed a lofty Virgilian stance, his motives as well as his arguments were dubious. Though pro-Soviet, rather than anti-Soviet like Brodsky, Yevtushenko was a formidable rival. The tall, handsome Siberian was a flamboyant, theatrical and popular performer. The author of "Babi Yar" (1961), about the massacre of Jews in the Nazi-occupied Ukraine, had an international reputation. The two temperamental Russians had had bitter personal, poetical and political quarrels, and Brodsky had called him a self-promoter, a lackey and a shit. Brodsky had been expelled from Russia; Yevtushenko was admired in both Russia and

America. Jealous as well as disdainful, Brodsky wanted to be the only honorable and superior Russian poet, and leading candidate for the Nobel that year. As Alexander Pope said of Joseph Addison, Brodsky bore "like the Turk, no rival near the throne."

By contrast to this vitriol, Heaney described congenial, stimulating evenings in Boston with Brodsky and Derek Walcott, when the three poets were teaching in Massachusetts and had not yet won what Hemingway called "the Swedish thing": "It was like being back in your first clique as a young poet with all your original greed for the goods and gossip of poetry instantly refreshed. Poems being quoted and poets being praised or faulted, extravagantly; anecdotes exchanged; jokes told; but underneath all the banter and hilarity there was a prospector's appetite in each of us for the next poem we ourselves might write. We were high on each other's company and that kept the critical standard-setter alive and well in each of us."

Heaney and Brodsky met again in Ireland early in 1988, soon after Brodsky had secured the glittering prize in Stockholm. He was then less combative and more confidential about his permanently distant family. Heaney remarked that "the mouth of the River Liffey reminded Joseph a lot of the quays of St. Petersburg, and he spoke more intimately than he'd done before about his family and his first life in Russia. I don't mean he shared secrets, just that his tenderness and loss were more evident, readier to reveal themselves."

A few years earlier, in June 1983, Heaney had sent Brodsky a condolence letter on the death of his mother, whom he'd not been allowed to see when she was moribund: "A pang of unexpected shock occurred. I had never taken into account that your parents were still behind you all that time. Stupidly I had assumed that your spiritual state . . . of solitude and beyond-ness was some sort of absolute condition."

Heaney had seen Robert Lowell only six days before his death in September 1977, and met Brodsky for the last time in New York in January 1996, three weeks before he died. (Was he getting superstitious?) Though well aware of his poetic genius, Brodsky refused to take proper care of himself. Heaney recalled that "dear, undaunted and endangered Joseph" was in terrible shape and destined for an early grave: "He looked awful, stooped, pale, out of breath, still smoking, and we knew, of course, that his heart condition was very bad: he couldn't settle at the [dinner] table, just kept coming in and out between cigarettes. . . . Even though I knew he was living under a threat, even though I knew he'd had several bypass operations and had seen with my own eyes the state he was in, something in me just refused to consider his death an imminent possibility." He just didn't want to lose his precious friend.

Heaney's obituary of Brodsky appeared in the *New York Times* (March 3, 1996). He recalled Brodsky's "igneous and impetuous sensibility," his rare mixture of brilliance and sweetness. Remembering his "shared secrets" in Ireland, Heaney said their friendship was like meeting a Conradian "secret sharer." He also observed that since Brodsky, despite his weak heart, always seemed indestructible, "it was difficult for friends to admit that he was in danger. The intensity and boldness of his genius plus the sheer exhilaration of being in his company kept you from thinking about the threat to his health. . . . Having to speak of him in the past tense feels like an affront to grammar itself." Echoing "your gift survived it all" in Auden's elegy on Yeats, Heaney observed with a striking simile, "print is what we have of him now, and he will survive behind its black lines, in the pace of its poetic meter or its prose arguments, like Rilke's panther pacing behind black bars."

The following week Heaney read Brodsky's late poem "Reveille" at the Cathedral of St. John the Divine in New York. At first Brodsky wakes hopefully in a gentle dawn to winged creatures, clouds, sun, sky and oceanic ejaculation:

Birds acquaint themselves with leaves.
Hired hands roll up their sleeves.
In a brick malodorous dorm
boys awake awash in sperm.

The intensely compressed and convoluted poem then turns dark as the poet stoically faces, with scant consolation, the harsh reality of human existence. It ends with four strong monosyllables that echo Robert Frost's "Nothing Gold Can Stay." Brodsky concludes:

putting up with nothing whose
company we cannot lose
hardens rocks and—rather fast—
hearts as well. But rocks will last.

It's unclear why Heaney chose this gnomic poem or whether the audience understood it. As Dennis O'Driscoll observed, Brodsky's English poems "could be linguistically clotted, syntactically confused, totally misjudged, not to mention rhythmically unconvincing." In June 2003, while reading and lecturing in Saint Petersburg, Heaney visited Akhmatova's House on the Fotanka and Brodsky's family apartment—an utterly "solemn, sweet, sorrowful, unforgettable moment."

Heaney wrote two poems about Brodsky. The first, "Lauds and Gauds for a Laureate" on prayers and celebrations, introduced Brodsky's reading at the American Repertory Theater in Cambridge, Massachusetts, on February 15, 1988. Instead of the usual formal and familiar presentation, the poem was like a witty prologue to a play, written with many off-rhymes (hotshots / glasnost) in the balladic style of Robert Burns. The poem mentions Stalin and Orwell's Big Brother, Shakespeare and Walcott, and includes Heaney's favorite image of "The digger working against time."

Heaney said that the poem originated in Brodsky's talk "about how he had once defied the labour-camp authorities in Siberia [i.e., the Arctic Circle] by refusing to stop when they deemed one of his punishments had gone on long enough. He'd been given a task of splitting logs, but when they indicated that he'd done his bit, Joseph refused to lay down the axe, and went on and on, splitting and splitting, furious at the absurdity, exposing it by his excessiveness. In my mind, that axe got mixed up with Kafka's remark that 'a book must be the axe for the frozen sea inside us.'" Heaney later explained that Brodsky's "muse was essentially a lie-detector."

> Yet Joseph's tool is not the spade.
> The axe with ice upon its blade
> Is more his thing.
> It splits the frozen sea inside
> And then, You lied! You lied! You lied!
> The echoes ring.

Heaney also recalls their memorable meeting in Dublin:

> In Ireland, on a harbour wall,
> Among the shipping lanes and all

Those gulls and gannets,
Joseph, I won't forget the day
We spent last year in Dublin Bay
Discussing sonnets.

The last stanza directly addresses the eager audience as Brodsky magically appears on stage to release the genie from the bottle of his Slavic art:

So let your expectations tremble
Now these real presences assemble
And lights are lowered,
As they unearth the jars and click
The locks wide open on the Slavíc
Poet's word-hoard.

Heaney's elegy on Brodsky, "Audenesque" (2001), is a brilliant and witty tour de force that uses the seven-syllable rhymed couplets of the third part of Auden's "In Memory of W. B. Yeats":

Earth, receive an honoured guest:
William Yeats is laid to rest:
Let the Irish vessel lie
Emptied of its poetry.

Yeats and Brodsky both died on January 28: Yeats in 1939, Brodsky at the age of fifty-five in 1996. Adapting some of Auden's memorable phrases, Heaney captures Brodsky's lively and lovable personality. He repeats the ice-axe-frozen images from "Lauds and Gauds" and mentions Archangel, where Brodsky did forced labor. As in Auden's poem, the icy weather matches the condition of the dead poet:

Dublin airport locked in frost,
Rigor mortis in your breast. . . .
Ice of Archangelic strength,
Ice of this hard two-faced month,

Ice like Dante's in deep hell
Makes your heart a frozen well.

Heaney then revives Brodsky through memories of their friendship when
they gave readings in Amherst. Brodsky would have liked the rough rhyme of
the first couplet:

Pepper vodka you produced
Once in western Massachusetts
With the reading due to start
Warmed my spirits and my heart.

Liberated from the oppression of Russia, where he'd been a political prisoner, Brodsky rejoiced in

Politically incorrect
Jokes involving sex and sect,
Everything against the grain,
Drinking, smoking like a train.

Repeating "train" in the next line, Heaney also recalls that they reversed the
direction of Lenin's return to the Finland Station in Petrograd:

In a train in Finland we
Talked last summer happily,
Swapping manuscripts and quips,
Both of us like cracking whips.

In a gentle rebuke, Heaney noted that in the self-indulgent peculiarities of
Brodsky's English verse "the English ear comes up against a phonetic element
that is both animated and skewed . . . a certain metrical oddity, especially in
the matter of enjambment":

Jammed enjambments piling up
As you went above the top,

Nose in air, foot to the floor,
Revving English like a car.

Heaney saw that the artful and idealistic Brodsky commanded a formidable intelligence, erudition and intuition. He displayed an absolute belief in the supreme value of great art and showed precisely "what makes the whole enterprise of poetry so valuable for our species."

18

DIANE ARBUS

—— AND ——

SYLVIA PLATH

I

Sylvia Plath is the Diane Arbus of poetry, the verbal equivalent of her visual art. Since Arbus and Plath had strikingly similar lives, it's surprising that they never mentioned each other and that their biographers have not compared them. They were self-destructive sexual adventurers, angry and rebellious, driven and ambitious. Both suffered extreme depression, had nervous breakdowns and committed suicide. But they used their mania to deepen their awareness and inspire their art, and created photographs and poetry to impose order on their chaotic lives. They shared an ability to combine the ordinary with the grotesque and monstrous, and expressed anguished feelings with macabre humor. Arbus was consciously and deliberately bohemian, Plath outwardly conventional yet inwardly raging. Both explored the dark side of human existence and revealed their own torments.

Arbus (1923–1971) and Plath (1932–1963) were contemporaries for thirty years. Arbus was Jewish; Plath imaginatively identified with the Jewish holocaust victims. Dorothea Krook, Plath's Jewish tutor at Newnham College, Cambridge, noted her unusually "passionate feeling for Jews and her sense of belonging with them." Both women rejected their parents' values and wanted to obliterate the traits they had inherited. Arbus' family owned Russeks department store in Manhattan, lived on Park Avenue and had seven servants. But she earned little as a photographer, was always short of funds and descended from an upper- to a lower-class life. She either wouldn't ask her father for cash or he wouldn't give her any. He spent lavishly and left little money in his will.

Plath's father was a scientist who died when she was nine and left her family in straitened circumstances. But like Arbus, she had the requisite lessons in ballet, piano and painting. Supported by scholarships and her patron at Smith College and Cambridge University, Plath clung to the middle class and remained angry at her father for abandoning her in death. Their mothers were problematic in different ways: Arbus' mother was self-absorbed, hysterical and depressed, Plath's was ghoulish, domineering and possessive.

Reading about Arbus in Arthur Lubow's excellent biography (2016) seems like reading about Plath. And Robert Lowell's description of Plath applies equally to Arbus: "She was willowy, long-waisted, sharp-elbowed, nervous, giggly, gracious—a brilliant tense presence embarrassed by restraint." In the conformist 1950s the two women wore pageboy hairstyles and dresses with Peter Pan collars. From high-school days to the end of their lives they were beautifully turned out when working well, dirty and disheveled when depressed. They aspired, as Arbus ironically said of herself, "to be competent, cheerful, serene and virtuous," but lacked the last three qualities. For a time both were teachers: Arbus at the Parsons School of Design in New York, Plath at Smith College in Massachusetts. Both had broken marriages and two children, and were torn between domestic duties and professional life.

Extremely competitive, ambitious and often unpleasant, they rebelled early on against their traditional backgrounds. Arbus' photos of glamorous models and Plath's formulaic stories both appeared in the young women's magazine *Seventeen*. In her novel *The Bell Jar* (1963) Plath describes the heroine posing for a fashion photograph and ruining it by bursting into tears. Her face, as if beaten, "looks bruised and puffy and all the wrong colors." After they both had achieved commercial success they realized that they loathed this glossy world. They had to break away from conventional work to discover their individuality and become real artists.

They shared a certain ruthlessness in their dealings with other people and had a savage wit. Arbus was sensitive and responsive to the people she photographed. But she admitted that she would assume a fake and ingratiating persona, lie to and deceive her subjects in order to get them to submit to her demands. Plath, as if talking about Arbus as well as about herself, confessed her own duplicity: "I can lie successfully; I have a direct honest look; I am plausive as the devil with my reasons; my actress-side is sensitive to mood and situation and, without calculation on my part, responds as the occasion demands."

Arbus and Plath had sharp tongues, flaunted their sexual power and mocked the absurdities of their friends. Arbus observed, "Sometimes I feel sorry for men. Their big ideas, and their trousers ready to burst!" She had done extensive fieldwork and was seriously interested in compiling "an atlas of penises; she marveled at the inexhaustible variations in them." In one of the funniest scenes in Plath's *The Bell Jar* the clean-cut, preppy boyfriend of the autobiographical heroine, Esther Greenwood, is proud of his penis and thinks his erection would excite her. He strips naked but provokes the wrong response. She recalls, "he just stood there in front of me and I kept staring at him. The only thing I could think of was turkey neck and turkey gizzards and I felt very depressed." In this detumescent episode his cock and balls resemble a fowl's stretched neck and sack of innards. She's repelled by them—and by him.

Like Arbus, addicted to the thrill of danger, Plath took risks. She tried daredevil skiing, galloping on horseback and crashing cars. Twice she attempted suicide. Arbus described her own sense of being driven by "an almost pathological need to have it all. . . . I get hysterical, fierce, like I'll try anything to get my way." Desperate to be famous, Plath was also aggressive and willing to do whatever was necessary for success.

Arbus photographed the corpses of her grandmother and her father, visited the morgue and pinned to her walls "gruesome photographs of body parts and deformities." Plath also wanted to confront ugliness and mortality. A morbid passage in *The Bell Jar* describes the image of Esther's face after she had attempted suicide in the rocky crawl space under her house: "You couldn't tell whether the person in the picture was a man or a woman, because their hair was shaved off and sprouted in bristly chicken-feather tufts all over their head. One side of the person's face was purple, and bulged out in a shapeless way, shading to green along the edges, and then to a sallow yellow. The person's mouth was pale brown, with a rose-colored sore at either corner." This chromatic picture of herself as a person of indeterminate sex who's referred to in the plural recalls the self-alienation in Arthur Rimbaud's famous declaration, "I is another."

Arbus' life was a series of personal disasters. As a teenager she had married her high-school boyfriend, the photographer Allan Arbus, in 1941. She was devastated when Allan began his six-year affair with the stunning Jewish actress Zohra Lampert and their marriage broke up in 1959. But Diane continued her photographic work with Allan from their separation until his move to Los Angeles to become an actor. They had two children: Doon, born in 1945 and named for a river in Scotland evoked in the poetry of Robert Burns; and Amy, born nine years later in 1954. Arbus' photo of a young girl in her early twenties, *Sitting on her bed with her shirt off, N.Y.C. 1968*, looks remarkably like Doon, who was twenty-three that year. The girl has a huge crown of wild dark hair cascading down to her eyebrows, pointed nose, thin lips, tiny breasts and a grim expression. Doon aroused Arbus' jealousy by working as an assistant for her artistic rival Richard Avedon.

Arbus replaced Allan with a lover, the short, bald, ugly Marvin Israel, who remained married and devoted to his wife. He encouraged and inspired Arbus, but was also an evil genius, a malign influence who had sexual relations with Doon, her daughter and rival. Arbus felt cheated and betrayed by both Allan and Marvin and spoke bitterly about both of them.

Arbus' sexual life was worthy of Casanova and De Sade. She was persistently in search of sex but never satisfied. She had lifelong incestuous relations, from adolescence until just before her death, with her older brother, the poet Howard Nemerov, and treated her deepest and most forbidden emotional connection as if it were a casual affair. She envied her younger sister who'd been raped by a Black man with a knife. As a teenager she posed naked in her bathroom for a voyeur who stared at her from across the narrow courtyard. She slept with any man who ever asked her—and seduced those who didn't ask. She had sex in her hospital room, sex with lesbians, sex in anonymous orgies, tourist sex with a Black waiter in Jamaica and sex with strangers in the back of a Greyhound bus. She even gave a helping hand to men masturbating in sleazy 42nd Street movie houses. She didn't seem to get much pleasure out of all this frantic activity, unromantically described sex as "wet and hairy," and was once infected by hepatitis that made her seriously ill for a year.

Her polymorphously perverse and reckless sexuality, her eagerness to engage in pathological adventures with sick strangers, had complex motives. She wanted to break out of her isolation and make physical contact with other people; confirm, after being jilted by Allan, that she was still desirable; free herself from conventional restrictions; achieve the instant pleasure of a cheap thrill; get hedonistic rewards for her depression; and reach the extremes of experience by trying every possible sexual permutation without considering the consequences. She confessed, "my favorite thing is to go where I've never been."

In 1956 Arbus abandoned her successful fashion photography career, and made a radical change in subjects and style from glamor and beauty to deformity and ugliness. For her (as for the fashion photographer Richard Avedon) beauty was commerce, ugliness was art. Arbus' photos seemed to confirm traditional beliefs about physical appearance. According to Neo-Platonic thought in the Renaissance, the human face reflected the inner soul. A beautiful face revealed a good person, an ugly face betrayed an evil one. Shakespeare's villainous hunchback Richard III bitterly complains that he's been "Cheated of feature by dissembling nature, / Deformed, unfinished, sent before my time / Into this breathing world, scarce made up," and swears to take revenge by acting as evil as he looks.

Our preference for the power of beauty endures and we assume that the portrait painter and photographer will enhance the subject. In Arbus' pictures, however, babies are screaming, children repulsive, young couples grotesque, older people hideous. Her stigmatized victims have everything but holes in their hands. She shot all manner of wretched outcasts: strippers, carnival performers, sword swallowers, tattooed men and dwarves; nudists, homosexuals, lesbians, cross-dressers, female impersonators and the mentally ill. She flayed them into harsh reality and adorned them with weird props, bizarre makeup and grotesque costumes. Her exact delineations of biological disasters, her taxonomy of terror, are forbidden and alluring. Satire, not sympathy, cruelty, not compassion give them a fierce emotional charge.

Arbus' aphoristic and perceptive comments on her work in the *Aperture* volume of 1972 are often quoted but rarely explained. She said, "A photograph is a secret about a secret. The more it tells you, the less you know." The photo was her secret that revealed her subject's secret, and she tried to remain as objective as possible to let the viewers form their own impressions. She also said you had to prepare your face to meet the faces that you meet: "everybody has that thing where they need to look one way but they come out looking another way and that's what people observe. You see someone on the street and essentially what you notice about them is the flaw." Her comment reveals the difference between appearance and reality, between how people want to look and how they actually look when her scalpel eye reveals their fatal flaw. Her brutal, full-frontal close-ups intensify people's physical imperfections and create the opposite impression they hope to make. In Arbus' pictures even people trying to appear normal—the suburban couple sunbathing on their lawn and the older couple smiling and dancing—look alienated and isolated, increase each other's misery and reflect the sick American society of the 1960s.

Staring at Arbus' beguiling nightmares is like handling barbed wire, seeing a car crash or watching an epileptic fit. These imaginative projections of her own tortured self were, as T. S. Eliot wrote, "as if a magic lantern threw the nerves in patterns on a screen." Her subjects craved attention and attention must be paid. She managed to win their trust by seducing them with flattery, but was afraid she'd end up like one of them—or already had.

A close look at eight of her best photos gives some idea of her formidable achievement. Arbus' nudists ignore the admonition of Gulliver in Lilliput and "exposed those parts that nature taught us to conceal." Middle-aged, naked and wearing forced smiles, the husband and wife are seated on cushioned chairs and dressed only in casual footgear. Nude photos hanging on the wall and resting on the blank television between them suggest they live in a self-enclosed world. Fat and flabby, they are nourished by a bulging sandwich just visible on the side table. Unlike the idealized naked bodies of Adam and Eve in Western art, the man's brown, cigar-like cock and the woman's drooping dugs are repulsive.

Arbus made a rare political statement in two photos. The boy wearing a bright straw hat pulled low on his forehead, has a thick nose, thin lips, protruding ears and blank stare. His buttonhole displays a bow-shaped American flag, enlarged in the tall flag that he holds on a tall stick. One pin on his lapel urges the military to lift restraints and "Bomb Hanoi"; the other states, "God Bless America. Support our boys in Vietnam." Ignorant and easily manipulated by patriotic slogans, this mindless youngster advocates the hopeless war. He's either too feeble to serve in the army or, if drafted, destined to be destroyed in the tropical mud. Complementing this photo is another young man with tousled hair, wild staring eyes, gaping mouth, sharp incisors and pitted, freckled face. Also sporting an "I'm Proud" patriotic pin and holding a drooping flag, he seems equally manipulated and mindless, even lobotomized.

The seven-year-old boy clutching a toy hand grenade (and eager to get a real one) has a child's clothing and adult's rage. In the sylvan setting of Central Park with tranquil pedestrians in the misty background, he wears a patterned shirt with a little round collar, short pants with one shoulder strap hanging down, sinking socks and white-laced dark sneakers. His blond head is tilted sideways, his knees are dirty and his grimacing mouth is smeared. He radiates fury while grasping the grenade in one hand and twisting his other hand into an animal's claw. If not confined in a mental asylum, he seems destined to become a bomb-throwing mass murderer. This photo inspired Norman Mailer's remark about how Arbus emphasizes extreme behavior and destroys common perceptions about strange people: "Giving a camera to Diane is like putting a live grenade in the hands of a child."

Arbus observed, "Freaks was a thing I photographed a lot. . . . Most people go through life dreading they'll have a traumatic experience. Freaks were born with their trauma. They've already passed their test in life. They're aristocrats"— a notable non sequitur. These freaks were professionals who exhibited themselves in a circus. The three Russian midgets attempt to look normal with housedresses, aprons and sensible shoes. Their reflections appear in a tall triple-mirror and their room is cluttered with a pussy-cat lamp and other tchotchkes. But the constricted setting only intensifies their squashed bodies, and wide, wrinkled, weird Slavic faces.

The seated Mexican dwarf, sustained by a liquor bottle at his elbow, has a cheap tilted hat and pencil-mustache to camouflage his thick upper lip. Brown-skinned, bare-chested and cut off at the waist, he reveals his stunted arms and stubby fingers, and allows three toes of his hidden leg to creep out from under the covers. His massive head and defiant expression challenge the viewer to deny his right to exist. In *The Bell Jar* Esther, also fascinated by repulsive figures, wittily describes an unfortunate blind date, "some pale, mushroomy fellow with protruding ears or buck teeth or a bad leg. I didn't think I deserved it. After all, I wasn't crippled in any way." She also recalls in a letter a hunchbacked neighbor who was "apparently born without parents of either sex."

Arbus' nine-foot-tall Jewish giant brings Brobdingnag into Lilliput. The blunt-featured giant, wearing huge orthopedic shoes and unsteadily supported by a cane, bends over as his thick curly hair brushes against the low, cracked ceiling. In this distorted perspective either the giant is unable to fit into his parents' house or the midgets cannot fit into his room. Gazing up at him, his shocked progenitors wonder how they managed to create the monster who could suddenly topple over and crush them. Arbus called the giant "tragic with a curiously bitter, somewhat stupid wit." He convincingly claimed she made sexual overtures toward him, but she missed that great opportunity.

Under a dark, cloud-swept sky seven mentally defective mongols (to use the word current in 1970) wear Halloween costumes with masks, painted faces, false noses and inflated bosoms. Clutching hands, they struggle blindly and hopelessly toward an unknown destination. Arbus' photo has a rich genealogy. It was influenced by Pieter Bruegel's *The Blind Leading the Blind* (1568), which portrays a string of six beggar-like men wearing capes and hoods, staring upwards with sightless eyes and stumbling through a bleak landscape. Another source, also called *The Blind Leading the Blind* (1918), was one of the most poignant photos of World War I. This progression of sightless British soldiers blinded by chlorine gas shuffles with bandaged eyes toward the refuge of a field hospital. This war photo probably inspired the most memorable scene in Ingmar Bergman's *The Seventh Seal* (1957). In this dance of death, seven linked figures in black capes, one of them holding a sharp scythe, are silhouetted on a hill beneath a cloud-filled, doom-laden sky and express the same morbid mood as Arbus' photo.

II

Anne Dick and Robert Lowell formed a personal link between Arbus and Plath. Lowell's sexual relations with his college girlfriend, the mentally unstable debutante Anne Dick, provoked a violent quarrel in which he punched and knocked down his father. Anne, a close friend of Arbus, later married Alex Eliot, and Arbus was godmother to their daughter May. But in 1949, when Arbus had a sexual encounter with the persistent Alex, Anne felt betrayed and broke off their friendship. (After attempting suicide, Anne finally killed herself in 1981.) In 1959, when Path had a job typing psychiatric records at Massachusetts General Hospital, she was seeing her own psychiatrist and auditing Lowell's poetry course at Boston University. Connecting Plath's poetic powers to her mental illness, Lowell told Elizabeth Bishop, "whatever wrecked her life somehow gave an edge, freedom and even control, to her poetry."

Sexually sophisticated, voracious and domineering, Sylvia Plath claimed her vagina was an organ of perception. My friend Peter Davison, her sometime lover, told me that she became very angry and critical if she did not achieve orgasm. Plath began her sex life with a number of clean-cut, blond-beast Yalies, and graduated to the sinister Richard Sassoon and the crazy rapist Edwin Akutowicz. Sassoon was born in Paris and played the French card—wine and Rimbaud—for all it was worth and it was worth a lot to Plath. He conned her with phony statements, abandoned her in Paris and jilted the pretty girl who'd always been pursued. Alluding to Gregor Samsa in Franz Kafka's "The Metamorphosis," she told her college roommate that when Sassoon "holds me in his arms, I feel like Mother Earth with a small brown bug crawling on me." Her roommate added that Plath (like Arbus) needed to feel physically desirable at all times and "could not resist exploring the bizarre or ugly, even when it frightened and sickened her."

Plath liked to have simultaneously competing lovers. She was excited by dangerous sex, but felt more pain than pleasure. As Oscar Wilde remarked of illicit homosexuality in De Profundis, "it was like feasting with panthers, the danger was half the excitement." Plath, who needed some kind of punishment to assuage her guilt for hating her parents, had a morbid taste for the extremes of experience. Betrayal, cruelty, mutilation, madness, rape, attempted suicide and the threat of death pervade her life and work.

While still an undergraduate at Smith, Plath attended summer school at Harvard and met Edwin Akutowicz, a brilliant mathematics professor at MIT. Tall, myopic, emaciated, balding and repellently ugly (like Marvin Israel), he suited her perverse needs. He raped her and she had to rush to the emergency room in a spurt of blood, an episode she used in The Bell Jar. Instead of feeling violated and outraged, she was proud that she had abandoned her puritanical inhibitions and went on a picnic with him the next day.

As a graduate student at Cambridge, Plath seemed to have found the perfect husband in the handsome, virile and gifted English poet Ted Hughes. Though they inspired and sustained each other's work, their idealistic love contained the seeds of destruction. Despite Plath's beauty and brilliance, many people found her personally unappealing and were even repelled by her Arbus-like qualities: her quest for perfection, unrelenting egoism and naked ambition combined with the horrors and self-pity in her work. A fellow student recalled, "she had a fierce competitive edge that made one rather afraid of her." Hughes confirmed that "people who met her were alarmed or exhilarated by the intensity of her spirits. . . . Once she had set her mind to it, nothing was too much trouble for her." She did not want to forget her traumas, the rich mine of her poetry, and repeatedly hurt herself so she'd always remember them. Fascinated by her own suffering, she forced readers to see her work as a reflection of their own misery.

Both Arbus and Plath adored their husbands, who were talented artists and worked with them. Punning on his name, Plath recorded that Hughes "even fills somehow that *huge*, sad hole I felt in having no father." But she was always insecure and intensely suspicious, flew into jealous rages and constantly needed reassurance. Arbus slept with women and men when she was married. Plath always remained faithful to Hughes, even when he left her for his Jewish lover, Assia Wevill. She turned Plath into an innocent victim who could no longer identify with Jews. (In 1969, after Hughes left her, Assia killed her child by Hughes and herself.)

Hughes knew that Plath was mentally unstable and suicidal, but was remarkably insensitive—or indifferent—to her precarious emotional state. Even before her marriage she recognized Hughes' ironclad egoism and accurately prophesized that she would love not wisely but too well: "he has never thought about anything or anyone except himself and his will . . . and has done a kind of uncaring rip through every woman he's ever met." Plath had two children with Hughes. Frieda was not yet three at the time of Plath's death, Nicholas was just one year old. Frieda became a poet and writer of children's books. Nicholas, a fish-biologist who retreated to Fairbanks, Alaska, became deeply depressed and hanged himself there in 2009 at the age of forty-seven. The suicides of Arbus and Plath punished their husbands for betraying them and left them with an intolerable burden of guilt.

The pictorial and literary influences on Arbus and Plath reveal their similar intellectual background. We have seen that Bruegel's *The Blind Leading the Blind* had a powerful impact on Arbus' photo of the stumbling mentally defective people. In Bruegel's *Triumph of Death* (1562) two doomed lovers, unaware of the devastating army of death and the menacing skeleton hovering above them, inspired Plath's equally morbid "Two Views of a Cadaver Room":

> In Bruegel's panorama of smoke and slaughter
> Two people only are blind to the carrion army. . . .
> Both of them deaf to the fiddle in the hands
> Of the death's-head shadowing their song.
> These Flemish lovers flourish; not for long.

The German Expressionist painters used the same disfigured subjects and threatening tone as Arbus and Plath. Egon Schiele's tormented vision of life, depiction of the body in agony and emphasis on human misery give the viewer what Immanuel Kant called the "negative pleasure" of vicarious suffering. Otto Dix painted the mutilated and patched-up faces of German soldiers wounded in World War I. Like Schiele and Dix, George Grosz was satiric and angry, advocated "deep digging behind things" and created art that had "toughness, brutality and a clarity that hurts!" He portrayed a decapitated corpse in *Sex Murderer* (1916), and his *Portrait of Max Hermann-Neisse* (1925) exposed a shriveled, dwarfish creature with claw-like hands and gigantic bald head sunk into his narrow chest.

Kafka was another soulmate and powerful literary influence on Arbus and Plath. He exclaimed, lamenting his psychological pain, "I consist of nothing but spikes that go into me," compared his words to "raw meat cut from my body," felt his life of anguish and alienation was a series of unfinished suicides. Kafka suffered for the higher purpose of art, which he called "the axe that shatters the frozen sea within us." He said he "knew how to bear pain and come out with the truth because he stayed in close touch with his innermost self." On his deathbed he told his doctor, with absurd black humor: "Kill me, or else you are a murderer!"

Both Arbus and Plath were attracted to Kafka's "In the Penal Colony," which describes the spiky needles of a torture machine that engraves the crime on the flesh of a condemned prisoner. In "A Hunger Artist" a well-fed crowd watches the spectacle of an anorexic performer and then ignores this sacrificial artist who starves himself to death. Similarly, in Plath's "Lady Lazarus" the parasitic spectators observe the officials uncover her mummified body: The peanut-crunching crowd

Shoves in to see
Them unwrap me hand and foot—
The big strip tease.

In this poem Plath recounts her suicide attempts and tells what it was like to come back from her close calls with death. She's thrilled by approaching the edge of extinction and drawing back just in time. For Plath life itself is a kind of death and she returns from death to try to get dead once again. "Lady Lazarus" expresses Plath's hatred of all her enemies: her oppressive parents, doctors, husband, Ted's lover and, most of all, herself. In our time the disturbing display closest to Arbus and Plath was the Chinese *Bodies* exhibition of 2005. The flayed, preserved and anatomically revealing cadavers once belonged to tortured and murdered Chinese political prisoners.

Plath's poems in *Ariel* (1965), like Arbus' photos, pick open the scar of her wound instead of hiding or healing it, and her portrayal of extreme emotional states sucks us into the vortex of her morbid world. "Cut," a study in self-mutilation, suggests the tragic aspect of a kitchen accident:

What a thrill—
My thumb instead of an onion.
The top quite gone
Except for a sort of hinge
Of skin.

Both victim and executioner, she's intensely personal yet surprisingly dissociated from herself, and resembles Dostoyevsky's Underground Man who doesn't care about his pain and is even glad that his liver hurts.

Hospitals to Plath were like daffodils to Wordsworth. "Death & Co." recalls her miscarriage in February 1961. The morbid messenger "tells me how badly I photograph" when she's depressed and won't pose properly or reveal herself:

He tells me how sweet
The babies look in their hospital
Icebox.

Each baby has two little feet sticking out of their classical toga-shrouds. These miniature corpses recall Esther Greenwood examining in a hospital a display of miscarried fetuses, which she degrades to amphibians and calls babies, as if they were still alive: "glass bottles full of babies that had died before they were born. The baby in the first bottle had a large white head bent over a tiny curled-up body the size of a frog."

In *The Bell Jar* Esther "had a great yearning, lately, to pay my father back for all the years of neglect, and start tending his grave." She means, with deliberate ambiguity, that she will either repay him for neglecting his grave or take revenge on him for neglecting her. When Plath actually visited his grave in a Boston cemetery, she had a necrophiliac desire to dig him up and examine the decomposed remains of his body. "Daddy," her most savage poem, portrays her German father as a Nazi and herself as his Jewish victim. She kills Otto Plath in her poem for killing himself in life. Both her father and husband abandoned her; and the poem twists suddenly at the end to attack the vampiric father of her children, who ruined her life and eventually drove her to suicide:

There's a stake in your fat black heart
And the villagers never liked you.
They are dancing and stamping on you.
They always *knew* it was you.
Daddy, daddy, you bastard, I'm through.

In the last line "Daddy" also refers to the treacherous "Teddy."

Plath published *The Bell Jar* under the pseudonym of Victoria Lucas in January 1963, four weeks before her suicide, and the novel received only lukewarm praise. The surname of the heroine, Greenwood, is the English translation of Grunewald, the maiden name of her maternal grandmother. In this novel Plath rivals Arbus in gruesome scenes and gallows humor. Writing from the eye of a tornado and with a voice sounding from her bones, she looks hard at a series of disasters: poisoning and puking, pickled fetuses, carved cadavers, painful defloration and vaginal hemorrhage as well as depression, attempted suicide, shock treatments, lobotomy, insane asylums and hanging. To alleviate the agony, Plath combines sardonic comedy with caustic wit.

The Bell Jar portrays the rebellious life of a conventional young woman. Defying the norms of reticence and reserve, she attacks the counterfeit lives of the Eisenhower 1950s. She even describes, with her favorite fetus image, Richard Avedon's portrait of the seventy-four-year-old former president, "bald and blank as the face of a fetus in a bottle." Like Arbus, Plath is paradoxically engaging and offensive, charming and cruel, sensitive and masochistic. Her vitriolic fury, as gentle as a razor blade, is her weapon against the demons of sex and death.

Arbus attacked her parents indirectly with satiric portraits of rich New York Jews; Plath practiced the assault direct. She writes, "My German-speaking father, dead since I was nine, came from some manic-depressive hamlet in the black heart of Prussia. . . . Each time I picked up a German dictionary or a German book, the very sight of those dense, black, barbed-wire letters made my mind shut." In fact, Otto Plath came from Pomerania, and she was eight when the scientist who taught at Boston University refused to recognize his diabetes, had his leg amputated and died prematurely at fifty-five. Plath did not struggle through works in thick Gothic type, which were not published in Germany after 1941, but read much clearer modern print.

Her mother, Aurelia, accompanied Plath on her honeymoon, witnessed the breakup of her marriage and urged her to get divorced when Plath really wanted a reconciliation with Hughes. Only after Plath had destroyed the part of her mother in herself, exhausted her feelings of gratitude, and rejected the maternal concepts of work, love, marriage, home and family, could she finally express her hatred of Aurelia in *The Bell Jar*. In the novel Esther expresses her murderous desire to throttle her mother's neck and says that when she was sleeping near her snoring mother, "the piggish noise irritated me, and for a while it seemed to me that the only way to stop it would be to take the column of skin and sinew from which it rose and twist it to silence between my hands." Like Plath, Esther is ecstatic when her psychiatrist gives her permission to hate her mother. Despite this literary catharsis, Plath finally transferred her destructive impulse from her mother onto herself. After Plath's death, Aurelia spent the rest of her life censoring her daughter's *Letters Home* and pretending she was a happy and healthy girl who loved her mom.

Esther attempts to kill herself by slitting her wrists, by hanging, by drowning and by taking an overdose of sleeping pills. She plans to jump from a building, and considers the Japanese method of disembowelment, which Yukio Mishima used to kill himself. After the Japanese samurai cut a circle through their intestines with sharp knives, "their stomach skin would come loose, like a plate, and their insides would fall out, and they would die."

Two scenes—Esther's shock treatment and massive hemorrhage—come closest to the mood of Arbus' photos. In the novel electroconvulsive therapy, which electrically induces seizures and is supposed to alleviate depression, becomes a form of torture and punishment. As with Hemingway at the Mayo Clinic, this treatment intensified Plath's illness, and she feared if she went mad that she would have to endure the shocks all over again. Esther's shock treatment, the classic account of a helpless victim, recalls the electrocution, mentioned in the first sentence of the book, of the convicted communist spies, Julius and Ethel Rosenberg (though Ethel, like Esther, may actually have been innocent). Esther says that in the hospital, when she's connected to the metal plates, "something bent down and took hold of me and shook me like the end of the world. Whee-ee-ee-ee-ee, it shrilled, through an air crackling with blue light, and with each flash a great jolt drubbed me till I thought my bones would break and sap fly out of me like a split plant. I wondered what terrible thing it was that I had done?" Like Joseph K. in Kafka's *The Trial*, Esther suffers the punishment but doesn't understand the crime.

But Esther's troubles are not over. After being violently deflowered by the brutal Irwin, Esther (like Plath in real life) starts to bleed uncontrollably. She feels "a warm liquid seeping out between [her] legs" and her saturated towel starts to drip. As she's driven to the hospital, the warm seepage falls onto her skirt, and she sees "the blood trickling down my legs and oozing, stickily, into each patent leather shoe." Arbus also violated a taboo by discussing her periods at a time when they were unmentionable. She menstruated in a nudist colony with her Tampax string hanging out and (Lubow writes) described "a time she was teaching a class and felt a sudden heavy flow of blood running down her leg." A friend told her she would have been horrified; Arbus was delighted and laughed about her public display of blood.

III

Both Plath and Arbus attempted suicide before their final closure. Though they abandoned all hope of happiness and tried to absorb themselves in work, their existence was doomed. Everything in their lives led up to their creative achievement and everything afterward led to their precipitous death. Suicide, which authenticated their depth and pain, was a great career move.

Plath's realization of what all the treacherous years were leading to and really meant was too tragic to bear. After her shock treatments had failed to minister to a mind diseased, she feared another breakdown, inevitably followed by shock treatments, lobotomy and a straitjacket—permanently locked up with the other crazies. She confessed in a letter, "The only doubt in my mind was the precise time and method of committing suicide. The only alternative I could see was an eternity of hell for the rest of my life in a mental hospital."

Since Plath was explicit about her motives for suicide, her other reason—overwhelming guilt—has scarcely been noticed. She felt guilty about hating her father and her mother; shaming her family after her first suicide attempt; condescending to students less brilliant than herself; being sexually promiscuous; expressing her jealousy of Hughes; failing to cope at the end with freezing weather, small children, physical illness and unbearable depression, without any help from her husband, friends or doctors; and emotionally damaging her children after her death. After preparing bread and milk for her infants, she sealed the room, put her head in the stove and gassed herself, aged thirty, on February 11, 1963.

William Wordsworth observed these emotional heights and depths in "Resolution and Independence":

> But, as it sometimes chanceth, from the might
> Of joy in minds that can no further go,
> As high as we have mounted in delight
> In our dejection do we sink as low.

Arbus described this kind of depression in a letter of 1968, three years before her death: "quite suddenly either through tiredness or a disappointment or something more mysterious the energy vanishes, leaving me harassed, swamped, distraught, frightened by the very things I thought I was so eager for." She felt her life was hanging by a thread and as her depression deepened asked, as Plath had done, "How long should you wait if you can't tolerate being alive?" Again like Plath, Arbus gained few insights from years of analysis, was not given antidepressants and went straight from psychiatrist to suicide. After twice attempting to kill herself, she made sure she would die on July 26, 1971, aged forty-eight, by taking a handful of barbiturates and slashing both wrists with a razor blade.

Arbus' self-proclaimed dissatisfaction with her work does not begin to explain the reasons for her suicide. There were more complex motives. In her childhood her father was absorbed in business, her mother was egoistic and severely depressed. Her husband left her for another woman. Her more serious lovers were married, distant and not fully committed. Marvin Israel remained with his wife and had sexual relations with Doon. Arbus felt betrayed by everyone except her incestuous brother, and continued her lifelong search for sexual compensation.

Plath and Arbus achieved almost mythical status after they killed themselves and were taken up by feminists, who accused their husbands of murdering them. Like the impoverished Rimbaud, Van Gogh and Modigliani, the posthumous reputations of Arbus and Plath were far greater than in their lifetimes. Plath died at the peak of her powers. *The Bell Jar*, and the poems in *Ariel* written in a creative surge two months before her death, are now greatly admired. The first edition of the novel now costs as much as $10,000 and her books sell millions of copies, but she had to go through agony to compose them.

In 1969 Arbus offered a portfolio of her ten best photos in a specially made box for $1,000, but sold only four of them (three were bought by friends). No one wanted to keep looking at her disturbing images or thought they would ever become a valuable investment. Nevertheless, her original vision was extremely influential. In 2015 a single print was sold at auction for $785,000. Both sacrificial figures were portrayed in recent films: Plath in *Sylvia* (2003) and Arbus in *Fur* (2006).

Plath and Arbus had a similar molten core beneath a frail carapace. They wanted a normal marriage as well as an extraordinary career, but broke the constraints of social behavior and bravely sacrificed themselves for art. They reflected our own misery and the sickness of American society. Their tormented existence confirmed the connection between creativity and insanity that began with Plato's concept of *furor divinus* and verified Friedrich Nietzsche's bold assertion: "one must still have chaos in oneself to be able to give birth to a dancing star. With my own blood I increased my own knowledge." Their broken lives and wasted talents exemplified the ancient Greek belief, "Those whom the gods wish to destroy they first make mad."

BIBLIOGRAPHY

1. SIGMUND FREUD AND ADOLF HITLER

Bullock, Alan. *Hitler: A Study in Tyranny*. Rev. ed. NY: Harper and Row, 1964.

Fest, Joachim. *Hitler*. Tr. Richard and Clara Winston. NY: Vintage, 1975.

Freud, Sigmund. *Civilization and Its Discontents*. Tr. James Strachey. NY: Norton, 1966.

———. *Letters, 1873–1939*. Ed. Ernst Freud. Tr. Tanya and James Stern. London: Hogarth, 1961.

———. *Moses and Monotheism*. Tr. Katherine Jones. NY: Vintage, 1967.

Hamann, Brigitte. *Hitler's Vienna: A Dictator's Apprenticeship*. Tr. Thomas Thornton. NY: Oxford UP, 1999.

Janik, Allan and Stephen Toulmin. *Wittgenstein's Vienna*. NY: Simon & Schuster, 1973.

Johnston, William. *The Austrian Mind: An Intellectual and Social History, 1848–1938*. Berkeley: University of California Press, 1972.

Jones, Ernest. *The Life and Work of Sigmund Freud*. 3 vols. NY: Basic Books, 1953–57.

Schorske, Carl. *Fin-de-Siècle Vienna: Politics and Culture*. NY: Vintage, 1980.

Zweig, Stefan. *The World of Yesterday*. London: Cassell, 1943.

2. FREUD AND THOMAS MANN

Mann, Thomas. *Death in Venice and Seven Other Stories*. Tr. H. T. Lowe-Porter. NY: Vintage, 1954.

———. *Diaries, 1918–1939.* Ed. Hermann Kesten. Tr. Richard and Clara Winston. NY: Abrams, 1982.

———. *Freud, Goethe, Wagner.* Tr. H. T. Lowe-Porter. NY: Knopf, 1937.

———. *Joseph and His Brothers.* Tr. H. T. Lowe-Porter. NY: Knopf, 1958.

———. *Letters, 1889–1955.* Ed. and tr. Richard and Clara Winston. NY: Knopf, 1971.

———. *The Magic Mountain.* Tr. H. T. Lowe-Porter. London: Secker & Warburg, 1957.

———. *Past Masters.* Tr. H. T. Lowe-Porter NY: Knopf, 1933.

———. *Tables of the Law.* Tr. H. T. Lowe-Porter. NY: Knopf, 1945.

Meyers, Jeffrey. *Thomas Mann's Artist-Heroes.* Evanston, IL: Northwestern University Press, 2014.

Schur, Max. *Freud: Living and Dying.* NY: International Universities Press, 1972.

3. ANNE FRANK AND AUDREY HEPBURN

Frank, Anne. *The Diary of a Young Girl.* Ed. Otto Frank and Miriam Pressler. NY: Bantam, 1997.

Matzen, Robert. *Dutch Girl: Audrey Hepburn in World War II.* Pittsburgh, PA: GoodKnight Books, 2019.

Müller, Melissa. *Anne Frank: The Biography.* Tr. Rita and Robert Kimber. NY: Henry Holt, 1998.

Paris, Barry. *Audrey Hepburn.* NY: Putnam, 1996.

4. ARTHUR RIMBAUD AND PAUL VERLAINE

Auden, W. H. "Rimbaud." *Collected Shorter Poems, 1927–57.* London: Faber and Faber, 1966.

Nietzsche, Friedrich. *The Portable Nietzsche.* Ed. and Tr. Walter Kaufmann. NY: Viking, 1954.

Petitfils, Pierre. *Rimbaud.* Tr. Alan Sheridan. Charlottesville: University of Virginia Press, 1987.

Plato. *Phaedrus.* Tr. Walter Hamilton. London: Penguin, 1973.

Richardson, Joanna. *Verlaine.* London: Weidenfeld and Nicolson, 1971.

Rimbaud, Arthur. *Rimbaud: Complete Works, Selected Letters.* Ed. and tr. Wallace Fowlie. Chicago: University of Chicago Press, 1966.

Robb, Graham. *Rimbaud: A Biography*. NY: Norton, 2000.

Verlaine, Paul. *The Cursed Poets*. Tr. Chase Madar. Los Angeles: Green Integer, 2003.

———. *Selected Poems*. Tr. C. F. MacIntyre. Berkeley: University of California Press, 1948.

Wilson, Edmund. *Axel's Castle*. NY: Scribners, 1931.

5. T. E. LAWRENCE AND ANDRÉ MALRAUX

Boak, Denis. *André Malraux*. Oxford: Clarendon, 1968.

Frohock, W. M. *André Malraux and the Tragic Imagination*. Stanford, CA: Stanford UP, 1952.

Lacouture, Jean. *André Malraux*. Tr. Alan Sheridan. NY: Pantheon, 1975.

Lawrence, T. E. *Seven Pillars of Wisdom*. Garden City, NY: Doubleday, 1935.

Malraux, André. "Lawrence and the Demon of the Absolute," *Hudson Review*, 8 (Winter 1956), 519–532.

———. *The Walnut Trees of Altenburg*. Tr. A. W. Fielding. London: John Lehmann, 1955.

Meyers, Jeffrey. *The Wounded Spirit: A Study of "Seven Pillars of Wisdom."* London: Martin, Brian & O'Keeffe, 1973.

6. WYNDHAM LEWIS AND T. S. ELIOT

Eliot, T. S. *Complete Poems and Plays, 1909–1950*. NY: Harcourt, Brace, 1952.

———. "A Note on *Monstre Gai*," *Hudson Review*, 7 (Winter 1955), 522–526.

Gordon, Lyndall. *T. S. Eliot: An Imperfect Life*. NY: Norton, 1998.

Kirk, Russell. *Eliot and His Age*. NY: Random House, 1971.

Lewis, Wyndham. *Blasting and Bombardiering*. London: Eyre & Spottiswoode, 1937.

———. *The Demon of Progress in the Arts*. Chicago: Regnery, 1955.

———. *Letters*. Ed. W. K. Rose. Norfolk, CT: New Directions, 1963.

———. *Men Without Art*. London: Cassell, 1934.

———. *One-Way Song*. London: Faber and Faber, 1933.

Meyers, Jeffrey. *The Enemy: A Biography of Wyndham Lewis*. London: Routledge & Kegan Paul, 1980.

Tate, Allen, ed. *T. S. Eliot: The Man and His Work*. NY: Delta, 1966.

7. EVELYN WAUGH AND ROBERT BYRON

Byron, Robert. *Europe in the Looking Glass*. London: Hesperus, 2012.

———. *Letters Home*. Ed. Lucy Butler. London: John Murray, 1991.

———. *The Road to Oxiana*. London: Cape, 1937.

Knox, James. *Robert Byron: A Biography*. London: John Murray, 2003.

Stannard, Martin. *Evelyn Waugh*. 2 vols. NY: Norton, 1987.

Sykes, Christopher. *Evelyn Waugh: A Biography*. Boston: Little, Brown, 1976.

———. *Four Studies in Loyalty*. NY: Sloane, 1948.

Waugh, Evelyn. *Diaries*. Ed. Michael Davie. Boston: Little, Brown, 1976.

———. *Letters*. Ed. Mark Amory. NY: Ticknor & Fields, 1980.

———. *A Little Learning*. London: Sidgwick and Jackson, 1973.

8. WAUGH AND RANDOLPH CHURCHILL

Churchill, Winston S. *His Father's Son: The Life of Randolph Churchill*. London: Weidenfeld & Nicolson, 1996.

Maclean, Fitzroy. *Eastern Approaches*. Alexandria, VA: Time-Life Books, 1980.

Roberts, Brian. *Randolph: A Study of Churchill's Son*. London: Hamish Hamilton, 1984.

Unpublished material from the National Archives and Public Record Office, Kew, England, and Churchill College, Cambridge University.

9. ROBERT FROST AND KAY MORRISON

Frost, Robert. *Poetry*. Ed. Edward Connery Lathem. NY: Henry Holt, 1975.

———. *Selected Letters*. Ed. Lawrance Thompson. NY: Holt Rinehart Winston, 1964.

———. *A Witness Tree*. NY: Henry Holt, 1942.

Interview with Anne Morrison Smith.

Meyers, Jeffrey. *Robert Frost: A Biography*. Boston: Houghton Mifflin, 1996.

Lawrance Thompson Papers, University of Virginia, Charlottesville.

10. EDMUND WILSON AND SCOTT FITZGERALD

Fitzgerald, Scott. *Correspondence*. Ed. Matthew Bruccoli and Margaret Duggan. NY: Random House, 1980.

———. *The Crack-Up*. Ed. Edmund Wilson. NY: New Directions, 1945.

Meyers, Jeffrey. *Edmund Wilson: A Biography*. Boston: Houghton Mifflin, 1995.

———. *Scott Fitzgerald: A Biography*. NY: HarperCollins, 1994.

Turnbull, Andrew. *Scott Fitzgerald*. London: Bodley Head, 1962.

Wilson, Edmund. *Dear Bunny, Dear Volodya: The Nabokov-Wilson Letters*. Ed. Simon Karlinsky. Berkeley: University of California Press, 2001.

———. *The Fifties*. Ed. Leon Edel. NY: Farrar, Straus and Giroux (FSG), 1983.

———. *The Forties*. Ed. Leon Edel. NY: FSG, 1986.

———. *Letters on Literature and Politics, 1912–1972*. Ed. Elena Wilson. NY: FSG, 1977.

———. *The Sixties*. Ed. Lewis Dabney. NY: FSG, 1993.

———. *Upstate*. NY: FSG, 1971.

———. *A Window on Russia*. NY: FSG, 1972.

11. WILSON AND ALLEN TATE

Bishop, John Peale, and Allen Tate. *The Republic of Letters in America: Correspondence*. Ed. Thomas Daniel Young and John Hindle. University Press of Kentucky, 1981.

Jonza, Nancylee Nowell. *The Underground Stream: The Life and Art of Caroline Gordon*. Athens: University of Georgia Press, 1995.

Sullivan, Walter. *Allen Tate: A Recollection*. Baton Rouge: Louisiana State University Press, 1988.

Tate, Allen. *Essays of Four Decades*. Chicago: Swallow Press, 1999.

Underwood, Thomas. *Allen Tate: Orphan of the South*. Princeton, NJ: Princeton UP, 2000.

12. WILSON AND VLADIMIR NABOKOV

Boyd, Brian. *Vladimir Nabokov*. 2 vols. Princeton, NJ: Princeton UP, 1990, 1996.

Nabokov, Vladimir. *The Annotated "Lolita."* Ed. Alfred Appel. NY: McGraw-Hill, 1970.

———. *Selected Letters, 1940–1977*. Ed. Dmitri Nabokov and Matthew Bruccoli. Harcourt Brace Jovanovich, 1989.

———. *Speak, Memory*. Rev. ed. NY: Putnam, 1966.

———. *Strong Opinions*. NY: McGraw-Hill, 1973.

Pushkin, Alexander. *Eugene Onegin.* Ed. Vladimir Nabokov. 2 vols. Rev. ed. Princeton, NJ: Princeton UP, 1975.

13. NABOKOV AND BALTHUS

Bal, Mieke. *Balthus: Works and Interview.* Tr. Sue Brownbridge. Barcelona: Ediciones Polígrafa, 2008.
Balthus. *Vanished Splendors: A Memoir.* Tr. Benjamin Ivry. NY: Ecco, 2001.
Joyce, James. *Ulysses.* NY: Vintage, 1986.
Rewald, Sabine. *Balthus.* NY: Abrams, 1984.
Weber, Nicholas Fox. *Balthus: A Biography.* NY: Knopf, 1989.

14. ERNEST HEMINGWAY AND JOHN HUSTON

Hemingway, Ernest. *Complete Short Stories.* NY: Scribners, 1987.
———. *Green Hills of Africa.* NY: Scribners, 1935.
———. *Selected Letters, 1917–1961.* Ed. Carlos Baker. NY: Scribners, 1981.
———, ed. *Men at War.* NY: Crown, 1942.
Huston, John. *An Open Book.* NY: Da Capo, 1980.
———. Unpublished screenplay of *Across the River and into the Trees.* Margaret Herrick Library, Beverly Hills, California.
Long, Robert Emmet. *John Huston: Interviews.* Jackson: University Press of Mississippi, 2001.
Meyers, Jeffrey. *Ernest Hemingway: A Biography.* NY: Harper & Row, 1985.
———. *John Huston: Courage and Art.* NY: Crown Archetype, 2011.

15. HEMINGWAY AND GARY COOPER

Meyers, Jeffrey. *Gary Cooper: American Hero.* NY: William Morrow, 1998.
Swindell, Larry. *The Last Hero: A Biography of Gary Cooper.* Garden City, NY: Doubleday, 1980.

16. SEAMUS HEANEY AND ROBERT LOWELL

Hamilton, Ian. *Robert Lowell: A Biography.* NY: Random House, 1982.
Heaney, Seamus. *Finders Keepers: Selected Prose, 1971–2001.* NY: FSG, 2002.

———. *Poems, 1965–1975*. NY: FSG, 1980.

———. *Selected Poems, 1966–1987*. NY: FSG, 1990.

Lowell, Robert. *Collected Poems*. Ed. Frank Bidart and David Gewanter. NY: FSG, 2003.

———. *Collected Prose*. Ed. Robert Giroux. NY: FSG, 1990.

———. *Letters*. Ed. Saskia Hamilton. NY: FSG, 2005.

Meyers, Jeffrey. *Manic Power: Robert Lowell and His Circle*. London: Macmillan, 1987.

———. *Robert Lowell in Love*. Amherst: University of Massachusetts Press, 2016.

———, ed. *Robert Lowell: Interviews and Memoirs*. Ann Arbor: University of Michigan Press, 1988.

O'Driscoll, Dennis. *Stepping Stones: Interviews with Seamus Heaney*. NY: FSG, 2008.

17. HEANEY AND JOSEPH BRODSKY

Brodsky, Joseph. *Collected Poems in English*. NY: FSG, 2000.

———. *Less Than One: Selected Essays*. NY: FSG, 1982.

Loseff, Lev. *Joseph Brodsky: A Literary Life*. Tr. Jane Anne Miller. New Haven, CT: Yale UP, 2011.

Volkov, Solomon. *Conversations with Joseph Brodsky*. Tr. Marian Schwartz. NY: Free Press, 1998.

18. DIANE ARBUS AND SYLVIA PLATH

Bosworth, Patricia. *Diane Arbus: A Biography*. NY: Avon, 1984.

Koren, Yehuda, and Eilat Negev. *A Lover of Unreason: The Life and Tragic Death of Assia Wevill*. London: Robson, 2006.

Lubow, Arthur. *Diane Arbus: Portrait of a Photographer*. NY: Ecco, 2016.

Plath, Sylvia. *Ariel*. NY: Harper & Row, 1966.

———. *The Bell Jar*. NY: Harper & Row, 1971

———. *Letters*. Ed. Peter Steinberg and Karen Kukil. 2 vols. NY: Harper, 2017–18.

———. *The Unabridged Journals*. Ed. Karen Kukil. NY: Anchor: 2000.

Rollyson , Carl. *American Isis: The Life and Art of Sylvia Plath*. NY: St. Martin's, 2013.

Printed in the USA
CPSIA information can be obtained
at www.ICGtesting.com
CBHW060052051124
16919CB00001B/63